Acing

Contracts

A Checklist Approach to Contracts Law

Suzanne Darrow-Kleinhaus

Associate Professor of Law
and Director of Academic Development

Touro College
Jacob D. Fuchsberg Law Center

Series Editor
A. Benjamin Spencer

WEST®

A Thomson Reuters business

Mat #40516222

© 2010 Thomson Reuters
   610 Opperman Drive
   St. Paul, MN 55123
   1-800-313-9378

Printed in the United States of America

ISBN: 978-0-314-17171-9

To my parents, Bernice and Albert Darrow,
for their unwavering love and support.

This book is in loving memory of my father, who taught me
early the meaning of promise—and what it meant
to never make a promise one could not keep.

ACKNOWLEDGMENTS

This project has been a major enterprise and would not have happened without the support and assistance of others. Thanks to my husband, Murray, for his love and support. Thanks to Meredith, who demonstrates daily what it means to be a loving mother and daughter. And thanks to Benjamin, who is always eager and delighted to learn something new.

My deepest appreciation to Dean Larry Raful and to the Touro Law Center for providing a stipend in support of this work. I would also like to thank Professor Louise Harmon, Associate Dean for Academic Affairs & Faculty Development, for her receptivity to new ideas and encouragement of faculty scholarship. She truly cares about our projects and helps us make them happen.

I wish to thank my former law teachers and now colleagues, Professors Heather Melniker and Sidney Kwestel, who model by example the art of teaching, the process of legal thinking, and the type of professionalism that comes only from within. But a very special thank you is owed to Sidney Kwestel, my Contracts professor, without whom this book would not have been written. I realized early in his class that what was important was learning to identify the relevant questions because the answers I sought were to be found in the questions I asked. It is wholly appropriate and right to recognize his enormous contribution to a book which shows how to organize the rules into a series of logical questions that guides the thought process to resolve the legal issue.

Finally, I would like to thank my students. There are far too many to name individually, but a couple made very real contributions. First, Nancy Chanin, class of 2010, without whom this manuscript would never have been completed. Thank you for your careful reading, editing, and unbelievable skill with the Blue Book. Your suggestions and presence during the final phases of this book have been a comfort and true source of support. I am forever grateful. I would also like to thank Daniel Podhaskie, class of 2010, who contributed significantly to the sample analyses for several of the illustrative problems.

SUZANNE DARROW-KLEINHAUS

Bellmore, New York
April 2010

Table of Contents

Introduction

Many students find contracts to be the most challenging of their first year subjects. It seems that the combination of the common law, the Restatement, and the Uniform Commercial Code can be confusing and makes the subject appear more difficult than it needs to be. This book should clear up that confusion and be a useful learning tool. It does not attempt to explain contract principles in great detail, but rather, it seeks to provide a summary overview of the relevant law with a comprehensive set of checklists to guide you through a reasoned analysis of the types of fact patterns you are likely to encounter on your exam.

Each chapter presents a different topic, beginning with a brief review of the subject followed by the checklist for that subject. There are problems at the end of each chapter to give you an opportunity to see how the checklists can be used to work through such problems. I wrote the problems very carefully to provide a range of content, style, and format. As you will soon learn, professors' exam styles vary widely. I have tried to provide a variety of formats—there are single issue problems and multi-party, fact-laden hypotheticals. There are targeted questions and general, open-ended inquiries.

Each question is followed by a sample answer. I provide these answers with a number of caveats. First, since it is possible to write a solid answer in so many ways, a single "sample" answer can be misleading. There are any number of possibilities and the ones you find here are just examples to let you see how the IRAC elements transform into complete sentences and how the checklist questions transition from one issue to another. Second, while each question is grounded in doctrine, you should answer the questions according to the law as presented by your professor. If you do so, you will probably notice differences in emphasis and approach in your answer as opposed to that provided in the sample analysis. If there is a difference between the sample answer's articulation of the controlling rule (for example, it identifies four factors for a given cause of action or principle and your professor has identified six), then use your professor's articulation of the rule. The same is true of the checklists: make sure that you modify them according to your professor's presentation of the material. In doing so, you will gain a thorough understanding of the substantive material and make the checklist reflective of your individual course.

At the end of the book, there is an Appendix where you will find two summary checklists: one for the common law and one for the sale of goods. Each is an analytical outline of leading questions to guide you through analysis of a problem. The framework of questions moves from one issue to the next as though you were answering a hypothetical that raised every possible issue covered in the course, from formation through remedies for breach. You can use these checklists to provide a summary outline for a final review, to help you finalize a framework for the overall structure of the course, and to create a topic checklist for issue-spotting on the exam.

After teaching Contracts for a number of years, I found that my students benefitted greatly from the overview provided by the Contracts TimeLine. I recommend it as your starting point to get a sense of the whole subject. When you look at the big picture, it does not matter where your professor begins the course—whether it's formation or damages—you can see where all the pieces fit and it is much easier not to get lost in the details. The Contracts

TimeLine, when combined with the topical checklists, provides a blueprint for preparing for and taking your contracts exam.

I have tried not to over-document the source materials, but this has not always been possible. All references to the Restatement mean to the Restatement Second. Article 2 of the Uniform Commercial Code is referenced where applicable to provide the sales counterpart to a common law rule but it is well beyond the scope of this book to discuss all the rules under UCC Article 2. Consequently, it covers only the basic topics likely to be covered in a general contracts course and not one specifically dealing with the Uniform Commercial Code.

CHAPTER 1

Introduction to Contract Law

R2d § 1-8
UCC 1-201(11), 2-104

Contract law is one of the foundation courses you take in the first year of law school. All law school schools require it and for good reason: the subject matter of contracts—the mechanics of exchange—is at the center of our lives for most of our lives. The simple fact is that the act of trading one thing for the other—money for goods or services or vice versa—is at the heart of what we do everyday in business, at work, and in our personal lives. Even the simplest transaction is about an agreement between the parties. The question for contract law is whether that agreement is legally enforceable.

Consider the following three examples: first, your favorite uncle promises to give you his extensive collection of sports memorabilia. When you call to tell him you've cleaned off your shelves and you're ready to pick up the collection, he tells you he's really sorry but can't bear to part with it. Second, your friend Jessica agrees to meet you for dinner on Thursday evening and doesn't show up, leaving you to have dinner at the restaurant by yourself. Finally, you agree to cut your neighbor's lawn in the summer and, in exchange, he promises to shovel the snow from your driveway in the winter. You cut his lawn all summer and he refuses to clear your driveway after the first snowfall.

Do you have a cause of action in any of these cases? The answer is "no" to the first two and "yes" to the third. Why the differing results? Each of these situations involves promises and even performances, yet only the last is recognized as an enforceable agreement. How do we know when a promise will be accorded the status of contract?

Determining whether a promise or set of promises will be enforced is a recurring question in contract law. Because a contract creates a legal relationship resulting in rights and obligations for the parties, the law is careful to recognize only such relationships as the parties intended to create. This is because freedom of contract is essential to a market economy such as ours and only such agreements which have been freely and voluntarily entered into will be recognized. Consequently, when such agreements are found, courts will enforce them and refrain from undoing that which the parties themselves have undertaken.

WHAT IS A CONTRACT?

It makes sense to begin with a definition of "contract" but this is not as easy as it sounds. Most of us already have some idea of what a contract is so the challenge is not to allow our lay understanding to interfere with its precise legal definition. This is true of many of the words you will encounter in your legal studies—they have ordinary, non-legal meanings as well as legal ones. But now your task is to learn and apply the legal definitions.

Having said that, it is *still* not easy to provide a single definition of contract. Some definitions focus on a contract's promissory basis while others look to the resulting consequences. For example, the promissory element figures prominently in the definition provided by Restatement Second § 1: a contract is "a promise or a set of promises for the breach of which the law gives a remedy, or the performance of which the law in some way recognizes as a duty[,]"[1] while the Uniform Commercial Code omits

---

1. Restatement (Second) of Contracts § 1 (1979).

any reference to promises and defines a contract as "the total legal obligation which results from the parties' agreement[.]"[2]

Perhaps the best approach is to consider a contract's characteristics: generally, a contract can be defined as an exchange relationship created by an agreement, which can be either oral or written, between two or more parties, and involves at least one legally enforceable promise. We will explore each of these concepts in greater detail in subsequent chapters of this book.

CENTRAL THEMES OF CONTRACT LAW

This book is not a hornbook and does not attempt to explain doctrine or theory in great detail. However, it is useful to identify the basic ideological values at the core of contract doctrine to inform your reading and understanding of course materials.

The freedom of parties to contract, to make their own promises and agree to be bound is at the core of contractual liability. The power to determine the terms of the contractual relationship is deemed an exercise of individual liberty and autonomy. Consequently, contract law seeks to enforce only those agreements which have been freely and voluntarily entered into since no one should be bound absent their true assent.

However, the individual's freedom to contract is not without limits. It is subject to the state's right to protect the rights and needs of all its citizens. As a result, the individual's freedom to contract is balanced against the need to protect weaker, more vulnerable parties from unfair and overreaching practices. For now, it is sufficient to note that contract liberty is a critical value but one which is subject to a variety of limitations based on the rights of others and competing public interests.

Individual sovereignty is but one theory you will encounter in your study of contract law. You will also learn about the following: the sanctity of promises, both for providing certainty in future planning as well as upholding ethical obligations; the needs of the free market and economic efficiency; and the reliance principle for ensuring fairness by providing relief to promisees.

---

2. U.C.C. § 1–201(11) (2009).

SOURCES OF CONTRACT LAW

Common Law

Contracts is a common law subject because it is based largely on the decisions of judges as opposed to legislative enactment. This is not to say, however, that there is no statutory law governing contracts because there is a strong legislative component, most notably in the form of the Uniform Commercial Code ("UCC") governing the sale of goods. But quite apart from the UCC, individual states have enacted legislation dealing with all aspects of contract law. Consequently, any client issue involving a contracts question requires a careful review of the relevant jurisdiction's statutory code.

The law of every state but Louisiana is based on the common law of England. Louisiana follows a civil system based on the Napoleonic Code. Whether common law or statutory, contract law is principally a matter of state law. Even if a rule originates as a statute, once a court is called upon to interpret and decide a matter concerning that statute, it becomes part of the state's common law. Although each state develops its own body of contract law, there is enough similarity between states because of their common law heritage to allow for a general study of contract principles.

Restatement (Second) Of Contracts

The Restatement was written by the American Law Institute ("ALI"), a private, non-profit group of law professors, lawyers, judges, and practitioners, to provide guidance as to what the law is and perhaps should be. Although the Restatement consists of summaries of the existing law, it is not "the law" itself and therefore is not binding on any jurisdiction. However, it is persuasive, secondary authority and highly influential. It is cited frequently in judicial opinions, thus becoming part of that jurisdiction's common law. What is important to remember is that the Restatement is not a statute, although it is numbered like one and is written to sound like statements of black letter law.

You will find citations to the Restatement Second throughout this book. In addition, there is a reference box at the beginning of each chapter which identifies the principal Restatement sections (and UCC provisions) associated with the topics reviewed in the chapter. The list is by no means exhaustive and it is very likely that your professor will emphasize additional or different provisions as you work through the assigned cases. It might be helpful to add them to the list as you discuss them in class.

Uniform Commercial Code (UCC)

In addition to the Restatement Second, the other main source of contract law is the Uniform Commercial Code. It is the product of a Permanent Editorial Board under the joint auspices of the ALI and the National Conference of Commissioners on Uniform State Laws (NCCUSL).

The UCC is a statute adopted by the legislatures of 49 states (Louisiana is the exception) and is binding law. It has separate articles, each one covering a specific type of commercial transaction. Typically, your contracts course will be concerned with only one of the types of transactions covered by the UCC: Article 2 for the sale of goods. You will also deal with some of the provisions of Article 1 because it contains the general provisions and definitions that apply to all articles of the UCC, including Article 2.

As you will soon learn, a threshold question for contracts analysis is whether the transaction involves a sale of goods: if it does, then the UCC applies, otherwise, it does not. For example, a construction contract, an employment agreement, and a sale of land are covered by the state's common law and not the UCC.

It is also important to note that Article 2 governs contracts for the sale of goods whether the seller is a merchant or not. There are some provisions which treat merchants differently, but it is not a requirement that one be a merchant to fall within the Code. UCC 2–104 defines a merchant as one who "deals in goods of the kind or otherwise by his occupation holds himself out as having knowledge or skill peculiar to the practices or goods involved in the transaction[.]"[3] For example, suppose I sell my car to Meredith and a dispute subsequently arises. The matter will be decided according to the UCC because the transaction involves a sales of goods, a car,

---

3. U.C.C. § 2–104(1) (2004) (the 2003 Proposed Revision of U.C.C. § 2–104(1) has substantially the same definition.).

and it does not matter whether I am a merchant or not. In this case, I am not a merchant with respect to vehicles but only an ordinary, or casual seller.

Although Article 2 is applicable only to transactions involving the sale of goods, it has been highly influential in the development of the common law. As you will see, the Restatement Second has adopted many provisions of Article 2 in formulating its own rules. Courts often apply the UCC by analogy to non-sales transactions in view of the underlying policies to be served. Sometimes a case involves both goods and services. These are referred to as "hybrid cases." Here, a court has several options: a minority of courts apply Article 2 to only the sale of goods aspect of the transaction whereas a majority of courts apply Article 2 only if the *predominant purpose* of the whole transaction was a sale of goods, and in that event, the majority applies Article 2 to the whole. If the sale of goods is not the predominant purpose, then Article 2 does not apply at all.

It is important to note that even if a contract is for the sale of goods, it does not mean that the common law is irrelevant—in fact, quite the opposite. Since Article 2 does not address every issue which might arise in a transaction involving the sale of goods, the general principles of law and equity are applicable to supplement the Code provisions.[4] Consequently, where the Code is silent, the common law rules fill the gap. For example, the Code does not have specific provisions regarding agency, estoppel, mistake, misrepresentation, or capacity. In such cases, common law rules are used.

Revisions To The UCC

Article 1 was revised in 2001 and Article 2 in 2003. However, just because the National Conference of Commissioners on Uniform State Laws and the American Law Institute have approved the changes does not make them law: each state legislature must adopt the revisions for them to take effect as the law of that jurisdiction. As of January 1, 2009, Revised Article 1 is in effect in thirty-four states whereas no state has yet enacted revised Article 2.

---

4. *See* U.C.C. § 1–103 (2004); *see also* U.C.C. § 1–103(b) (Proposed Revision 2003).

This makes for a rather difficult situation: contracts professors have to decide whether to teach the pre-revision version or the post-revision version, or both. The same is true with your casebook. This book relies on the pre-revision versions of Articles 1 and 2 for its discussions and analysis. However, both Code versions are accommodated with citations to the corresponding provision in the revised version and an explanation of any differences between them where applicable.

In addition to the UCC, you may encounter references to two additional sources of contract law. They are two international documents. The first is the United Nations Convention on Contracts for the International Sale of Goods (CISG), which has been ratified in 65 countries, including NAFTA. The main exceptions are Japan and the United Kingdom. CISG applies to contracts for the sale of goods between parties who do business in different countries when both countries have ratified the Convention. When applicable, it preempts the domestic law regarding the sale of goods, which in the United States is Article 2 of the UCC.

The other source is the UNIDROIT Principles of International Commercial Contracts. This document is a restatement of international contract principles and its legal effect is comparable to the Restatement.

Classifying Contracts

The following are some basic contracts concepts you should take the time to understand at the beginning of your studies. Doing so now will make the task of learning the substantive law much easier as you proceed.

Void, Voidable, And Unenforceable Contracts

The terms void, voidable, and unenforceable are easily confused and often mistakenly used interchangeably. However, they refer to distinctly different contractual situations. You must be sure to understand the distinctions since they result in significantly different consequences for the parties, specifically with respect to the right to enforce the agreement and seek damages.

Let's begin with an enforceable contract. A contract is said to be enforceable when its breach entitles the non-breaching party to damages, either legal or equitable.

A contract is considered void when it results in no legal obligation on the part of the promisor. It is also accurate to say that no contract has been formed. For example, if the parties' exchange of promises lacks consideration, then the contract is said to be "void for lack of consideration."

A contract is voidable if one or more of the parties have the power to avoid the legal obligations imposed by the contract. For example, a contract made by a party while under a legal incapacity is voidable. One such incapacity is based on age where a person under the age of 18 has the capacity to incur only voidable contractual duties. Here, the minor may choose either to avoid or perform the contract. Other instances where a party has such power to avoid performance exist where the person has been induced to contract by means of fraud, duress, or mistake.

An unenforceable contract is one that may be valid but which the court will not enforce. This can be for any number of reasons, including, for example, an agreement which satisfies all the requirements for a contract but is lacking a signed writing to satisfy the Statute of Frauds. Some contracts are unenforceable because they arise out of illegal bargains[5] while others may be unenforceable due to the government's sovereign immunity.[6] And still others are deemed unenforceable because they are "against public policy" in that the contract offends the public interest either because of improper conduct in the bargaining process, the subject matter of the contract, or both.

Express, Implied, And Quasi–Contracts

An express contract is formed when the parties manifest their agreement explicitly by words. When the agreement is manifested by conduct, the contract is said to be implied-in-fact. For example, if Carly takes her shoes to the shoemaker to have new heels and soles put on them, it may be inferred that Carly has agreed to pay the shoemaker a reasonable price. In this case, the contract is partly express and partly implied-in-fact. It does not matter that express words of contract were not spoken. The parties' conduct manifested mutual assent.

---

5. Restatement (Second) of Contracts § 8   6. *Id.* § 8 cmt. c.
cmt. b (1979).

Conceptual difficulties arise with respect to a contract implied-in-law, which is not really a contract at all. Here, the court creates an obligation in law (quasi-contract) to do justice even though no promise was ever made or intended. The main purpose of a quasi-contract is the prevention of unjust enrichment. A common example is the case where a doctor provides necessary medical care to someone in dire need. The doctor will be able to recover in quasi-contract the value of his or her services, even though the party receiving the benefit of those services did not expressly or impliedly promise to do so at the time.

The requirements for a quasi-contract claim are: first, the defendant received a benefit; second, there is an appreciation or knowledge by the defendant of the benefit; and third, the circumstances make it unjust for the defendant to retain the benefit without paying for it. For a complete discussion of quasi-contractual remedies, refer to Chapter 12, Contract Remedies.

Structure of This Book

Contracts casebooks can be organized in a number of ways. Some begin with an overview of the theories underlying contract law and the bases for enforcing promises. Others begin with the breach of a contract and are organized around the possible remedies. Still others begin with a discussion of contract formation and leave remedies for the end, a structure we will follow. Ultimately, every casebook covers all of these areas and in the end it matters little where you begin. You will want to use this book to follow the material covered in your class and in the sequence in which it is covered. This will be easy enough to do because each chapter is structured to cover a particular topic.

A major challenge in studying contracts is not losing sight of the relationships between the individual concepts and the whole. I strongly recommend that you take a few minutes to review the Contracts TimeLine in this chapter to get a sense of the "big picture" and then review it again when you begin each new chapter. The TimeLine will help you understand where the individual concepts "fit" in relation to the whole and this will let you keep things straight, i.e., whether you are in the offer, acceptance, performance, or damages phase of the contractual relationship.

The Contracts Timeline

FORMATION ➤

AVOIDING THE DEAL ➡

Do we have a deal?

We have a deal, but

Mutual Assent		+ Consideration
Offer +	Acceptance	Bargained-for exchange

Statute of Frauds
Misunderstanding
Mistake
- Unilateral
- Mutual

Objective Test	Power of acceptance	"Peppercorn" theory	Incapacity
"Master" of offer	Unilateral contract	Benefit/detriment	Fraud/Misrepresentation
Contractual intent	Bilateral contract	Illusory promises	Duress
Certainty of terms	"Mirror-image Rule"	Gratuitous promises	Undue influence
Prelim negotiations	"Mail Box Rule"	Past consideration	Unconscionability
Terminating an offer	"Battle of the Forms"	Moral obligation	• Procedural
• Revocation	Irrevocable offers	Promissory Estoppel	• Substantive
• Rejection/	• Option contract	Contract modification	Illegality/Public policy
Counter-offer	• "Firm offer"	• Pre-existing Duty Rule	
• Lapse of time		• UCC 2-209	
• Death or incapacity		Requirements/output contract	
		Accord and satisfaction	

Additional formation concepts:
    Implied-in-fact contracts
    Implied-in-law or "quasi contracts"

Notes: These terms and category delineations represent a way of
        looking and thinking about contract law; they are not definitive, nor
        by any means the only way to look at the subject. The chart is meant
        as a way to begin looking at the parts and trying to make
        sense of the whole. But know that the whole is greater than the
        sum of these parts!

PERFORMANCE ➡ **THIRD PARTIES** ➡ **REMEDIES**
/NONPERFORMANCE

Who has to do what and when,   *Is there another party*   *Someone failed to perform*
or maybe not?   *to the deal?*   *when required, now what?*

Finding the Contract Terms	At formation?	Subsequently?	Measuring money damages:
• Parol Evidence Rule			• Expectation interest
• Interpretation	3rd Pty Beneficiary	Assignment	Loss in value
• Ambiguity	• Intended	Delegation	Cost of repair/completion
Implied Terms	• Incidental	Novation	Diminution in value
• Good faith			• Reliance interest
Warranties			• Restitution interest

Finding the Contract Terms
• Parol Evidence Rule
• Interpretation
• Ambiguity
Implied Terms
• Good faith
Warranties
Conditions
• Express/Implied
• Constructive
Excuse/Waiver of Condition
Modification
Impossiblity/Impracticability
Frustration of purpose
Anticipatory Repudiation & Adequate Assurances
Material Breach
• Substantial Performance
• UCC Perfect Tender Rule

At formation?

3rd Pty Beneficiary
• Intended
• Incidental

Subsequently?

Assignment
Delegation
Novation

Measuring money damages:
• Expectation interest
    Loss in value
    Cost of repair/completion
    Diminution in value
• Reliance interest
• Restitution interest
Consequential damages
Incidental damages
Liquidated damages

Limitations on money damages
• Foreseeability
• Mitigation/avoidability
• Certainty

Equitable remedies
• Specific performance
• Injunctive relief

Formation ➡	Avoiding ➡ the Deal	Performance ➡	Third ➡ Parties	Remedies
Do we have a deal?	We have a deal, but	Who has to do what and when, or maybe not	Is there a third party to the deal?	Someone failed to perform when required, now what?
Mutual Assent + Consideration				

Excerpts of Contracts Time-line

FORMATION
DO WE HAVE A DEAL?

Mutual Assent

Offer   +   **Acceptance**

Offer	Acceptance
Objective Test	Power of Acceptance
"Master" of offer	Unilateral Contract
Contractual Intent	Bilateral Contract
Certainty of Terms	"Mirror–Image Rule"
Prelim negotiations	"Mail Box Rule"
Terminating an offer	"Battle of the Forms"
• Revocation	Irrevocable offers
• Rejection/Counter-offer	• Option Contract
	•"Firm offer"
	• Lapse of time
	• Death or incapacity

Additional Formation Concepts:

Implied-in-fact contracts

Implied-in-law or "quasi contracts"

Close-up on Formation

CHAPTER 2

Offer and Acceptance

> R2d § 17, 18, 19, 22

The first requirement to form a contract is an agreement between the parties, generally referred to as a mutual manifestation of assent. Both parties must intend to contract and must agree to the same terms. Typically, mutual assent is found through the process of offer and acceptance.[1] The proposal to enter into a contract is called an offer and the person who makes it is called the "offeror." The party to whom the offer is made is called the "offeree." Upon receiving the offer, if the offeree wishes to enter the agreement proposed by the offer, she must manifest her assent to it. The offeree's assent to the terms of the offer is called the acceptance.

THE OBJECTIVE TEST

In finding assent, the courts apply an "objective test" which looks to the parties' words and actions (outward manifestations) and not to what they may have subjectively believed. The test of a party's intent is viewed from the perspective of a reasonable person

---

1. Restatement (Second) of Contracts § 22(2) (1979). In some cases, mutual assent may be found even though the precise moment of formation cannot be determined. Here, which party made the "offer" and which made the "acceptance" is less important because of the conduct of the parties.

in the position of the other party.[2] By looking to the other party's *reasonable* understanding, the objective test takes into account her experience, training, the relationship between the parties, and the context of the specific transaction. As a result, subjective components are not entirely excluded from consideration which makes sense since the goal of the objective test is to protect the party's reasonable expectations.

UNILATERAL AND BILATERAL CONTRACTS

Restatement Second does not use the terms "bilateral" and "unilateral."[3] However, since many of the cases you will read use these terms as well as many Contracts professors, it is best to be acquainted with them and understand the distinction. In forming a bilateral contract, each party makes a promise—the offeror's promise is contained in the offer and the offeree makes a return promise in the acceptance. "Bilateral," therefore, refers to the fact that both parties have made promises. For example, Jon offers to pay $1000 in return for Jessica's promise to sell her car. As soon as Jessica accepts Jon's offer with her return promise, a bilateral contract is formed and both parties are bound.

On the other hand, in forming a unilateral contract, only one party makes a promise—the offeror's promise is in the offer and the offeree renders a performance as the acceptance. For example, Ben offers $1000 to anyone who finds and returns his laptop computer. If Emma finds his computer and returns it to him, she is entitled to the $1000. Ben is not seeking Emma's return promise to find his computer, but the actual performance of returning it to him. If Emma returns the computer, then her acceptance is her act of performance. In short, if the exclusive means of acceptance is to render the performance under the proposed contract, then the

---

2. *Embry v. Hargadine, McKittrick Dry Goods Co.*, 105 S.W. 777 (Mo. Ct. App. 1907) ("though McKittrick may not have intended to employ Embry . . . , yet if what McKittrick said would have been taken by a reasonable man to be an employment, and Embry

so understood it, it constituted a valid contract").

3. Restatement (Second) of Contracts § 1 cmt. f (1979).

offeror has proposed a unilateral contract. We will revisit these concepts in greater detail as we examine the mechanics of assent.

REVIEW OF OFFER

R2d § 24, 26, 27, 33, 41, 43

Restatement Second § 24 defines an offer as "the manifestation of willingness to enter into a bargain, so made as to justify another person in understanding that his assent to that bargain is invited and will conclude it."[4] This follows the standard formula for forming a contract in which one party (the "offeror") makes a proposal (the "offer") to the other party (the "offeree"), indicating an intent to enter into a deal on the proposed terms. The offeree's assent to the terms of the offer is invited, and if given, is called the acceptance and concludes the deal. For example, Amy says to Ben, "I will sell you my computer for $1000." Ben is delighted and says, "Great. I will buy your computer for $1000."

Here, Amy and Ben have formed a contract. But it might have gone differently. Suppose Amy had said instead, "I am thinking of selling my computer but would not take less than $1000. Let me know if you are interested." Unlike the earlier exchange, where it could not be clearer that Amy has made a plain promise to sell her computer if Ben agrees to pay the offering price of $1000, here Amy is expressing an invitation to Ben to make an offer. Amy has identified the subject matter of the transaction and mentioned a price—the specific terms that a genuine offer would be expected to include—but the use of such equivocal language as "I am thinking of selling" and "let me know if you are interested" lacks the promissory certainty of "I will sell" or "I offer" and is instead indicative of preliminary negotiations.

Things might just as easily have progressed differently at Ben's end. For example, in response to Amy's offer, Ben might have

---

4. Restatement (Second) of Contracts § 24 (1979).

said, "I think $1000 is too much for a used computer. How about $900?" In this case, Ben would not have accepted the offer but terminated it and made a counter-offer of his own. Now it would be up to Amy whether to accept the new offer.

This example shows that not every proposal is an offer and not every response from the offeree is an acceptance. While a contract may be formed after a single set of communications between the parties, more often there is a series of communications over a period of time. In some instances, a contract may be formed only after considerable "dickering" over the terms and negotiations back and forth between the parties. A dispute may arise when the parties disagree over "timing": at what point during the negotiations was the offeree justified in believing her assent was invited and would conclude the deal?

Whether a party has made an offer capable of acceptance is the classic starting point for analysis of a contract claim. As "master of the offer," the offeror controls the person (or persons) to whom the offer is made and the manner of acceptance. Only the offeree has the power to accept the offer and must do so on the offeror's terms.

To qualify as an offer, the terms must be certain and definite. It must be reasonably clear to the offeree that her acceptance will bind the parties as soon as it is given. If the offeror appears to retain the right to make the final decision, then it is not an offer but an invitation to the other party to start negotiating or to make a proposal. Similarly, in situations where the parties "agree to agree" or agree to negotiate further concerning material terms, no contract will be found. Here the indefiniteness of material terms prevents formation. In some situations, the parties may reach an agreement orally, but do not intend to be bound until they have executed a final writing.[5] These situations are distinguishable, however, from instances where parties reach an agreement but

---

5. Restatement (Second) of Contracts § 27 (1979).

leave out a term or terms to be decided later with the understanding that they will negotiate and use reasonable efforts to reach agreement.[6]

Another issue that comes up under the topic of offer relates to the effect to be given to proposals to the public such as advertisements, catalogs, and circulars. These are generally held not to be offers because they would expose the maker to the risk of liability for performance well beyond the maker's ability. For example, suppose a retail store advertised to sell premium designer jeans on the following terms, "nationally advertised at $250, for the price of $75." When Carly went to the store, the manager refused to sell her any jeans saying that they had no more at that price. Is Carly entitled to purchase the jeans for $75? Most likely the answer is "no" because the advertisement did not state a quantity and there is no language of commitment. Instead, the cases interpret such ads as invitations to the public to purchase or a preliminary proposal inviting offers.

As always, there are exceptions as in the famous case of *Lefkowitz v. Great Minneapolis Surplus Store, Inc.*,[7] where an ad for a fur piece was found to be an offer. The court found that the department store's ad containing the words, "1 Black Lapin Stole * * * worth $139.50 * * * $1.00[.] First Come First Served[.]"[8] was sufficiently clear, definite, and explicit and left nothing open for negotiation. There was only one stole and only the first person who came to claim it could accept the offer. The words "First Come First Served" indicate language of promissory commitment.[9]

Since not every expression qualifies as an offer, it is critical to distinguish offers from other kinds of statements. For example, if a statement is not an offer, it might be an expression of opinion, a statement of intent, an inquiry, or an invitation to deal. In determining whether an offer has been made, the court looks first to the language of the particular proposal. It will also consider the

---

6. James M. Perillo, *Calamari and Perillo on Contracts*, § 2.9 (5th ed. 2003).

7. 86 N.W.2d 689 (Minn. 1957).

8. *Id.*, at 690.

9. Restatement (Second) of Contracts § 26 cmt. b (1979); *see also id.* at illustration 1.

surrounding circumstances, any prior communications between the parties, relevant trade practices, and the completeness of the suggested exchange. Because of the voluntary nature of the contractual relationship, courts are reluctant to find an offer and impose liability when the parties are at the formation stage. Consequently, the more definite the terms and whether the proposal contains language suggesting that it is within the power of the recipient to close the deal through acceptance, the more likely an offer will be found.

Terminating an Offer

For an acceptance to be valid, it must become effective while the power of acceptance is still in effect. An offeree's power of acceptance may be terminated in any of the following ways: (1) revocation by the offeror; (2) rejection or counter-offer by the offeree; (3) lapse of time; (4) death or incapacity of the offeror or offeree.[10]

Revocation

The offeror is free to revoke her offer at any time before it is effectively accepted unless the offer qualifies as an option or is otherwise made irrevocable. The offeror has the power to revoke even though the offer plainly states the opposite and promises to be held open for a specific period of time. This is because an agreement is binding as a bargain only if supported by consideration.[11] So unless the promisor receives something in exchange for the promise to keep the offer open, the offeror is not bound and can revoke the offer at any time before it is accepted.

A revocation must be communicated to the offeree to be effective. Communication may be direct or indirect. An indirect communication of revocation occurs when the offeror acts in a way that is inconsistent with an intent to enter the contract and the

---

10. Restatement (Second) of Contracts § 36 (1979).

11. Restatement (Second) of Contracts § 42 cmt. a (1979).

offeree acquires this information through a reliable source.[12] In this case, there is a revocation, even though the offeror never communicated directly with the offeree. For example, suppose Spencer offers to sell Adam a parcel of land and gives him a week to consider the proposal. The next day, Spencer contracts to sell the same land to Dan and Adam learns about it from a tenant on the premises. The offer is effectively revoked as to Adam and he no longer has the power to accept Spencer's offer.

Revocation of a general offer made by newspaper or other general notification made to the public may be revoked by using the same medium in which the offer was made.[13] Unless a better means of notification is reasonably available, a notice of termination by a means equal to that given to the offer is acceptable.

Rejection or Counter-Offer

Rejection of the offer by the offeree terminates the power of acceptance and the offeree can no longer accept the offer. Should the offeree subsequently attempt to accept the offer, this purported acceptance might itself be an offer.

If the offeree attempts to add to or vary the terms of the offer, then it is not an acceptance but a counter-offer and rejection of the offer. To be effective, the acceptance must be the "mirror-image" of the offer or it is a counter-offer and terminates the power of acceptance. Any deviation, even the slightest or unintentional, is considered a counter-offer and terminates the offeree's power of acceptance.[14]

Lapse of Time

As master of the offer, the offeror may set the time for acceptance and the offeree's power to accept is terminated at the time specified in the offer. If no time is specified, then the offer

---

12. Restatement (Second) of Contracts § 43 (1979).

13. Restatement (Second) of Contracts § 46 (1979).

14. E. Allan Farnsworth, *Contracts*, § 3.21 (4th ed. 2004).

lapses at the end of a reasonable time. What is a reasonable time depends on all the surrounding circumstances at the time the offer and attempted acceptance was made.[15] Such circumstances can include the following: the nature of the proposed contract, the parties' course of dealing, and any relevant usage of trade.

When parties are engaged in direct negotiations (bargaining face-to-face), the power of acceptance continues only during the conversation, unless a contrary intent is indicated.[16] If the offer is by mail, then it is "seasonably accepted if an acceptance is mailed at any time before midnight on the day on which the offer is received."[17] However, the Restatement commentary adds that "in the absence of a significant speculative element in the situation, a considerably longer time may be reasonable."[18]

Death or Incapacity

The offeror's death terminates the power of acceptance—whether or not the offeree has notice of the death. The offeror's lack of capacity terminates the power of acceptance in the same manner as the offeror's death. Since only an offeree has the power of acceptance, when the offeree dies or lacks capacity, acceptance is no longer possible. These rules do not affect option contracts.

REVIEW OF ACCEPTANCE

R2d § 30, 39, 40, 41, 45, 50, 51, 53, 54, 56, 58, 59, 60, 61, 63

As we've seen, the offeror is the "master of her offer" which means, among other things, that she has the right to determine the manner in which her offer can be accepted. She can insist that it be accepted in only one way or in a particular way. For example, she can specify that the acceptance be made by return promise, by mail, by phone, or by standing on one's head and reciting the preamble

---

15. Restatement (Second) of Contracts § 41(2) (1979).

16. *Id.* § 41 cmt. d.

17. *Id.* § 41(3); *see also id.* cmt. e.

18. *Id.* § 41 cmt. e.

to the Constitution! Once the offeree accepts the offer in the manner and on the terms required by the offer, a contract is formed and both parties are bound.[19]

Offerors do not always prescribe a particular form of acceptance when they make an offer. Of course if they do, the offeree can only accept by complying with the requested manner of acceptance. If an offeror merely suggests a particular manner of acceptance, then "another method of acceptance is not precluded."[20] If the offeror does not specify the form of acceptance, then the offeree may accept "in any manner and by any medium reasonable in the circumstances."[21]

The concept of reasonableness is flexible and, in the absence of specific language in the offer, courts are reluctant to find a prescribed method or medium of acceptance.[22] The Code approach to acceptance is similar. Section 2–206(1)(a) states that an offer "shall be construed as inviting acceptance in any manner and by any medium reasonable in the circumstances"[23] unless otherwise indicated. Comment 1 explains that any reasonable manner of acceptance is available unless the offeror has made it clear that it would be unacceptable.[24] If it is not specified in the offer or there is doubt, an offeree may choose to accept either by promising or rendering the promised performance.[25] However, some offers may only be accepted by performance—the doing of the requested act—and not a return promise. This is a unilateral contract where the offer is limited to acceptance by performance only.

Acceptance by Promise

Generally, the offeror seeks a commitment from the offeree in the form of a return promise in advance of performance. Under

---

19. Restatement (Second) of Contracts § 50 (1979).

20. Restatement (Second) of Contracts § 60 (1979).

21. Restatement (Second) of Contracts § 30(2) (1979).

22. Perillo, *Calamari and Perillo on Contracts*, § 2.23.

23. U.C.C. § 2–206(1)(a) (2004).

24. *Id.* § 2–206 cmt. 1.

25. Restatement (Second) of Contracts § 32 (1979).

the objective theory, the offeree's subjective intent is irrelevant and what matters is whether the offeree's conduct gives the offeror reason to believe that the offer has been accepted. The language or conduct sufficient for acceptance by promise depends on the circumstances but there are three general requirements. First, the promise must be an expression of commitment. It cannot merely acknowledge receipt of the offer but must indicate an intent to be bound. Second, the commitment must be unconditional and not require any further action on the part of either the offeror or offeree. Finally, the return promise must not vary the terms of the offer. For this reason, a valid acceptance is said to be the "mirror image" of the offer. If the acceptance contains terms that are different from those of the offer, then it is not an acceptance but a rejection or counter-offer.

Notice of acceptance is generally required if the offeree accepts an offer by a return promise. The offeree must take appropriate steps to let the offeror know that the offer has been accepted. If an offer is accepted by "any medium reasonable" in the circumstances, it is effective when it is put out of the possession of the offeree.[26] It is sufficient for the offeree to exercise reasonable care to let the offeror know of acceptance, even if the offeror never actually learns of it.[27]

Acceptance by Performance

In forming a unilateral contract, the offeror is seeking an act, and not a promise to perform. Therefore, if the offer seeks acceptance by performance and not a return promise, then a contract can be formed only by performing the requested performance. The offer is not accepted until performance is

---

26. *See* Restatement (Second) of Contracts § 63 (1979).

27. Restatement (Second) of Contracts § 56 (1979) ("it is essential to an acceptance by promise either that the offeree exercise reasonable diligence to notify the offeror of acceptance or that the offeror receive the acceptance seasonably").

completed; moreover, there is no contract and legal liability does not attach until the offeree has fully performed.[28]

For example, suppose Carly says to Ashley, "I must have lost my watch. I will give you $100 if you find it." Carly does not want Ashley to promise to find her watch. Carly wants her watch. Ashley can accept this offer *only* by finding the watch and returning it to Carly. Carly is then required to pay Ashley the $100.

The offeree need not give notice of an intent to perform, but must render the performance for an effective acceptance.[29] However, if the offeree who accepts by performance has reason to know that the offeror will not learn of the acceptance within a reasonable time, then the offeree has a duty to exercise reasonable diligence to notify the offeror of acceptance.[30]

"The Mailbox Rule"

Generally, an acceptance takes effect when it is communicated to the offeror and it is not difficult to determine when this has occurred if the parties are in each other's presence or otherwise in instantaneous communication by phone or electronic means. However, when parties are not in instantaneous communication, i.e., corresponding by mail, there is a delay between the sending and receipt of acceptance. Often, it is critical to determine which of these two times constitutes the legally effective acceptance: is it the time of dispatch or that of receipt?

When the contract is formed by correspondence, the mechanics of assent follow "the mailbox rule" from the celebrated case of *Adams v. Lindsell*.[31] This rule holds that an acceptance is effective upon dispatch. The rationale is that the offeree should be able to

---

28. There is some "legal liability" in the sense that where an offer requires acceptance by performance only, an option contract is created when the offeree begins the invited performance. The offeror is no longer free to revoke the offer and must allow the offeree a reasonable time to complete performance. We will discuss this concept in greater detail when we consider option contracts and irrevocable offers.

29. Restatement (Second) of Contracts § 54(1) (1979).

30. *Id.* § 54(2).

31. 106 Eng. Rep. 250 (1818).

rely on the contract and be protected against a revocation by the offeror following dispatch of the acceptance. At this time, the offeror's power to revoke is terminated and the offeror is bound, even though the offeror does not know that the offer has been accepted. Of course the offeror, as master of the offer, can depart from the mailbox rule by providing otherwise in the offer.

Upon dispatch, the mailbox rule also binds the offeree to the acceptance and it now becomes too late for the offeree to either reject the offer or revoke the acceptance.[32] However, an acceptance is not effective on dispatch if it is not "made in a manner and by a medium invited"[33] by the offer. If the offeree chooses an acceptance not invited by the offer, the mailbox rule does not apply and the acceptance is not effective until receipt.

It is important to note that the mailbox rule applies only to *acceptances* by mail, not revocations. As stated earlier, a revocation is not effective until received by the offeree; hence, a revocation by mail or telegram is not effective until receipt. This means that if an offeror mails an offer and the next day mails a revocation, the offeror may still be bound if the offeree puts an acceptance in the mail after receiving the offer but before receiving the revocation. The mailbox rule binds the offeree as well: once the offeree has mailed an acceptance, it is too late for the offeree to then reject the offer or withdraw the acceptance.

So when does a rejection or counter-offer by mail or telegram terminate the power of acceptance? Restatement Second § 40 states that the power to accept ends on the offeror's receipt of the rejection so that the offeree is bound. This protects the offeror that has relied on an acceptance overtaking a rejection and has passed up another deal. On the other hand, assume that the offeree's acceptance does not overtake the rejection. In this case, it would be unfair to bind an offeror who has accepted another deal before the acceptance arrives. Under the Restatement Second, this purported

---

32. Farnsworth, *Contracts*, at § 3.24.

33. Restatement (Second) of Contracts § 63(a) (1979).

acceptance is not an acceptance but only a counter-offer unless the acceptance is received by the offeror before receiving the rejection or counter-offer.

A limitation to the mailbox rule is that it does not apply to communications that are relatively simultaneous such as phone conversations, telexes, and electronic email.[34] With most modern communications using one of these other means, the significance of the "mailbox rule" is probably greatest on law school exams!

Silence and Dominion as Acceptance

Since notice of acceptance is necessary to form a contract and bind the offeror, it makes sense that an offeree's silence does not ordinarily constitute acceptance. Consequently, the general rule is that mere silence is not acceptance. A promise of acceptance, however, may be inferred by an offeree's exercise of dominion over the offered property.[35] Another exception to the general rule that silence is not acceptance is when the offeree takes the benefit of offered services with the opportunity to reject them, knowing that they were made with the expectation of payment. The other cases where silence has been held to be acceptance are where the offeror has stated or given the offeree reason to believe that assent may be given by silence or inaction and the offeree in so doing intends to accept, and where previous dealings of the parties make it reasonable for the offeree to notify the offeror if she does not intend to accept.[36]

REVIEW OF OPTION CONTRACTS AND IRREVOCABLE OFFERS

R2d § 25, 37, 45, 62, 87

As discussed earlier, most offers are freely revocable. Even an offeror's promise not to revoke the offer or a statement that the

---

34. Farnsworth, *Contracts*, at § 3.24.

35. Restatement (Second) of Contracts § 69(2) (1979).

36. *Id.* § 69(1).

offer is not revocable is unenforceable unless it is supported by consideration. For example, suppose Spencer makes an offer to sell his car to Adam for a specified price and tells him that the offer is open for a week to let Adam think about it. Under the common law rule, Spencer can sell the car to someone else even though he promised to keep the offer open.

The result would be different, however, if Spencer had made the offer irrevocable by forming an option contract. Suppose that Adam had given Spencer $100 to hold the offer open for a period of one week. Now Spencer cannot sell the car to someone else but must wait one week until Adam decides what he wants to do. This is referred to as an option contract—it meets the requirements for the formation of a contract, i.e., there is mutual assent and consideration, and limits the offeror's power to revoke the offer during the time period of the option.[37]

Basically, there are two ways in which an offer can be made irrevocable when dealing with bilateral contracts. One way applies only to contracts for the sale of goods and is known as a "firm offer." This is discussed later in the section on Formation Under the UCC. Another way to make an offer irrevocable is with an option contract as we've just seen with Spencer and Adam and typically requires the giving of consideration.

Under the Restatement Second, the consideration require-ment is flexible in that even nominal consideration can be found sufficient to support a short-term option proposing an exchange on fair terms.[38] Moreover, the recital of a "purported consideration" may be sufficient as well as in section 87(1)(a) where an offer may be binding as an option contract if it is in writing, signed by the offeror, "recites a purported consideration" and "proposes an exchange on fair terms within a reasonable time[.]"[39] Even a relatively small amount may furnish consideration for the irrevo-

---

37. Restatement (Second) of Contracts § 25 (1979).

38. Restatement (Second) of Contracts § 87 cmt. b (1979).

39. Id. § 87(1)(a).

cability of an offer involving a transaction for a much greater sum.[40] Courts differ in the effect to be given to the situation where there is a recital of consideration but no actual payment is made. Some have held it to be of no effect since a false recital is not consideration. Others have found that it makes the offer irrevocable, either as an acknowledgment of the payment or as a promise to pay.[41] In answering an exam question on this issue, it would be appropriate to note the split in authority and identify the differing views.

Irrevocable offers also arise in the context of unilateral contracts when the offeree begins the performance invited by the offer. Where the offer invites acceptance by performance only and does not allow for a promissory acceptance, an option contract is created to protect the offeree when the offeree "tenders or begins the invited performance or tenders a beginning of it."[42] The offer becomes "irrevocable" and the offeree must be allowed a reasonable time to complete the performance. Naturally, the offeree must complete the required performance before the offeror's duty of performance under the contract arises.[43]

Typically, questions arise as to whether the offeree's actions constitute the "beginning of performance" or are mere "preparations." To avoid revocation, what is begun or tendered must be part of the actual performance. Although beginning preparations may be essential to accepting the offer and accomplishing the performance, they are not sufficient to make the offer irrevocable.[44] However, preparations to perform may constitute reliance, thus making the offeror's promise binding under Restatement § 87(2). Here, an offer may become binding as an option contract where there has been justified reliance under the principle of promissory estoppel.[45]

---

40. *Id.* § 87 cmt. b.

41. *See* Farnsworth, *Contracts*, § 3.23 n. 13 and 14.

42. Restatement (Second) of Contracts § 45(1) (1979).

43. *Id.* § 45(2).

44. *Id.* § 45 cmt f.

45. Restatement (Second) of Contracts § 87(2).

A reliance theory is also applied in connection with bids on construction contracts to make the subcontractor's bid an option contract to the extent necessary to avoid injustice.[46] Unless the parties have agreed otherwise, where a subcontractor makes a bid to the general contractor, the subcontractor's offer is irrevocable until the general contractor has had a reasonable opportunity to notify the subcontractor of the award and accept the subcontractor's offer.[47]

Finally, unless the offer provides otherwise, acceptance of an option contract is not effective until it is received by the offeror.[48]

Consequences Of Irrevocability

There are several effects of irrevocability. As already discussed, if the offer is irrevocable, then a purported revocation by the offeror does not terminate the offeree's power of acceptance. The offeree may still accept and if the offeror refuses to perform, then the offeree may bring suit for breach. Moreover, the offeree's power of acceptance under an option contract is not terminated by rejection, revocation, or death or incapacity of the offeror or offeree.[49] While the modern view is that the rejection should not terminate an irrevocable offer, if the offeror has detrimentally relied on the rejection, then the offeree should be estopped from later accepting the offer.[50]

REVIEW OF FORMATION UNDER THE UCC

UCC 1-103, 2-204, 2-205, 2-206, 2-207

The UCC follows a very liberal policy for formation of a contract and departs from the common law in several respects,

---

46. *See id.* (this provision generalizes from the case of *Drennan v. Star Paving Co.*, 333 P.2d 757 (Cal. 1958)).

47. *Id.* § 87 illustration 6.

48. Restatement (Second) of Contracts § 63(b).

49. Restatement (Second) of Contracts § 37 (1979); *see also,* Restatement (Second) of Contracts § 48 cmt. d (1979).

50. *Id.* § 37 illustration 2.

beginning with allowing parties to form a contract through conduct and not relying solely on the mechanics of offer and acceptance. The emphasis is on the existence of a contract and not the mechanics or technicalities of the formation process. Under the Code, a contract for sale may be found even though the precise moment of its making is undetermined and it may be formed in any manner sufficient to show agreement.[51] Since the Code is practically silent with respect to formation, issues arising in this context are supplemented by the principles of the common law regarding offer and acceptance.[52]

The Code also allows for contract formation when one or more terms are left open. While the common law requires that the terms of an offer be certain and definite to be capable of acceptance, under the UCC, an agreement may be found even if terms are missing. Section 2–204(3) states, "Even though one or more terms are left open a contract for sale does not fail for indefiniteness if the parties have intended to make a contract and there is a reasonably certain basis for giving an appropriate remedy."[53] If the parties intend to make an agreement, it will not fail for indefiniteness if terms are missing. Sales contracts must contain a quantity term whereas almost all other terms can be supplied by the UCC's "gap filler" provisions. There are gap filler provisions for price, delivery, and payment terms.

---

51. *See* U.C.C. §§ 2–204(1)—(2) (2004). U.C.C. § 2–206 is the other Code provision which addresses formation and deals with the manner and medium of acceptance. There are minor changes to the provisions of §§ 2–204 and 2–206 in the 2003 revision to the Code. The main change to § 2–204 is the recognition of contract formation through the interaction of electronic agents. An electronic agent is defined in revised § 2–103(g) as "a computer program or an electronic or other automated means used independently to initiate an action or respond to electronic records or performances in whole or in part, without review or action by an individual." The text of § 2–206 (1) and (2) are unchanged in the 2003 revision but there is a new subsection, 2–206(3), which imports its text from existing § 2–207(1). Section 2–206(3) provides that "[a] definite and seasonable expression of acceptance in a record operates as an acceptance even if it contains terms additional to or different from the offer."

52. *See* U.C.C. § 1–103 (2004). This is section 1–103(b) in the 2003 revision.

53. U.C.C. § 2–204(3).

"Firm Offers"

Under the Code, section 2–205[54] limits the offeror's power to revoke thereby making the offer irrevocable. However, this section only applies if (1) there has actually been an offer (2) it has been made by a merchant (3) to buy or sell goods (4) which gives assurances that it will be held open (4) in a signed writing (5) which is for the time stated, or for a reasonable time if no time is stated, up to a maximum of three months.

"Battle of the Forms"

The more significant departure between the common law and the UCC occurs in situations where the acceptance varies from the offer. Under the common law, an acceptance that varies from the terms of the offer is a rejection and a counter-offer and no contract is formed. Under UCC 2–207,[55] however, a contract may be formed even if the acceptance has different or additional terms than the offer. The usual issue in section 2–207 cases is not whether a contract was formed but what the terms are after the parties exchange documents, perform, or start to perform and a dispute arises.

There are numerous cases with which section 2–207 must deal—far too many for us to review here. Instead, I will describe the most typical situations you can expect to find on a law school exam and take you through a basic analysis.

For example, the phrase "battle of the forms" refers to the typical scenario in which a purchaser, perhaps a retailer, orders a

---

54. U.C.C. § 2–205 (2004). The 2003 revision of Article 2 makes no significant changes to this section except for a few minor language changes and the substitution of the word "record" for "writing."

55. U.C.C. § 2–207 has undergone substantial changes in the 2003 revisions to the Code—in fact, far too extensive to discuss in a footnote. Consequently, I strongly recommend that you read the revised version for yourself should you require a working knowledge of the revisions for your contracts class. For our purposes, it is important to note the following: first, that the 2003 revision to Article 2 has not been enacted in any state at this time so that the current version of 2–207 is still the law; and, second, the revisions remove the formation issue and limit the section to the question of what to do with additional or different terms. The discussion and examples in this chapter are limited to the current version of 2–207.

quantity of goods from a supplier at a stated price and for delivery by or at a specified time. Usually, the order takes place orally with the seller's representative, either in person or over the phone, and the seller follows up by sending a written confirmation to the buyer. Here is where the problem begins: the confirmation reflects the main items of the exchange, i.e., the price and quantity, but adds some additional information, maybe delivery or payment terms, that were not mentioned in the earlier discussion. Or, on the other hand, the purchaser may send a printed order form to the seller and, in return, receive the seller's own acknowledgment form. Once again, the forms agree as to the basics of the transaction but each includes a number of paragraphs, usually in small print on the back, written by attorneys and included to protect the interests of their respective parties. In most cases, the parties do not bother to read the boiler-plate material and simply file the papers. Still, the provisions become part of the parties' agreement.

Frequently, this situation presents no problem and the deal goes forward. But sometimes the parties fall into dispute before performance is even due. More often, one or both will perform or begin to perform and then a dispute arises. Now the parties go back to review the original papers and find that their forms differ. Is there a contract? If so, what are its terms?

Section 2–207 is supposed to provide the solution to this problem. Commentary on this section is voluminous and much of it critical, finding the provision confusing and poorly drafted. For example, subsection (2) mentions only "additional" terms. But suppose the seller's confirmation contains a "different" term, one that directly conflicts with a term in the buyer's offer? Some commentators interpret section 2–207(1) to resolve this conflict in favor of the purchaser-offeror and the "different" term is rejected.

Other commentators apply the so-called "knockout" rule under which conflicting terms in the offer and acceptance simply knock each other out and do not become part of the contract. However, the "knockout" rule has been criticized and courts have been urged not to adopt it because it lacks support both in the statutory scheme and under general contract principles.[56] While it is beyond the scope of this book to delve deeply into legal theory, it is nonetheless critical to your understanding of basic formation doctrine to be able to evaluate arguments raised with respect to the "knockout" rule. Let's consider one commentator's analysis which led him to conclude that "courts adopting the knockout rule in effect are adopting a rule that flies in the face of a basic contract concept—that the offeror is the master of the offer—and the express language of subsection (1)."[57] Professor Kwestel begins his discussion with a hypothetical which sets up a classic "battle of the forms" dispute:

> B sends S a written offer to purchase 10 computers, Model No. 2100, at a cost of $5,000 for a computer. The offer states: "you warrant that your Model No. 2100 computers have the same features and capabilities as your competitor's Model AB700." The warranty is critical because Model 2100 was worth only $2,000 to B without the warranty. S sends a seasonable written acknowledgement that contains a definite expression of acceptance but adds: "S makes no express warranty and disclaims and excludes any express warranty."[58]

If the "knockout" rule is applied to this problem, then the offeree's acceptance is an acceptance only of the terms on which the documents exchanged between B and S agree. As a result, the contract terms would not include the express warranty in B's offer that the Model No. 2100 have the same features and capabilities as the competitor Model AB700 even though the warranty term is critical since the Model 2100 was worth only $2,000 to B without the warranty.

Professor Kwestel turns to the express language of the statute itself for guidance. Accordingly, he begins with subsection (1) of 2–207 which provides that "a definite and seasonable expression of

56. Sidney Kwestel, *Unrevised Section 2–207—Different Terms Revisited*, 67 No. 4 U.C.C. Bulletin 1 (May 2009).

57. *Id.*

58. *Id.*

acceptance . . . operates as an acceptance" even though it states different terms from those "offered or agreed upon[.]" [59]Since the UCC does not define acceptance, it is appropriate to turn to the common law. Applying the law, Professor Kwestel reasons that "the offeree's acceptance is an expression of assent to the terms offered—and not to the terms of the offer minus the different terms. Nothing in contract law permits an offeree to selectively accept the terms of the offer and nothing in section 2–207 or the comments indicates that the UCC was so radically departing from the effect of an acceptance, namely that it constitutes an assent to the terms offered."[60]

While there is more to the analysis, it is important for you to appreciate Professor Kwestel's argument that while subsection (1) changes the common law's mirror image rule, it does not dispense with the rule that the offeror is master of the offer.[61] Accordingly, subsection (1) provides the offeree with two choices: the offeree can accept the terms offered or if he does not want to assent to the terms offered unless the additional or different terms contained in his acceptance become part of the deal, then he can choose to expressly make his acceptance conditional on the offeree's assent to the additional or different terms. According to Professor Kwestel, there is no third choice—"to accept the terms of the offer with which the offeree agrees and to simultaneously reject the terms in that offer with which he differs."[62] This option would lead to the preposterous result where the offeror might be forced into a contract on terms different from those offered. Instead, the plain language of subsection (1) and common law doctrine assures that the offeror will not be forced into a contract on terms different from those offered.[63]

Despite the issues surrounding section 2–207, you will be able to work your way through the statute for the purposes of your

---

59. U.C.C. § 2–207(1) (2004).

60. Kwestel, *Unrevised Section 2–207— Different Terms Revisited.*

61. *Id.*

62. *Id.*

63. *Id.*

Contracts class. Working through a Code provision means beginning at the top and proceeding step by step:

1. UCC 2–207(1): varies the "mirror-image" rule by treating the seller's confirmation as an acceptance of the offer rather than a counter-offer even though it contains terms that are "additional to or different from" those that appear in the buyer's order form (or that were agreed to orally).
    This means that unless the seller expressly conditions its acceptance on the buyer's assent to the additional or different terms, there is a "contract" and it contains, at the least, all the terms offered.

    There is one critical point to be made before continuing: you must first pass the hurdle of whether there was a "definite and seasonable expression of acceptance." Despite the Code's liberal policy of contract formation, if the second form or document does not agree on the "dickered terms" or the essential material terms, then it does not constitute an "expression of acceptance" and the inquiry ends here.

2. UCC 2–207(2): this section addresses the question of what to do with the additional terms. There are two possibilities. First, the additional terms are considered mere "proposals for addition" to the contract and are excluded (unless accepted). Second, if the parties are merchants, such terms become part of the contract unless: (1) the offer expressly limited acceptance to the terms of the offer; (2) they materially altered it; or (3) notification of objection was already given or given within a reasonable time after notification.

    Note: There is a problem with what to do with the "different" terms since subsection (2) speaks only of "additional" terms. Courts vary in their treatment of different terms in the acceptance, formulating three approaches: one approach treats different terms the same as additional terms and applies subsection (2) to different terms; a second approach simply disregards different terms contained in the acceptance since they are not mentioned in subsection (2) and therefore are not to be construed as proposals that can become part of the contract; and a third approach applies the "knockout rule" where the conflicting terms on the parties' offer and acceptance "knock each other out" and neither term becomes part of the contract.[64] What is left are the terms on which the two writings do not conflict, presumably the dickered terms among them.

3. UCC 2–207(3): this section is applicable when the parties' writings do not establish a contract but one is evidenced by their conduct. Here, the goods may have been shipped, accepted, and paid for before a dispute arises and there is no question that a contract had been formed. In such cases, the terms of the contract consist of "those terms on which the writings of the parties agree" together with the UCC's "supplementary terms." The additional or different terms fall by the wayside.

Formation Issues in the Internet Age

A discussion of contract formation would be incomplete without mentioning the formation issues involved in internet transactions. The scenario is familiar: you order and pay for something over the phone or by computer. Then the item arrives together with lots of papers in the box or online instructions when the accompanying software is loaded—instruction manuals and documents with various notices, setting forth terms and conditions, warranty disclaimers, and limitations on available remedies. The additional terms which are included in the product's packaging are referred to as "shrinkwrap" agreements and the ones you encounter when loading a program's software on your computer are known as "clickwrap" agreements.

Usually, you don't bother reading this stuff and maybe even throw it all away with the rest of the packaging. But serious questions can and do arise: do the new terms on or in the seller's packaging become part of the contract?

There are several formation questions which are likely to arise in internet transactions and you should be aware of them. The first

---

64. Kwestel, *Unrevised Section 2–207— Different Terms Revisited.*

is whether a valid contract was concluded between computers involving electronic signatures and records; second, if a valid contract was formed by electronic commerce, when was it formed; and third, if a contract was formed, what are its terms? The last two questions clearly implicate section 2–207 and it should come as no surprise, therefore, that this section has figured prominently in court decisions. While courts appear to be split as to whether terms received with a product become part of the parties' agreement,[65] the usual analysis is to apply section 2–207 in resolving the dispute.[66]

OFFER AND ACCEPTANCE CHECKLIST

Here is a checklist for analyzing problems presenting questions regarding the agreement process. The first question you must always ask when approaching a contracts problem is whether the transaction involves the sale of goods or the common law. If the transaction involves the sale of goods, then Article 2 and the Code's provisions apply. Proceed to Section II. If the common law controls, proceed with Section I.

I. Common Law

A. **Offer**—has the offeror made an offer? Has a manifestation of willingness to enter a bargain been made so as to justify the offeree in understanding that her assent to the bargain is invited and, if

---

65. *Klocek v. Gateway, Inc.*, 104 F. Supp. 2d 1332 (D. Kan. 2000). Compare *Step-Saver Data Systems, Inc. v. Wyse Technology*, 939 F.2d 91 (3d Cir. 1991) (printed terms on computer software package not part of the parties' agreement); *Hill v. Gateway 2000, Inc.*, 105 F.3d 1147 (7th Cir. 1997), cert., denied, 522 U.S. 808 (1997) (arbitration clause shipped with a computer binding on buyer); and *ProCD, Inc. v. Zeidenberg*, 86 F.3d 1447 (7th Cir. 1996) (shrinkwrap license contained inside a product box binding on buyer).

66. While the Seventh Circuit in *Hill v. Gateway 2000, Inc.*, found § 2–207 inapplicable because there was only one written form involved and not a "battle of the forms" between the two parties, this reasoning has been criticized by legal scholars. See Jean R. Sternlight, *Gateway Widens Doorway to Imposing Unfair Binding Arbitration on Consumers*, 71 Fla. B. J. 8, 10 (1997) (the outcome in *Gateway* is questionable on federal statutory, common law and constitutional grounds and as a matter of contract law).

given, would conclude it? To determine whether an offer capable of acceptance has been made, consider the following:

1. **Intent**—was there intent to make an offer? The words or conduct used in the proposal must be words of offer and not just words of preliminary negotiation.

   a. **Language**—what words were used? Were they words of promise and commitment or invitations to negotiate? "I bid" suggests an offer whereas "are you interested?" suggests preliminary negotiations.

   b. **Surrounding Circumstances**—what were the surrounding circumstances? Were the parties intoxicated or at a party? Words may sound like an offer but clearly be made in jest. Surrounding circumstances may alter the normal meaning of words.

   c. **Advertisements to the Public**—to whom was the offer made? Proposals made to the public or a large group of persons (such as advertisements, circulars, price quotations) are more likely to be considered invitations to make an offer.

2. **Definite and Certain Terms**—are the terms sufficiently clear and definite so that a court could determine what the parties intended and fix damages in the event of breach?

   a. **Yes.** If such significant terms as the parties to the contract, the subject matter of the contract, the time for performance, and the price to be paid are identified, then it is more likely to be an offer.

   b. **No.** If essential terms are missing or vague, then the offer may fail for indefiniteness unless it can be cured. Even if some terms have been left open, it may still be possible to meet the requirement for definiteness by the time for performance arrives. Ask the following:

      i. **Indefinite Term Cured**—can the indefinite term be cured by the conduct of the parties through full or part performance? R2d § 34.

      ii. **Missing Term Implied**—can the missing term(s) be implied from the usages of trade to which the parties are subject, by a prior course of dealing between the parties, or by a course of performance between them after the agreement?

    iii. **Gap Filler**—can the missing term be cured by the court with a "gap filler"?

3. Communicated—has the offer been communicated to one capable of acceptance?

    a. **Yes.** If so, then the power of acceptance has been created in the offeree.

    b. **No.** If not, then there is no power of acceptance.

B. Acceptance—has there been a valid acceptance? Has the offeree manifested assent to the offer? In order for a contract to be formed, there must be an acceptance of the offer on the same terms and in the manner requested or authorized by the offeror. To determine whether there has been a valid acceptance, consider the following:

1. Who is Accepting the Offer— is the proper party accepting the offer? Only the party with the "power of acceptance" can accept the offer. Ask the following:

    a. **Invited to Accept?** Only the party to whom the offer is made has the power of acceptance. A purported acceptance by one not invited by the offeror is not an acceptance but may itself amount to an offer.

    b. **Knowledge of the Offer?** Only one with knowledge of the offer and who acts with that knowledge has the power to accept. This is the case in reward claims: one cannot receive the reward unless she knew of the offer of reward and acted with intent to accept it.

2. Manner of Acceptance—has the offeree accepted the offer in the manner required by the offer?

    a. **Acceptance by Promise?** Does the offer invite acceptance by a return promise? If so, then ask if the following have been met to determine whether there has been a valid acceptance by a promise:

        i. **Was there an Expression of Commitment?** The offeree must express an unequivocal intent to be bound.

ii. **Was it Unconditional?** The offeree's expression of assent cannot be conditional on some further act by either party.

iii. **Was it a "mirror-image" of the Offer?** The acceptance must be on the same terms as proposed in the offer and cannot vary them. If the terms of the acceptance vary from the terms of the offer, then it is a counter-offer.

b. **Acceptance by Performance?** Does the offer invite acceptance by performance and no promise is invited?

     i. **Yes.** If so, then the offeree can accept only by performing the act the promisor is seeking and cannot accept by promising the performance. Here, the act requested and performed as consideration for the offeror's promise also constitutes acceptance.

     ii. **No.** If the manner of acceptance is not specified, then the offeree can choose whether to accept by promise or by performance.

c. **By Silence?** Has the offeree accepted by virtue of her silence?

     i. **No.** The general rule is that silence is not acceptance.

     ii. **Yes**, silence can act as acceptance but in a very limited set of circumstances. R2d § 69. Ask the following:

- Has the offeree taken the benefit of services when she has had a reasonable opportunity to reject them and reason to know that payment was expected and has not done so? If so, then there is an acceptance.

- Has the offeror stated or given the offeree reason to understand that assent may be manifested by silence or inaction and the offeree in remaining silent or inactive intends to accept? If so, then there is an acceptance.

- Have there been prior dealings between the parties such that it would be reasonable for the offeree to notify the offeror if she did not intend to accept? If so, then there is an acceptance.

- Has the offeree exercised dominion over the goods or property by acting in a way that inconsistent with the offeror's ownership? If so, then there is an acceptance.

d. **Manner Not Specified?** If the offer does not specify the mode of acceptance, then acceptance may be given "in any manner and by any medium reasonable in the circumstances." R2d § 30(2).

3. **Notice of Acceptance—** is the offeree required to give notice of acceptance to the offeror?

    a. **Acceptance by Promise?** Does the offer invite acceptance by promise?

        i. **Yes.** Unless the offer indicates otherwise, it is essential to an acceptance by promise either that the offeree "exercise reasonable diligence to notify the offeror that the offer has been accepted or that the offeror receives the acceptance seasonally." R2d § 56.

        ii. **No.** If not, then proceed to the next question.

    b. **Acceptance by Performance?** Does the offer invite acceptance by performance? If the offer invites acceptance by providing a performance, then no notification is necessary to make it effective unless one of the following is applicable. Ask:

        i. Does the offer request a notification? If so, notification is necessary for a valid acceptance. R2d § 54(1).

        ii. Does the offeree have reason to know that the offeror will not learn of the acceptance with "reasonable promptness and certainty" without notice? If so, the offeror's duty will be discharged unless: R2d § 54(2).

- The offeree exercises reasonable diligence to notify the offeror, or

- The offeror learns of the performance within a reasonable time, or

- The offer indicates that notification of acceptance is not required.

4. **When Acceptance is Effective**—when does acceptance take effect? This question is closely related to the method of acceptance but sufficiently separate to require its own consideration. To determine the effective date of acceptance, consider the following:

   a. **Instantaneous Communication**—were the parties in direct communication with each other at the time by phone, in person, or communicating by electronic means? If so, then acceptance occurs as soon as it is manifested.

   b. **Invited by the Offer**—was the acceptance made in a manner and by a medium invited by the offer? If so, it is effective as soon as it is put out of the offeree's possession, "without regard to whether it ever reaches the offeror." This is referred to as the "mailbox rule" where acceptance is effective upon dispatch if the letter was properly stamped and addressed. If properly dispatched, it is effective, even if it was received after the offer terminated or was never received by the offeror. R2d § 63.

   c. **Where Offeree sends both an Acceptance and Rejection**—has the offeree mailed a rejection and then changed her mind and mailed an acceptance or vice versa? Since a rejection terminates the power of acceptance, you must consider the question in terms of when a rejection becomes effective:

      i. **Rejection sent before Acceptance**? A rejection does not terminate the offeree's power of acceptance until it is received, but any acceptance dispatched by the offeree after she has dispatched the rejection is not effective unless the acceptance is received by the offeror before she receives the rejection. R2d § 40.

      ii. **Acceptance sent before Rejection**? The contract is binding as soon as the acceptance is dispatched and the subsequently dispatched revocation of acceptance does not undo the acceptance, whether it is received by the offeror before or after her receipt of the acceptance.

d. **Acceptance of Option Contract**—an acceptance of an option is effective upon receipt by the offeror, not upon dispatch. R2d § 63(b).

5. **Termination of the Power of Acceptance**—does the offeree have the power of acceptance? For an acceptance to be valid, it must be made while the power of acceptance is still in effect. Does the offeree still have the power of acceptance or has the offer terminated?

    a. **Lapse of Time**—has the offer lapsed either because the time specified in the offer for acceptance has passed or, if no time was specified, then a reasonable time has passed? Ask:

        i. **Was the Offer sent by Mail?** If so, then it is seasonably accepted if an acceptance is mailed at any time before midnight on the day on which the offer is received. R2d § 41(3).

        ii. **Was the Offer made during Direct Negotiations?** Where the parties bargain face-to-face or over the telephone, the time for acceptance ends with the conversation unless a contrary intention is indicated. R2d § 41 cmt. d.

    b. **Rejection**—has the offeree failed to accept the offer before it lapsed or has she communicated to the offeror that she does not intend to accept?

        i. **Yes.** If so, the power of acceptance is terminated and the offer can no longer be accepted.

        ii. **No.** If not, then the offeree may still accept unless the power of acceptance has terminated in another way. Proceed to the next question.

    c. **Counter-offer**—has the offeree declined the contract on the terms proposed in the offer and suggested different terms?

        i. **Yes.** If so, then the offeree's power of acceptance is terminated. A valid acceptance must be the "mirror-image" of the offer. However, is it possible it was not a counter-offer but a **mere inquiry**? A mere inquiry about the possibility of different terms or a comment about the terms is not ordinarily a counter-offer.

ii. **No.** If not, then the offeree still has the power of acceptance unless it has terminated in another way. Proceed to the next question.

d. **Death or Mental Disability**—has the offeror or offeree died or become mentally incapacitated before the offer has been accepted? R2d § 48.

   i. **Yes.** If so, then the power of acceptance is terminated unless it is an option contract. Notice of the offeror's death is not necessary to terminate the offeree's power of acceptance. R2d § 48 cmt. a.

  ii. **No.** If not, then the offeror has the power of acceptance unless it was terminated in another way.

e. **Revocation**—has the offeror revoked the offer? The offeror may revoke the offer at any time before acceptance, even if the offer says it will remain open, unless it is an option contract or a "firm offer" (if so, proceed to Part B.6.a. and Section II, Part A.2., respectively). If the offeror indicates an intent not to make the proposed contract, then it may be a revocation even without the words "I revoke." However, the revocation is not effective until it is received by the offeree. Ask:

   i. **Was the Revocation Received?**

     • **Yes.** If so, then the offeree's power of acceptance is terminated.

     • **No.** If not, then it is not effective unless it was an indirect revocation. Proceed to the next question.

  ii. **Was it an Indirect Revocation?** Has the offeror behaved in a way inconsistent with an intent to enter the contract and the offeree has acquired reliable information to that effect?

     • **Yes.** If so, there was a revocation and the offeree cannot accept.

     • **No.** If it was a mere rumor or heard from an unreliable source, then the power of acceptance is not terminated.

      iii. **Was it the Revocation of a General Offer?** Was it the revocation of an offer made by a newspaper or advertisement? If so, then the revocation should be made in the same manner in which the offer was made so as to give it equal publicity.

6. **Option Contracts and Irrevocable Offers**—was there a promise to keep an offer open for a stated period of time?

    a. **Was it an Irrevocable Offer?** While the general rule is that offers are freely revocable, there are certain conditions, which if met, make the offer irrevocable. Ask the following:

      i. **Consideration**—did the offeree give consideration in exchange for the promise to keep the offer open?

        • **Yes.** If so, then the offer is irrevocable. It may also be said that an option contract was formed.

        • **No.** If not, an option might be binding even without consideration. Proceed to the next question.

      ii. **Statute**—is there a state statute which permits the creation of irrevocable offers without consideration? For the UCC's "firm offer," proceed to Section II, Part A.2.

        • **Yes.** If so, as in the case of New York under N.Y.Gen.Obl.Law § 5–1109, then the offer is irrevocable without consideration if it is made in a writing signed by the offeror which states that it is irrevocable.

        • **No.** If not, then proceed to the next question.

      iii. **Restatement (Second) of Contracts**—does the jurisdiction follow the Restatement view which finds a valid option if the promise is in a writing signed by the offeror, recites a purported consideration, and proposes a fair exchange within a reasonable time? R2d § 87(1)(a).

        • **Yes.** If so, then the offer is binding as an option

contract. Even nominal consideration will be sufficient to support a short-time option proposing a fair exchange.

— **Recital and no Consideration?** Was there a recital of consideration and no payment was actually made? Courts differ in the effect given to a recital without actual payment. Some have held the recital to have no effect while others have found that the recital makes the offer irrevocable, either as a promise to pay or an acknowledgment of payment.[67]

— **Gross Disparity between Payment and Value of Option?** If so, then this may indicate it was a mere formality, pretense, or sham and will not constitute consideration. R2d § 87 cmt. b.

- **No.** If not, an option contract was not formed in this manner. However, an option might be formed under the rule in the next question.

iv. **Offer for a Unilateral Contract**—has the offeree partially performed the requested performance? Ask the following:

- **Common law?** Does the jurisdiction follow the traditional common law view? If so, then the offer may be revoked at any time before performance of the requested act has been completed.

- **Restatement (Second)?** Does the jurisdiction follow the Restatement view? If so, then once the offeree begins to perform the requested act, the offer becomes irrevocable. The Restatement uses the term "option contract" but the meaning is the same as making the offer irrevocable. However, the offeree must begin the actual performance and not make mere preparations to perform. The offeror's own duty to perform is conditional on the offeree's completing performance as specified in the offer.

---

67. Farnsworth, *Contracts*, at § 3.23.

- **Reliance that is not Part Performance?** Did the offeror make an offer which she should reasonably expect to induce reliance on the part of the offeree before acceptance and which did induce such reliance? If so, then it is binding as an option contract to the extent necessary to avoid injustice. R2d § 87(2).

v. **Bid on Construction Contract**—did a subcontractor submit a bid to a general contractor in connection with a bid on a construction contract?

- **No.** If not, the inquiry ends here.

- **Yes.** If so, is the subcontractor's bid revocable? Unless the parties have agreed otherwise, the subcontractor's offer is irrevocable until the general contractor has had a reasonable opportunity to notify the subcontractor of the award and accept the offer. This is based on a reliance theory. R2d § 87(2) illus.6.

b. **Was an Irrevocable Offer Accepted?** An acceptance under an option contract is not effective until received by the offeror. R2d § 63(b).

c. **Was an Irrevocable Offer Terminated?**

i. **Lapse of Time**—has the offer lapsed?

- **Yes.** If so, the irrevocable offer has terminated.

- **No.** If not, then the irrevocable offer has not terminated unless it has terminated in another way. Proceed to the next question.

ii. **Revocation**—has the offer been revoked? If the offer is irrevocable, then even a purported revocation by the offeror has no effect on the offeree's power of acceptance.

iii. **Death or Incapacity**—has the offeror died or become incapacited? The option survives the death or incapacity of the offeror.

iv. **Rejection or Counter-offer**—has there been a rejection or counter-offer? The power of acceptance under an option contract is not terminated by rejection or counter-offer.

II. Sale of Goods

A. **"Bargain of the parties in fact"**—is there an agreement between the parties? Have the parties, as a practical matter, reached sufficient agreement for contract liability to arise?

1. **Agreement**—has there been an offer and acceptance? A contract for the sale of goods may be made in any manner sufficient to show agreement. Consider the following:

   a. **Conduct**—does the conduct of both parties recognize the existence of a contract? UCC 2–204(1).

      i. **Yes.** If so, then there is a contract even if the moment of its making is undetermined.

      ii. **No.** If not, the parties may not have intended a contract and none will have been created.

   b. **Indefiniteness**—were one or more terms left open? A contract for the sale of goods does not fail for indefiniteness if the parties have intended to make a contract and there is a reasonably certain basis for giving an appropriate remedy. UCC 2–204(3).

   c. **Acceptance**—has the offeror specified a method of acceptance?

      i. **Yes.** If so, then the offer may be accepted only in the manner invited by the offer.

      ii. **No.** If not, then the offeror may accept "in any manner and by any medium reasonable in the circumstances." UCC 2–206(1)(a).

   d. **Acceptance by Promise to Ship or Shipment**—was an order or other offer to buy goods for prompt or current shipment accepted either by a prompt promise to ship or by the prompt or current shipment of conforming goods?

      i. **Yes.** If so, it was an acceptance.

      ii. **No.** It was a shipment of non-conforming goods. This is not an acceptance if the shipment of non-conforming goods is an accommodation to the offeror as allowed under UCC 2–206(1)(b). Ask: did the seller seasonably notify the buyer that the shipment of non-conforming goods was offered only as an accommodation to the buyer and not an acceptance?

- **Yes.** If so, then the seller's shipment of non-conforming goods is not an acceptance.

- **No.** If not, then the seller's non-conforming shipment is an acceptance and a breach of contract.

2. **"Firm Offer"**—did a merchant offer to buy or sell goods in a signed writing which promised to hold the offer open? UCC 2–205.

   a. **Yes.** If so, then the offer is not revocable for lack of consideration during the time stated or if no time is stated for not more than three months.

   b. **No.** If not, then the offer is revocable any time before acceptance unless it is made irrevocable under one of the other exceptions. See Section I Part B.6.a.

3. **"Battle of the Forms"**—have one or both parties used oral or written communications in the process of forming a contract where the writings exchanged may have been preprinted order and confirmation forms containing standard, boilerplate terms? If so, then a conflict between them is possible since such standard terms are usually designed to protect the interests of that party. In such cases, the provisions of UCC 2–207 may be implicated. Ask the following:

   a. **Acceptance**—is the response to the offer "a definite and seasonable expression of acceptance" or "a written confirmation" of a prior oral agreement?

      i. **Yes.** If so, proceed to Part A.3.b.

      ii. **No.** If not, then no contract has been formed by the writings of the parties. Proceed to Part A.3.c. to determine whether the conduct of the parties recognizes the existence of a contract.

   b. **Terms in Acceptance**—does the acceptance/confirmation state terms "additional to or different from" the offer?

i. **Yes.** If so, then ask: is acceptance of the offer "expressly conditional" on the offeror's assent to the additional or different terms?

- **Yes.** If so, then ask, did the offeror expressly assent?

  — **Yes.** If so, a contract has been formed. The contract terms are those that are agreed upon.

  — **No.** If not, then no contract has been formed by the writings of the parties. Proceed to Part A.3.c. to determine whether the conduct of the parties recognizes the existence of a contract.

- **No.** If the response is a definite and seasonable expression of acceptance and it is not expressly conditional on assent to new terms, it is an acceptance even though it states terms different from or additional to the those in the offer. There is a contract and the next question is to determine its terms. Ask: **are both parties merchants**?

  — **Yes.** If so, then the agreed upon terms are included and additional[68] terms become part of the contract as well *unless*:

    (a) The offer was expressly limited to its terms;

    (b) The additional term(s) materially alters the contract; *or*

    (c) The offeror has already given notice of objection to the additional term(s) or it is

---

68. Since subsection (2) refers only to "additional "terms," this checklist does so as well. However, if you are asked to deal with "different terms," then you should analyze the facts following the three approaches that courts follow with respect to different terms: one approach treats different terms the same as additional terms and applies subsection (2) to different terms; a second approach disregards different terms in the acceptance since they are not mentioned in subsection (2) and are not to be construed as proposals that can become part of the contract; and a third approach applies the "knockout rule" where the conflicting terms on the parties' offer and acceptance "knock each other out" and neither term becomes part of the contract.

given within a reasonable time after notice is received. UCC 2–207(2).

— **No.** If not, then the agreed upon terms are included and additional terms are merely proposals for addition to the contract.

ii. **No.** If not, then there is a contract and it consists of the agreed upon terms.

c. **Conduct**—does the conduct of the parties "recognize the existence of a contract"? Has there been a tender and acceptance of performance?

i. **Yes.** If so, a contract has been formed by the parties' conduct. Its terms are those upon which the parties' writings agree and the UCC's "supplementary terms." Missing terms may be supplied by an applicable trade usage or course of dealing or performance between the parties.

ii. **No.** If not, then no contract has been formed.

ILLUSTRATIVE PROBLEMS

■ PROBLEM 2.1 ■

Rob Coe, owner of an athletic-wear company, is a well-known sports enthusiast and world traveler. After returning from a prolonged exploration of the Australian outback, he realized that Americans were getting "soft." He decided to design a new line of sportswear to help Americans recapture their spirit and introduce them at the Coe Competitions, a series of endurance-type athletic events. Mr. Coe told Kim, his copywriter, that she should start writing the copy for the new athletic clothes. Then he added, "You know, Kim, there is nothing like exercise to keep in shape. I bet if you started to work out now, you could be ready for the Competitions. In fact, I will pay you a bonus of $1000 if you get in shape for the Coe Competitions."

Kim knew that Mr. Coe was serious about his commitment to physical fitness. It was also true that she had put on a few pounds recently. This was just the incentive she needed. She did not say a word to Mr. Coe or any of her co-workers but went out and bought a pair of sneakers and several exercise outfits. Every morning she went for a two-mile walk with her friend Carly and every night she exercised in the gym. As part of her new health regime, she drank only high energy, low-fat shakes for lunch and eliminated all muffins from her diet. After six weeks, Kim lost 15 pounds and several inches. She was in the best shape she had been in since high school and ready to compete in the Coe Competitions.

Kim went to see Mr. Coe to collect her bonus. Instead of giving her $1000, Mr. Coe laughed and said: "The only competition you are in shape for is the sale rack at the closest department store! Besides, I was only kidding." Kim is furious and wants to bring suit to collect the $1000. What is the likelihood of her success?

Analysis

Whether Kim can recover the $1000 depends on whether Coe made Kim an offer capable of acceptance. An offer is a proposal by one party to the other, manifesting a willingness to enter into a bargain and made in such a way by words or conduct that the other person is justified in believing that her assent to that bargain is invited and, if given, will create a contract.

Here, it is possible that Coe made an offer to Kim when he said, "I will pay you a bonus of $1000 if you get in shape for the Coe Competitions." These were words of offer because they were definite and certain since they indicated an amount for the bonus ($1000), set a defined goal ("get in shape") and identified a time for performance (the Coe Competitions). Further, the words were communicated directly to Kim. A reasonable person in Kim's position could believe that her assent was invited and would conclude a deal.

On the other hand, these words might not have been an offer because Coe's words to "get in shape" were not definite and specific. What kind of shape did he mean? What would be sufficient? As a result, this language might be considered indefinite and therefore not capable of acceptance. The stronger argument, however, would be that the words were definite because they referred to what would be necessary for Kim to get into a physical condition capable of competing in the Coe Competitions. Therefore, Coe made a valid offer.

The next question is whether the offer called for acceptance by a return promise or a performance. The acceptance must be in the same manner requested or authorized by the offeror because the offeror is the master of the offer. If it is not specified in the offer, an offer is interpreted as inviting the offeree to accept either by promising to perform what the offer requests or by rendering the performance, as the offeree chooses. However, some offers may only be accepted by performance—the doing of the requested act—and not a return promise.

Here, Coe was asking for Kim to get in shape. He was not seeking her promise to get in shape but the performance of getting in shape for the Competitions. His purpose can be inferred from his interest in keeping Americans from getting "soft" and his sponsorship of competitions to encourage such activity. Coe wanted Kim to be ready to compete in the athletic competitions and therefore was not seeking her promise to get in shape, but rather the act of getting in shape. Coe might claim that his offer was made in jest because he said, "I was only kidding," but the objective theory controls and the test is what a reasonable person in the position of the offeree would think were meant by the words. Kim had no reason to believe Coe was kidding when he made the offer of $1000 because he was fully committed to getting people in shape. He was a sports enthusiast himself and was sponsoring athletic competitions for this purpose. Kim would have no reason to believe Coe was joking in making her an offer to get in shape.

The next question is whether Kim had begun performance. If the offer calls for acceptance by return performance, once the offeree begins performance, the offer becomes irrevocable. The offeror's duty to render her return performance is conditional on the offeree's completing performance as specified in the offer but once performance has begun, the offeror is no longer free to revoke but must allow the offeree to complete performance within the time specified or within a reasonable time. Irrevocability takes effect only when actual performance is commenced, not when preparations for performance are begun.

Coe's power to revoke the offer became irrevocable when Kim began her performance by getting in shape for the Competition. She performed because she purchased sneakers and outfits to work out in and walked two miles every day and exercised every night. Further, she changed her diet and drank only high energy drinks for six weeks and lost 15 pounds. On the other hand, Coe will claim this simply signified preparations for performance and does not qualify as the actual performance of his promise. Still, even if buying clothes and sneakers could be seen as mere preparations, the actual acts of walking, exercising, eating properly, and losing weight would meet the criteria of "getting in shape." The offer did not require Kim to win the Competitions, but only to get in shape to compete. Further, it did not specify what kind of shape—only enough to compete. Kim said she was "in the best shape she had been in since high school and ready for the Coe Competitions." Hence, she got in shape and accepted Coe's offer by this performance.

> [The following analysis would be appropriate if you had learned about other bases of promissory liability. While we discuss the principle of promissory estoppel in a subsequent chapter, it is appropriate to include it here based on the facts of the problem. If you had not yet learned the doctrine, however, you would not be expected to discuss it on your exam.]

Assuming, however, that a court fails to find a valid offer and acceptance, Kim can seek recovery based on a reliance theory. There are some promises which, although the promisor makes them without bargaining for anything in return, nonetheless induce the promisee to rely to her detriment. In such cases, the doctrine of promissory estoppel offers some relief.

There are four requirements to meet to induce the doctrine: first, there must have been a promise. Here, Coe made Kim a promise to pay her $1000 if she got in shape. Second, the promisee's reliance must have been reasonably foreseeable to the promisor, even though the promisor may not have bargained for it. It would be foreseeable to Coe that Kim would rely on his promise because he offered a monetary incentive of $1000 which is a rather large amount of money. Third, there must have been actual reliance on the promise. Kim relied on the promise by going out and buying exercise clothes, dieting, and exercising. And finally, the circumstances must be such that injustice can be avoided only by enforcement of the promise. Kim relied to her detriment because she spent money on the clothes and foregoing her favorite muffins for a period of six weeks. Consequently, the court should enforce the promise to avoid injustice. While it might not be possible for a court to place a money value on the deprivation of muffins, it can, at the very least, reimburse her for the out-of-pocket expenses she incurred for exercise clothes.

On the other hand, Coe can argue that Kim benefitted by losing weight and getting in shape and that he really did her a favor. Consequently, he will claim there was no injustice. Nonetheless, Kim gave up something she had a legal right to do in reliance on his promise—eat muffins—and therefore he is liable on a promissory estoppel theory.

■ PROBLEM 2.2 ■

Until last year, Nancy worked for a catalog company as a copywriter and was quite happy in her job. But then she decided she could do more with her life and that she was meant to be a great author. She quit her job and began to devote all her time and energy to writing the great American novel. She made the appropriate filings with the State Attorney General's office to incorporate so she could deduct household expenses while writing and formed "The Pointed Pen, Inc."

Nancy needed writing supplies. On April 2, she sent a letter on her new corporate letterhead to Hemingways, a stationery supplier, requesting a catalog of supplies and prices. On April 10, she received the company catalog and, in addition, Hemingways enclosed a form letter that stated: "Available to our first-time customers: standard white typing-quality paper at $15 per ream. Ready for immediate delivery. 5 ream minimum. Reduced price with orders of 15 reams or more." Nancy wrote back on April 15: "I accept your offer. Please ship 10 reams of paper and deliver by May 1."

On April 18, Hemingways sent a letter to Nancy stating: "Confirming shipment to The Pointed Pen, Inc. of 15 reams of paper at a special price of $12 per ream, delivery to take place as requested."

On May 1, Nancy received a delivery of 15 reams of paper together with an invoice for $180 plus shipping charges. Nancy is livid. She does not need so much paper nor can she afford it. She called Hemingways and they said that because she failed to respond to their letter of April 18, she is stuck with the 15 reams. Nancy seeks your advice.

Analysis

The first question is whether this was a contract for the sale of goods or services. Since the agreement involves the sale of paper, which is a "good" according to the UCC definition where goods are all things which are movable at the time of identification to the contract, then Article 2 is applicable.

The next question is whether a contract was formed and if so, what are its terms. Since Article 2 does not define an offer, common law principles apply. Nancy's request on April 2 for a catalog and prices was not an offer but merely an inquiry because it was a general request for information. In response, Hemingways sent its company catalog and form letter which she received on April 10. Such a form letter and catalog would not constitute an offer on Hemingways' part but was merely a general invitation or advertisement.

Nancy's letter of April 15 was an offer. It was an offer because she set out the terms on which she proposed to buy paper. She asked for 10 reams of paper, a definite quantity, and identified a specific delivery date of May 1. The price term was not necessary since Nancy was responding to Hemingways' form letter which stated the price term of $15 per ream with a 5 ream minimum.

The next question is whether Hemingways accepted this offer. Under UCC 2–207(1), a response operates as an acceptance if it is a "definite and seasonable expression of acceptance" and sent within a reasonable time, even though it states terms additional to or different from" those of the offer. It is possible that Hemingways' letter to Nancy of April 18 was an acceptance. It was timely since it was only three days after her offer of April 15 and sent by return mail which would be reasonable under the circumstances since no particular manner for acceptance was required by the offer and all their prior communications had been by mail.

The question is whether this was an expression of acceptance when both the quantity and price terms differed: Nancy ordered 10 reams at $15 each and Hemingways "accepted" for 15 reams at $12 each. While 5 reams and $30 may not seem to be a big difference, it could be significant because it went to a material term of the agreement, which is quantity, and by extension, price. Hemingways increased Nancy's order by one-third, which could be significant. Despite the Code's liberal policy of contract formation, if the second document does not agree on the basic or "dickered terms," then it does not constitute an "expression of acceptance" and the inquiry ends here. In this case, there might not have been an acceptance since the quantity term in the acceptance differed from that of the offer.

Assuming, however, that an agreement was formed even though the acceptance contained different terms than the offer, the next question is whether the seller's term of 15 reams of paper or the buyer's term of 10 reams became part of the parties' agreement. Under subsection (2), the additional terms[69] are to be considered proposals for addition to the contract unless the parties are

---

69. U.C.C. § 2–207(2)(2004).

merchants, in which case other options are possible. Now we need to determine whether the parties are merchants. According to the Code, a merchant is one who deals in goods of the kind or otherwise by his occupation holds himself out as having knowledge or skill peculiar to the practices or goods involved in the transaction. "Between merchants" refers to any transaction with respect to which both parties are chargeable with the knowledge or skill of merchants.

Here, Hemingways is a merchant because it is a stationery supplier in the business of selling office supplies. The issue of whether Nancy is a "merchant" is more ambiguous. She may be a merchant because she incorporated as a business and used corporate letterhead in all her correspondence with Hemingways. Hemingways would have no reason to think she was not a business since the name of the company itself indicates that it is incorporated ("The Pointed Pen, Inc."). Further, the name is stationery-related and not that of an individual. "The Pointed Pen, Inc." could be a retailer of pens and stationary supplies. On the other hand, Nancy is just a person writing a book who incorporated for tax purposes. She does not deal in any goods since her goal is to write a book. She doesn't buy and sell pens or paper or anything else. The paper she ordered was for her personal use and this was merely a question of a basic, non-specialized business practice of answering mail (see section 2–104, Comment 2). If Nancy is not a merchant, then UCC 2–207(2)(a) controls and Hemingways' terms are mere proposals and do not become part of the deal. Consequently, Nancy's terms control and she is obligated to pay for only the 10 reams she ordered.

Still, it was reasonable for Hemingways to believe it was dealing with another merchant because Nancy always used corporate letterhead in her dealings with them and ordered a significant amount of paper. In this case, both parties would be merchants and Hemingways' quantity term would become part of the contract under 2–207(2) unless it was material. Nancy could argue that 15 reams was material because it increased her order by one-third and added $30 to the contract price. Conversely, Hemingways could claim that it was not a material term since the price increase was only $30 and she was enjoying a savings by getting the 15 reams at only $12 per ream instead of $15.

Under UCC 2–207(2)(c), where "notification of objection to [the terms] has already been given or is given within a reasonable time after notice of them is received," the term does not become part of the agreement. In order for Hemingways' quantity term not to become part of the agreement, Nancy would have to give notice of her objection in a reasonable time. While Nancy learned in the April 18 letter that the shipment would be 15 reams, she did not object until she received the delivery two weeks later. The question is whether it was reasonable for her to wait two weeks before objecting. Two weeks may be an unreasonable time to wait since she had a letter telling her what to expect. Further, only days had intervened between communications in her previous course of correspondence with Hemingways: when Hemingways sent a catalog on April 10, she wrote back on April 15. As a result, when Hemingways wrote to her on April 18, it would be reasonable to expect her to respond in approximately the same amount of time which would have been April 23 or April 24. Instead, she waited until May 1 when the delivery itself had been made. Since she did not respond for two weeks, Hemingways would be reasonable in believing that Nancy did not find the additional 5 reams to be objectionable. Consequently, it is likely that they would become part of the contract and Nancy would be held liable.

POINTS TO REMEMBER

- Always begin an analysis by determining the nature of the transaction—is it a sale of goods or one for services? If it is a sale of goods, then the problem will be analyzed under Article 2 of the UCC. If it is one for services, then the common law is applicable.

- Courts apply an objective test to determine whether there has been an offer and an acceptance. It does not matter what a party may have subjectively intended—the test is what a reasonable person in the other party's position would believe was meant by the promisor's words or conduct.

- Remember the limits of the "mailbox rule" which holds that an acceptance is effective upon dispatch. First, if the offeree chooses an acceptance not invited by the offer, the mailbox rule does not apply and the acceptance is not effective until receipt. Second, upon dispatch, the mailbox rule also binds the offeree to the acceptance. Third, as "master of the offer," the offeror can always depart from the mailbox rule by providing otherwise in the offer.

- It is also important to note that the mailbox rule applies only to *acceptances* by mail, not revocations. A revocation is not effective until received by the offeree; hence, a revocation by mail or telegram is not effective until receipt.

- Under the common law, an acceptance must be the "mirror image" of the offer or it is a rejection of the offer and may be a counter-offer. However, Article 2 is far more forgiving in finding an agreement and under 2–207, a contract may be formed even if the acceptance states terms additional to or different from the offer. Then the issue becomes what to do with those terms—are they mere proposals or do they become part of the agreement? Be sure you are comfortable in performing a "battle of the forms" analysis.

- While the general rule is that an offeror is free to revoke her offer at any time before acceptance, there are a number of ways in which an offer can be made irrevocable. One way is if the parties have formed an option contract where consideration is given in exchange for the promise to keep the offer open. However, there are exceptions to the consideration requirement and here is where you need to be aware of the possibilities, some of which include the following: the Restatement finds an option contract if the promise to keep the offer open is in writing, signed by the offeror, "recites a purported consideration" and "proposes an exchange on fair terms within a reasonable time"; an option contract arises when the offeree begins the invited performance where the offer invites acceptance by performance only and does not allow for a promissory acceptance; and a "firm offer" under UCC 2–205 which limits the offeror's power to revoke an offer if the offer is made by a merchant to buy or sell goods in a signed writing which gives assurances that it will be held open without consideration for the time stated, and if no time is stated, for a reasonable time, but not to exceed three months.

Formation ➡	Avoiding ➡ the Deal	Performance ➡	Third ➡ Parties	Remedies
Do we have a deal?	We have a deal, but	Who has to do what and when, or maybe not	Is there a third party to the deal?	Someone failed to perform when required, now what?
Mutual Assent + Consideration				

Excerpts of Contracts Time-line

FORMATION
DO WE HAVE A DEAL?

Consideration

Bargained-for exchange

"Peppercorn" theory

Benefit/detriment

Illusory promise

Gratuitous promise

Past consideration

Moral obligation

Promissory Estoppel

Contract modification

- Pre-existing Duty Rule
- UCC 2–209

Requirements/output contract

Accord and satisfaction

Close-up on Consideration

CHAPTER 3

Consideration

R2d § 17, 71, 73, 74, 76, 77, 79, 89
UCC 2-209, 2-306

REVIEW OF CONSIDERATION

The first requirement for the formation of a contract is the mutual assent of the parties; the second requirement is that of consideration. Having said that, you will find that consideration is not always necessary or sufficient to make a promise enforceable. For example, formal contracts under seal are recognized in some jurisdictions where the formality of the seal is a substitute for consideration. In addition, some promises lacking consideration may be enforceable to avoid injustice under alternate theories such as promissory estoppel or restitution. These other theories of recovery may assist a disappointed promisee when the consideration doctrine fails them. We will consider these alternate theories or "substitutes for consideration" after we examine the contours of the doctrine of consideration.

In the language of the Restatement Second, consideration consists of a performance or return promise that is bargained-for in exchange for the promise sought to be enforced. Originally, consideration was thought of as either a "benefit" conferred on the promisor, or a "detriment" suffered by the promisee. However, the

Restatement Second eliminated the requirement of a benefit or detriment and defines consideration simply as a "bargained for exchange."[1]

The Requirement of Exchange

As we discussed in Chapter 1, not all promises impose contract liability and the question for contract law is determining which promises should be enforced. One of the limitations on the enforcement of promises is the requirement of consideration.

The bargain theory of consideration recognizes that contracts are voluntary exchange relationships where a performance or return promise is said to be "bargained for" "if it is sought by the promisor in exchange for his promise and is given by the promisee in exchange for that promise."[2] This means that the promise and the consideration assume a reciprocal relationship of motive or inducement: "the consideration induces the making of the promise and the promise induces the furnishing of the consideration."[3]

Practically anything one would bargain for in exchange for a promise can be consideration for that promise. The same consideration can support a number of promises.[4] It can be a promise or act of doing something or it may be refraining from doing something that one has a legal right to do. Sometimes the consideration for a promise is a return performance by the promisee where the promise is made on only one side as in a unilateral contract. Usually, the consideration is a return promise as in a bilateral contract where promises are made on both sides.

The classic case on consideration is *Hamer v. Sidway*.[5] Here the New York Court of Appeals found consideration to support an uncle's promise to pay his nephew $5,000 if the nephew would "refrain from drinking liquor[,] using tobacco, swearing and play-

---

1. Restatement (Second) of Contracts § 17 (1979).

2. Restatement (Second) of Contracts § 71(2) (1979).

3. *Id.* § 71 cmt b.

4. Restatement (Second) of Contracts § 80 cmt. a (1979) ("A single performance or return promise may thus furnish consideration for any number of promises.").

5. 27 N.E. 256 (N.Y. 1891).

ing cards or billiards for money until [he became] twenty-one years of age[.]"[6] The nephew refrained from these activities until he was 21 and when the $5000 was not paid, brought suit. The problem for the court was whether there was consideration to support the uncle's promise. The defense claimed that there was no consideration because the nephew was not harmed but benefitted by not engaging in these activities and therefore the promisor did not enjoy a benefit. The New York Court of Appeals rejected the argument that the uncle needed to receive a benefit from the nephew's conduct to find consideration. Instead, it found that the nephew's forbearance from doing that which he had a legal right to do—drinking and smoking tobacco—was consideration to support the uncle's promise. [7]

What Is Sufficient Consideration?

Adequacy of Consideration

Because parties are free to make their own bargains, the consideration doctrine does not require the exchange of promises or performances to be of equal value. So long as the parties bargain for the exchange, the court will not review the adequacy of consideration—even if one party promises something of great monetary value in exchange for something as insignificant as a "peppercorn."[8]

In most commercial bargains, there is a rough equivalence in values exchanged so there is not much difficulty is finding the consideration. But in many situations, there is no reliable external standard by which to measure the exchange and valuation is left to the parties because they are in the best position to evaluate the particular transaction.[9] However, if the exchange is extremely unbalanced, a court may consider it a factor in determining

---

6. *Id.* at 257.

7. *Id.*

8. *See* Restatement (Second) of Contracts § 79 (1979) (A peppercorn is symbolic of something of insignificant value, but even a peppercorn can be consideration if it is bargained for); *see also* E. Allan Farnsworth, *Contracts*, § 2.11 (4th ed. 2004).

9. *Id.* § 79 cmt. c.

whether the bargain was tainted by fraud, duress, mistake, or unconscionability. We will consider such defenses in a subsequent chapter.

Sham and Nominal Consideration

The question often arises whether a promise is supported by consideration when there is payment of a nominal sum such as a dollar in a transaction worth considerably far more or when there is a recital of consideration and none is actually paid. For example, consider the seller's promise to sell a luxury sailboat for the buyer's promise to pay one dollar. Is the seller's promise supported by consideration? Such disparity in value may indicate that the purported consideration was not bargained for but was a pretense. In such cases, the consideration requirement may not be met.

The question of whether such a nominal sum can be effective as consideration arises most frequently in the context of a disguised gratuitous promise—where "a promisor really intends to make a gratuitous promise and casts the transaction in the form of a bargain in order to make it enforceable."[10] In this case, the question is really whether the donor's promise to make a gift of the boat is enforceable because the donee gives a dollar to the donor. The Restatement Second reflects the modern view which requires an actual bargain and not the pretense of an exchange. An extreme disparity in the exchange might be evidence of a sham and would not be consideration. Illustration 5 to Restatement Second § 71 gives this example: "A desires to make a binding promise to give $1000 to his son B. Being advised that a gratuitous promise is not binding, A offers to buy from B for $1000 a book worth less than $1. B accepts the offer knowing that the purchase of the book is a mere pretense. There is no consideration for A's promise to pay $1000."[11]

---

10. Farnsworth, *Contracts*, § 2.11.

11. Restatement (Second) of Contracts § 71 illustration 5.

Mutuality of Obligation

Frequently, courts refer to the consideration doctrine as imposing a "mutuality of obligation" on the parties where "both parties are bound, or neither is bound." This concept seems to follow from the consideration doctrine that requires both parties to give something of legal value in order to get something in exchange. However, the statement is overly broad and, if applied literally, would void several types of contracts that are routinely recognized. For example, consider the unilateral contract where a promise is exchanged for a performance. In these contracts where the consideration is the bargained-for performance, the promisor's duty does not arise until the performance is rendered. Typically in unilateral contracts, there is no one point in time where both parties will be obligated to do something. In short, unilateral contracts do not require "mutuality of obligation." The same can be said of bilateral contracts. There is no requirement that the parties obligations assumed by each party be precisely the same and to the same extent. According to Restatement Second § 79, if the require-ment of consideration is met, there is no additional requirement for the "mutuality of obligation." So what do courts mean when they say that a contract is unenforceable because it lacks a "mutuality of obligation?" All they are saying is that either or both of the promises made by the parties do not meet the consideration standard of a "bargained for" exchange.

Settlement of Claims

Public policy favors the settlement of disputed claims: if parties can resolve their disputes without litigating, it saves time, money, and court resources. Suppose that Julia asserts a claim against Dr. Mal and the doctor promises to pay $10,000 if Julia releases the claim or forbears from bringing suit. If the claim is valid and Dr. Mal has bargained with Julia for settlement of the claim for $10,000, then there is consideration to support the promise. What happens if the claim is invalid? Should the promise still be enforced?

While there is no dispute that a promise to settle a valid claim constitutes consideration, there is no consensus regarding the surrender of an invalid claim. This makes sense: if the party has no right to assert the claim because it is unfounded, then there is no "detriment" to the promisor in promising to do so. Thus, Restatement Second § 74(1) states that "[f]orbearance to assert or the surrender of a claim or defense which proves to be invalid is not consideration[.]"[12] As usual, there are exceptions. One exception is when the validity of the claim or defense is uncertain.[13] Even if the invalidity becomes clear later on, the bargain is judged as it appeared to the parties at the time it was made: the party asserting the claim must hold a good faith belief in its validity.[14]

Illusory Promises

A promise is not consideration if by its terms it makes performance entirely optional with the promisor. In this case, no words of commitment have been made. The statement may appear to be promising something, but in fact does not commit the promisor to anything at all. For example, suppose your friend Amy is moving after graduating from law school to a new house with all new kitchen appliances. You have always wanted a dishwasher and say to her, "if you give me the dishwasher when you move out of your apartment, I will pay you $100 next week unless I change my mind." Although you've used the words, "I promise," you have not obligated yourself to do anything at all. Such a promise is entirely illusory and would not be sufficient consideration for a return promise from Amy. So even if Amy agrees to give you the dishwasher, her promise would not be enforceable because she has received no consideration in exchange for it.

The question often arises whether a promise is illusory when the promisor retains discretion over her own performance. Depending on the surrounding circumstances, a court may find consideration by implying an obligation to exercise one's discretion in good faith. This means that while you may have agreed to exercise your discretion, that discretion is not unlimited: you must

---

12. Restatement (Second) of Contracts § 74(1) (1979).

13. *Id.* § 74(1)(a).

14. *Id.* § 74(1)(b).

do so reasonably and in good faith. The obligation to comport with the standard of good faith keeps your promise from being illusory.

Exclusive Dealings

A good example of promises which seem to be illusory but are not because of the implied obligation to use "reasonable efforts" are agreements for exclusive dealings. This rule is from one of contracts most celebrated cases—*Wood v. Lucy, Lady Duff–Gordon*.[15] Lady Duff–Gordon, a "creator of fashions," gave Wood the exclusive right for at least one year to place her endorsements and to sell or license her designs to others. In exchange, she was to receive half of "all profits and revenues" from any contracts he might make. Wood claimed that he kept his part of the bargain but that Lucy broke it by endorsing products on her own and keeping the profits to herself. Lucy argued that Wood had not bound himself to do anything to earn the profits. Judge Cardozo concluded that by granting an exclusive privilege to Wood where her sole compensation depended entirely on Woods efforts, an implication arose that he would "use reasonable efforts to bring profits and revenues into existence."[16]

In contracts involving the sale of goods, UCC 2–306(2) follows a similar approach by implying an obligation of "best efforts" in exclusive dealing contracts.[17]

Satisfaction Clauses

Another area in which consideration questions arise are in contracts with personal satisfaction clauses where the promisor's obligation to perform is conditioned on satisfaction with the other party's performance. In such cases, the promisor must act in good faith in determining its satisfaction or its promise is illusory. For example, suppose Carly enters a written contract with Ben for Ben to supply Carly with 100 personalized invitations on or before

---

15. 118 N.E. 214 (N.Y. 1917).

16. *Id.*, at 215.

17. U.C.C. § 2–306 (2004) (The 2003 revi-

sion of Article 2 makes no change to this section.).

January 15 for her annual Valentine Day's Party. The invitation is to consist of a photograph of Carly to be taken by Ben at Carly's house. Carly promises to pay $250 if she finds the photograph satisfactory. Ben takes her picture and delivers the completed invitations on January 15. Although the photograph on the invitations pleases everyone in Carly's family, Carly refuses to accept them because as she says, "I think the photograph makes me look old and frumpy. I hate it."

In this case, Carly's duty to perform, which is to pay the $250, is conditioned on her personal satisfaction with the photograph. Although a condition of satisfaction seems to be wholly discretionary, it is not. First, it depends on whether it is a matter of subjective or objective satisfaction. This in turn depends on the subject matter of the contract. If it is a commercial contract, such as one involving manufacturing or construction, then objective satisfaction, which requires the satisfaction of a reasonable person, is generally required. If the contract involves personal services, where the taste or judgment of the individual is involved, then subjective satisfaction is required. However, even personal satisfaction must be exercised in good faith which means honesty in fact. The party must be honestly dissatisfied with the performance.

Here, the subject matter of the contract is a personal photograph and therefore requires Carly's personal, subjective satisfaction. She can reject Ben's photo and not have to pay for it if it is truly dissatisfactory to her, even if it pleases everyone else, which is indeed the case since everyone likes the photograph but Carly. Her rejection appears to be in good faith since she says she looks old and frumpy. There are no facts to indicate that Carly was merely seeking to avoid the deal but honestly believed she didn't look good in the photograph. In this case, Carly has exercised good faith in failing to find the cards fully satisfactory and avoids liability.

Requirements and Output Contracts

In a *requirements* contract, the seller agrees to sell and the buyer agrees to buy all of the goods of a particular kind that the buyer may *require* in its business. This type of agreement assures the buyer of a steady supplier for the goods it needs. In an *output* contract, the seller agrees to sell and the buyer agrees to buy all of the goods of a particular kind that the seller may *produce* in its business. In this case, the seller is assured of a market for its goods.

As you can see, there is no set quantity for either the seller's output or the buyer's requirements. In these contracts, the parties create contractual obligations without committing to purchase a specific quantity. It would seem that the contract lacks definiteness because the quantity term is not defined but left to the discretion of the buyer or seller. While these agreements have often been disputed, it is not because of the contract requirement of definiteness but the question of consideration: is the buyer's promise illusory because it may choose to go out of business and thus not have any requirements? Similarly, is the seller's promise illusory because it, too, may choose not to have any output?

The Uniform Commercial Code addresses this issue by implying a duty of good faith. Unless the parties have agreed otherwise, the court will define the duty to have output or requirements in terms of good faith.[18] According to comment 2 of UCC 2–306, "a contract for output or requirements is not too indefinite since it is held to mean the actual good faith output or requirements of the particular party."[19] Consequently, the essential test of a party's conduct in having output or requirements, even to the point of zero, is whether the party is acting in good faith.

Modification and the Pre–Existing Duty Rule

Suppose a person promises to perform a duty that he or she already owes under an existing contract. Is it consideration to promise or perform that which one is already obligated to do? Generally, the answer is no. For example, assume that a contractor promises to construct a restaurant for $500,000 and, two months

---

18. *Id.* § 306(1) ("A term which measures the quantity by the output of the seller or the requirements of the buyer means such actual output or requirements as may occur in good faith, except that no quantity unreasonably disproportionate to any stated estimate or in the absence of a stated estimate to any normal or otherwise comparable prior output or requirements may be tendered or demanded.").

19. *Id.* § 2–306 cmt. 2.

into the construction, refuses to complete the job unless paid an additional $50,000. The frustrated owner promises to pay the additional amount so the contractor won't walk off the job. The owner's promise is not enforceable under the pre-existing duty rule because a pre-existing legal duty cannot serve as consideration to support a new promise.[20] Here, the contractor was already under a duty to construct the restaurant for $500,000. He offered nothing "new" to support the owner's promise to pay an additional $50,000 but is engaging in what is referred to as the "hold-up game."

Presumably, once parties have made a contract, each is bound to what was agreed and neither party has the right to unilaterally change the terms of the agreement. Any attempt to do so would be a breach of contract. However, parties should be able to make a subsequent agreement to amend that contract. The new agreement to modify the contract is itself a contract and subject to all the rules governing the formation of contracts, which of course includes the requirement of consideration.

Let's go back to our contractor. Suppose after working on the restaurant for two months, he finds that it will cost an additional $50,000 to install the ovens required in the contract because the building must be rewired to support the increased electrical demand. He asks the owner to pay the additional amount and the owner agrees. Assuming that this was an unanticipated and substantial difficulty but insufficient to discharge the contractor's duty under the theory of impracticability, then the owner's promise to pay the additional money will be enforceable as a valid modification.

The modern trend is away from a strict application of the pre-existing duty rule and is reflected in Restatement Second § 89. This section provides that "[a] promise modifying a duty under a contract not fully performed on either side is binding . . . if the modification is fair and equitable in view of circumstances not

---

20. Restatement (Second) of Contracts § 73 (1979) ("Performance of a legal duty owed to a promisor which is neither doubtful nor the subject of honest dispute is not consideration[.]").

anticipated by the parties when the contract was made[.]"[21] In this case, a modification to a contract will be enforced without consideration if a party encounters unanticipated difficulties, the modification is fair and equitable, and the contract is still executory on both sides—each side still owes a performance.

Modification Under the UCC

Uniform Commercial Code § 2–209[22] departs completely from the common law and eliminates the requirement of consideration for an agreement modifying a contract for the sale of goods. Although the Code abandons the consideration requirement, a modification must be made in good faith to be enforceable. A desire to escape a bad bargain or the extortion of a modification without legitimate commercial reason would be ineffective as a violation of the duty of good faith.[23]

Accord and Satisfaction

An accord and satisfaction occurs when the parties agree to modify the performance specified in their original contract. Typically, a lesser amount of money is offered by the debtor to the creditor to resolve a good faith dispute as to liability or the amount due. The new substitute agreement is the "accord." The consideration is the detriment of forbearance from suit on the original disputed contract. If the offer is accepted by the other party, an "accord" is created. The "satisfaction" is performance of the new agreement. When performed, the satisfaction discharges both the executory accord and the original contract. If, however, the executory accord is not performed, then the obligee may sue on either the original contract or on the accord agreement.

---

21. Restatement (Second) of Contracts § 89(a) (1979).

22. U.C.C. § 2–209 (2004) (The 2003 revision of Article 2 makes no significant changes to this section.).

23. *Id.* § 2–209 cmt. 2.

REVIEW OF PROMISES LACKING CONSIDERATION

> R2d § 82, 83, 86

Having determined what is required to make a promise enforceable, it is time to consider the types of promises that are unenforceable because they lack consideration. Such promises falls into two groups: those promises where there has been no exchange and those where there has been no bargain.

Gratuitous Promises

The most significant category of promises that are unenforceable for lack of consideration are gift promises. In this case, there is no exchange at all. For example, suppose Ashley promises to give a painting to her friend, Amy, as a present for her new house and then changes her mind. Ashley's promise is not supported by consideration because there was no exchange—Ashley did not receive anything from Amy in return for her promise. As a result, Ashley's promise to give Amy the painting is unenforceable.

It is important to note the distinction between a gift and a promise to make a gift. A gift is a present transfer of an interest in property and is conceptually different from a promise to make a gift. Suppose Ashley had given the painting to Amy and then had second thoughts and wanted it back. In this case, Amy's interest in keeping the painting is not a problem for contract law because Amy's right does not involve enforcement of a promise. Rather, it is a problem for property law because once Ashley has completed delivery of the painting, the transfer is irrevocable and Amy cannot recover it.

As we've seen, the bargain element requires that there be a reciprocal relationship between the promise and the consideration—that the one induced the other and vice versa. In the following types of promises, the bargain element is missing.

Past Consideration

A common example of where a promise lacks consideration is where it is given for an action that has already taken place or been performed. If the promisee has already taken the action, then the promisor cannot be said to have bargained for it when making the promise. While it is common to refer to this as past consideration, it is not really consideration at all. Consider the following example: Robyn's employer promises to send her on an all expense paid vacation to Hawaii for the "great work she did last year for the company." The employer's promise is not enforceable. Robyn already performed the work that is the subject of the promise and therefore cannot be said to have been induced by that promise. While the employer may have made the promise and Robyn performed the work, the promise did not induce the work and therefore was not the result of a bargain between the parties.

Moral Obligation/Material Benefit Rule

A promise to pay for a benefit previously received falls within the area of "past consideration" and is generally unenforceable. However, some promises fall within an exception to this rule, as in the cases where the promisor is said to be under a "moral obligation." The doctrine is extremely limited in scope and does not mean that a court will enforce a promise simply because the promisor has a moral obligation to perform what has been promised. Instead, courts have recognized the doctrine where a debtor promises to pay for a debt although there is no longer a legal obligation to do so because the debt has been discharged through bankruptcy[24] or barred by the statute of limitations.[25]

A debtor's promise to pay all or part of a debt, discharged or dischargeable in bankruptcy proceedings begun before the promise is made, is enforceable. However, it must be express and will not be inferred from a part payment or acknowledgment of the debt.[26] For example, Adam owes Ashley $5000 and is about to file for bankruptcy. He promises to pay Ashley the money despite any discharge he may get in bankruptcy. Here the promise is unen-

---

24. Restatement (Second) of Contracts § 83 (1979).

25. Restatement (Second) of Contracts § 82 (1979).

26. Restatement (Second) of Contracts § 83 cmt. a.

forceable because it was made *before* the bankruptcy proceedings were begun. If Adam had made the promise after the petition had been filed, it would have been binding.

Similarly, promises made to pay a debt otherwise barred by the statute of limitations may be binding under the moral obligation exception. Suppose that eight years ago, Cindy entered into a contract with Sam for services amounting to $3,000. Sam breached the contract by not paying Cindy for her performance. Cindy never brought suit and the six year statute of limitations has run. The claim is time-barred and Cindy can no longer sue. Sam now feels bad about not paying Cindy what he owed her. He promises to pay $2,000 of what he owes. Although Sam gives no consideration in exchange for this promise, the doctrine of moral obligation creates an exception and permits enforcement of the new promise. However, recovery is limited to the terms of the new promise—$2,000.

A promise may be inferred from a voluntary acknowledgment or part payment of the debt as will a statement that the statute of limitations will not be pleaded as a defense. However, the promisor is bound only to the terms of the new promise—if the promise is one to pay only part of the debt, then it is enforceable only to that extent.

Referred to as the "material benefit" rule, Restatement Second § 86, expands the application of the moral obligation exception to cover a wider range of promises in recognition of a prior benefit. Section 86 replaces the terms "past consideration" and "moral obligation" with "promise for a benefit received."[27] It was inspired by *Webb v. McGowin*,[28] a case many of you will read. The facts in *Webb* are compelling: Webb was an employee in a lumber company. In August 1925, he was clearing the upper floor of the mill and in the process of dropping a 75–pound pine block down to the floor below when he noticed McGowin standing right in its path. If Webb were to let the block go, it would fall on McGowin and crush him. To prevent this from happening, Webb held onto

---

27. Restatement (Second) of Contracts § 86 **28.** 168 So. 196 (1935).
(1979).

the block, falling with it and diverting its fall so that it missed McGowin completely. Webb was not so lucky: he was seriously injured and left permanently disabled by the fall. In gratitude for saving his life and to compensate him for his injury, McGowin promised to pay Webb $15 every two weeks for the rest of his life. McGowin made this payments until he died in 1934 but his estate discontinued the payments. Webb sued and the court of appeals upheld the promise. Although McGowin's promise came after Webb's performance and did not induce it, McGowin realized a benefit in being saved and had a moral obligation to compensate Webb for his loss. McGowin might have ignored this imperative but instead chose to affirm and ratify that obligation by promising to pay him a lifetime annuity. According to the court, a "moral obligation" and a "material benefit" is "sufficient consideration to support a subsequent promise to pay[.]"[29]

REVIEW OF PROMISSORY ESTOPPEL

R2d § 90

There are some promises which, although the promisor makes them without bargaining for anything in return, nonetheless induce the promisee to rely to her detriment. While the promisee would be unsuccessful on a breach of contract claim if the promisor failed to perform because of a lack of consideration, the doctrine of promissory estoppel offers some relief.

Restatement Second § 90 provides for recovery on the basis of reliance in a wide range of situations. There are four requirements which must be met to induce the doctrine: first, there must have been a promise. Second, the promisee's reliance must have been reasonably foreseeable to the promisor, even though the promisor may not have bargained for it. Third, there must have been actual reliance on the promise. And fourth, the circumstances must be such that injustice can be avoided only by enforcement of the promise.

---

29. *Id.* at 197.

The essence of promissory estoppel is the idea that the maker of a promise may be bound by that promise, even though it is not supported by consideration if the promisee relies upon the promise to her detriment and the promisor should have foreseen this reliance. In such cases, the promise is enforceable but "may be limited as justice requires."[30] Recovery is generally limited to damages based on the reliance interest which affords a lesser recovery than would a full measure of expectation damages.

Although promissory estoppel was seen originally as a substitute for consideration, the doctrine has developed to provide a remedy for promises that fail the test of enforceability by treating the promisee's reliance as an independent and adequate basis for recovery. The doctrine has been applied to several categories of cases: gratuitous promises to convey land if the promisee relied by moving onto the land and making improvements; gratuitous promises to procure insurance[31]; charitable subscriptions[32]; and gratuitous intra-family promises,[33] among others.

CONSIDERATION CHECKLIST

Here is the checklist for analyzing problems presenting consideration questions:

---

30. Restatement (Second) of Contracts § 90 (1979).

31. *Id.* § 90 cmt. e.

32. *Id.* § 90 cmt. f. (Courts favor promises made to charitable institutions and may find them enforceable even absent consideration or reliance. A seminal case in this area is *Allegheny Coll. v. Nat'l Chautauqua County Bank*, 159 N.E. 173, 175 (N.Y. 1927) (While Judge Cardozo decided the case on consideration grounds, it is his dictum concerning promissory estoppel that has been most influential with respect to charitable promises: "we have adopted the doctrine of promissory estoppel as the equivalent of consideration in

connection with our law of charitable subscriptions.").

33. *Ricketts v. Scothorn*, 77 N.W. 365, 367 (Neb. 1898) (While there was no consideration to support a grandfather's promise to his granddaughter to give her $2000 plus interest so she would not have to work like his other grandchildren, the court found the executor was "estopped" from alleging a lack of consideration. Having done what her grandfather induced her to do—quit her job—the court held that "it would be grossly inequitable" to resist payment on the ground that the promise was given without consideration.).

A. Consideration—is there consideration to support the promise?

    1. "Bargained For" Exchange—has something, either another promise or a performance, been sought by the promisor and given in exchange for that promise?

        a. **Yes.** If so, then the parties have bargained for the exchange of promises or performances such that each induces the other and the consideration requirement is met.

        b. **No.** If the performance or return promise is not sought by the promisor in exchange for her promise and given by the promisee in exchange for that promise, then there is no consideration.

    2. Promises that are not "Bargained For"—if the promise is not sought by the promisor and given by the promisee in exchange for that promise, then what type of promise is it?

        a. **Gratuitous Promise**—is the promise one to make a future gift where the promisor asks for and receives nothing in exchange? If so, then the promise is not legally enforceable. However, it is only the promise to make a gift, not the making of the gift, that is unenforceable for lack of consideration. Once made, the promisor cannot rescind the gift for lack of consideration.

        b. **Past Consideration**—has the promisee already taken the action before the promise is made? If so, then the promisor cannot be seeking to induce it and it is not consideration. However, there are exceptions for promises to perform what are considered "moral obligations." Ask: is the promise one made under the following circumstances?

            i. **Debt barred by Statute of Limitations**—has a debtor promised to pay a debt that has been barred by the statute of limitations? If so, the promise is enforceable absent the exchange element. R2d § 82(1).

            ii. **Antecedent Indebtedness**—has a debtor voluntarily acknowledged an antecedent debt? If so, any action is based on the new promise and recovery is limited to its terms. R2d § 82(2).

iii. **Debt Discharged in Bankruptcy**—has a debtor promised to pay a debt that has been discharged in bankruptcy or one that is not yet discharged but is dischargeable in bankruptcy proceedings begun before the promise is made? If the promise is express and voluntary, it is binding. R2d § 83.

      iv. **Material Benefit**—is the promise one made in recognition of a benefit previously received by the promisor from the promisee where enforcement is necessary to prevent injustice? If so, the promise is binding. R2d § 86.

  c. **Illusory Promise**—does the promise by its terms make performance entirely optional with the promisor? If so, then there is no commitment as to future behavior and the promise is illusory. However, if the promisor has limited its discretion in some way, then the promise is not illusory. Ask: are there limits to the party's discretion?

      i. **Requirements and Output Contracts**—is there a term which measures its quantity by the seller's requirements or the buyer's output? If so, it means such as may occur in good faith and is therefore enforceable.

      ii. **Reasonable Efforts**—is there an implied promise to use "reasonable efforts" as in an "exclusive dealings" agreement? If so, then the obligation to use best efforts prevents the promise from being illusory and the promisor is bound.

      iii. **Good Faith**—is there an obligation to act in good faith? Where a party is entitled to exercise discretion over its performance, that discretion is not unlimited because it must be done reasonably and in good faith. The obligation to act in good faith keeps the promise from being illusory.

  d. **Conditional Promise**—has the promisor conditioned its promise?

      i. On an **Event**? If the promise is based on a condition which must occur and the promisor knows at the time of making the promise that the condition cannot occur, then no commitment has been made because no duty of immediate performance can ever arise. R2d § 76.

ii. On **Personal Satisfaction**? If the promisor's obligation to perform is conditioned on satisfaction with the other party's performance, then the promisor must act in **good faith** where the performance involves matters of personal taste and must be **reasonable** where the performance is of a technical or commercial nature.

e. **Settlement of Claims**—is the promise one to forbear from bringing or to surrender a claim or defense which is invalid? If so, it is not consideration unless the claim or defense is doubtful or the forbearing party believes that the claim or defense may be found to be valid.

B. **Promissory Estoppel**—if there is no consideration, has there been reliance? There are some promises which, although the promisor makes them without bargaining for anything in return, nonetheless induce the promisee to rely to her detriment. In such circumstances, recovery may be available on a reliance basis. Ask: are the elements for promissory estoppel as set forth in Restatement Second § 90 satisfied?

1. **Promise**—has a promise been made? Did the promisor use clear and definite language such that a reasonable person in the position of the promisee would be justified in believing a commitment had been made?

   a. **No.** If not, then there is no basis for recovery.

   b. **Yes.** If so, then there may be a basis for recovery under promissory estoppel. If the promise is a **charitable pledge**, then the promise is enforceable under R2d § 90 without proof of reliance and your inquiry ends here. If your jurisdiction does not follow the Restatement view, then reliance on the promise by the charitable institution is required. Proceed to the next question.

2. **Foreseeability of Reliance**—did the promisor have reason to expect the promisee to rely on the promise?

a. **No.** If the promisor had no reason to expect any reliance or not the kind of reliance that resulted, then the promisor is not bound.

b. **Yes.** If so, then the promisor may be bound if the other requirements are met. Proceed to the next question.

3. **Justified Reliance**—did the promise induce actual reliance and was the reliance justified?

a. **No.** If the reliance was not induced by the promise, then it is not enforceable.

b. **Yes.** If the promisee actually relied on the promise and that reliance was reasonable based on the nature of the promise, then the promise may be enforceable if all the elements are satisfied. Proceed to the next question.

4. **Avoiding Injustice**—are the circumstances such that injustice can be avoided only by enforcement of the promise?

a. **No.** If not, then the promise is not enforceable.

b. **Yes.** If so, and all the other requirements are met, then the promise is enforceable. Proceed to the next question to determine the applicable remedy.

5. **Recovery may be Limited**—what is the appropriate form of relief? The remedy may be limited as justice requires. This means that the promisee may not receive full contractual relief which would include her expectation damages but may be limited to reimbursement of the actual loss expended in reliance on the promise.

C. **Modification**—is there consideration to support a promise modifying a duty under a contract not fully performed by either party?

1. **Pre-existing Duty**—is a party promising to perform a duty that she already owes?

a. **Yes.** If so, then the party has a pre-existing duty and there is no consideration to support the promise.

b. **No.** If not and the party is promising to perform a duty not already owed to the promisor, then there is consideration to support the promise.

2. **Modern Trend**—does the jurisdiction allow for a departure from a strict application of the pre-existing duty rule as reflected in R2d § 89 where a modification may be enforceable without consideration? If so, then a modification is binding absent consideration if all of the following requirements are met:

   a. **Voluntary**—did the parties voluntarily agree to the modification?

   b. **Executory**—is the contract still executory on both sides (each side still owes a performance)?

   c. **Unanticipated Circumstances**—were the underlying circumstances prompting the modification unanticipated by the parties?

   d. **Fair and Equitable**—is the modification fair and equitable?

3. **Sale of Goods**—is there a modification for a contract involving a sale of goods? If so, then consideration is not required under UCC 2–209 although the Code requires the modification to meet the test of **good faith**. Ask: was the modification made in good faith?

   a. **Yes.** If so, then the modification is enforceable.

   b. **No.** If the party acted in bad faith to escape a performance due under the original contract terms, then the modification is not enforceable.

ILLUSTRATIVE PROBLEMS

Consider the following problems. Here is an opportunity to apply the checklist to resolve questions involving consideration:

■ PROBLEM 3.1 ■

Julia was a copywriter for a catalog company. While she wrote product descriptions for camping equipment, she knew she had talent and was meant to be a great writer. Every night after work, she sat in front of her computer and wrote stories. She wrote about the people and places she knew from her childhood in the mid-west.

One day, she received an email from Mr. Spencer, the company president, complimenting her on copy she had written describing a pair of hiking boots. He wrote, "since you seem to have a true poetic sensibility, I'd like you to write a short story for the *Hemingway Hero* series. I am the editor of this anthology and we are always looking for new talent. I know how busy you are with your full-time job writing for my catalog company but I've read some of the stories you've written for the company newsletter, so if you write a story for *Hemingway Hero*, I will publish it and pay $5000."

Julia was overjoyed. She had been working on her writing and hoping for just such an opportunity. Julia thanked Mr. Spencer and said that she would be delighted to submit a story. She knew she had lots of stories already completed and worthy of submission. That night after work, she read through her stories and found one. It was a story about her grandfather. She revised it a bit by changing some of the names and locations and added some dramatic dialogue. When she finished, she thought it was her finest piece of writing. She sent her story to Mr. Spencer.

Is there consideration to support Mr. Spencer's promise of publication?

Analysis

The question is whether Julia's submission of a story she had written already was past consideration. A performance or return promise must be "bargained for" to constitute consideration. If the promisee has already taken the action, then the promisor cannot be said to have bargained for it when making the promise.

It is possible that Julia's promise might be past consideration because she had already written the story that she submitted to Mr. Spencer. His promise did not induce her to write the story because she wrote stories every night and had lots of completed stories worthy of submission. However, his promise did induce her to reread her stories, select one, and revise it by changing some of the names and locations and adding dialogue. Consequently, these actions would constitute consideration.

■   PROBLEM 3.2   ■

Nikolas Stone, a successful television producer, had the idea for a new television series based on the life stories of the contestants from *American Idol*, his current hit television show where ordinary people compete for a chance to win a recording contract with a major music label. In the past few seasons, there had been some very interesting contestants and sometimes the audience identified more with the losers than the winners. Nikolas thought that a television series about the lives of the losing contestants would be an instant hit.

Nikolas met with the contestants during a show rehearsal from the current season. He told them he would pay $10,000 for the exclusive use of each person's life story if he found it suitable for use in the new series, whether or not he actually used it in any episode, and if they agreed to forgo any further payments or royalties for his use of their story. Ten contestants agreed to his proposal and Nikolas tape recorded interviews with them. After several attempts at drafting a script for the new series, Nikolas concluded that the show needed a single story line because it was getting too confusing. Although many of the contestants had dramatic stories, Nikolas decided to concentrate on the story from only one of the contestants, that of a British woman named Lily.

Lily's tale was a real Cinderella story. As a child, Lily loved to sing and had a golden voice. She would sing every night with her mother. However, when Lily was only eight years old, her mother died in a car accident and Lily refused to sing another note. She grew up and became an accountant. She never thought about singing again until she heard her co-workers talking about *American Idol*. She watched an episode and decided to take a chance. She quit her job at the accounting firm, packed up her few belongings, and took the next flight from London to New York for an audition.

When Lily stepped on stage, everyone started to laugh—the audience, the other contestants, the show's producers, even the camera and stage crew. Lily did not look like any of the other contestants: she was a lot older, dressed oddly, and her hair had a life of its own. Then the music began and Lily started to sing. Suddenly, not a sound could be heard but Lily's voice. When she concluded, the entire audience stood up and cheered. Lily won several rounds in the competition but ultimately lost to another singer with more stage appeal.

Lily was upset but she got over it when the new series based on her life story was a huge success. Nikolas earned millions of dollars. Critics agreed that the show's success was based largely on Lily's compelling story. None of the contestants interviewed for the series except Lily has received any money from Nikolas. He paid Lily $10,000 but when the show became a hit, he feared that she might sue for additional compensation. He told her, "We couldn't have done this without your story" and he promised her "1% of the net profit from any use of her story." Lily was grateful and told Nikolas that this would make it possible for her to stop working as an accountant and begin a singing career. As it turned out, her singing career was exceedingly short-lived—although she had a terrific voice, she could sing only one song. There's not much a future for a one-song singer. Now poor Lily had no job.

Nikolas faithfully paid her throughout the original broadcast of the television series. When that ended, however, he refused to pay her anything derived from the reruns or a subsequent movie version that he produced.

Nikolas is concerned that Lily and the other contestants he interviewed may bring an action against him. Assuming you have been admitted to the bar, advise him.

Analysis

For purposes of analysis, we will consider Lily's claims before we consider those of the other contestants. Lily may seek to bring a claim for 1% of the revenue earned from the reruns and movie version of her life. The question is whether there is consideration to support Nikolas's promise to pay her 1% of the net profit from "any use of her story" or whether there was a pre-existing duty.

Originally, Nikolas promised to pay Lily $10,000 for the use of her life story "if he found it suitable for use in the new series." When Lily agreed, this constituted the bargained for exchange. Arguably, there is no consideration on Lily's part to support the new promise to pay her the 1% of the net profit since she had already promised her story for the television series. However, it may be possible to claim that there was a new promise—Nikolas made a new promise to pay for *any use* of her story and not just its use in the television series. In this case, there would be consideration.

Alternatively, it is possible for Lily to claim that there was a modification to the parties' agreement. A promise modifying a duty under a contract not fully performed on either side is binding if the modification is fair and equitable in view of circumstances not anticipated by the parties when the contract was made. Depending on whether there was still a performance due on Lily's part, then in exchange for her promise each time to forego further payments (the original promise), then she would receive the 1% of the net profits. Further, Nikolas's belief that she might have a claim for more money would be consideration for her promise to accept the 1% deal.

Assuming, however, that Lily's claim failed on these theories, she could bring a claim based on reliance. Here, Nikolas made a promise to pay her 1% of the net profit from any use of her story. It would be reasonably foreseeable to him that she would rely on this promise because she told him that this money would make it possible for her to stop working as an accountant and begin a singing career. She actually relied on the promise because she quit her job and pursued a singing career. Her reliance was to her detriment because she had a very short career as a singer and then had no job. Since the requirements for promissory estoppel have been met, the court could enforce the promise to avoid injustice.

The question with respect to the other ten contestants is limited to the issue of whether Nikolas's promise to pay each contestant $10,000 was an illusory promise. The analysis is identical for all of the contestants because there is no basis in the facts to differentiate between them.

A promise is illusory if by its terms it makes performance entirely optional with the promisor. However, if the promisor has limited its discretion in some way, then the promise is not illusory. Here, Nikolas promised to pay for the use of the person's life story "if he found it suitable for use in the new series." Such language would appear to be non-committal, leaving Nikolas with sole discretion as to whether or not he would use the story. However, such discretion is limited by the obligation of good faith. As a result, Nikolas was obligated to exercise his discretion in good faith in determining whether the candidate's life story was actually suitable for use in the series. This means that his promise was not illusory and he would be bound to pay those candidates with stories that were suitable. However, we do not have enough facts to make this determination. While the facts indicate that many of the contestants had "dramatic stories," this is insufficient to determine whether they satisfied the criteria. Additional facts would be necessary to make this assessment.

POINTS TO REMEMBER

- Many contracts professors choose to begin the course with an examination of consideration doctrine. This is an excellent starting point and usually provides an overview for understanding the bases for promissory liability: the expectation, reliance, and restitution interests.

- The classic formula for the formation of a contract is the mutual assent of the parties and consideration. However, consideration is not always necessary or sufficient to make a promise enforceable. Some promises lacking consideration may be enforceable under alternate theories such as promissory estoppel or restitution. Do not forget to consider these options when the traditional "bargained-for exchange" element is absent.

- Even if a party uses such traditional language as "I promise," be careful to assess the words carefully to determine whether a commitment has been made. Such language as "I promise to do it if I want to" is an illusory promise because the promisor has made her performance conditional on an event entirely within her own control.

- A promise may appear illusory where it is subject to the promisor's discretion as in requirements/output contracts, exclusive dealings, and contracts with satisfaction clauses. However, the promisor has an obligation to exercise her discretion in good faith and this prevents the promise from being illusory.

- Remember that promissory estoppel may not provide relief in every case of reliance. Be sure to examine the facts carefully to determine whether it was reasonably foreseeable to the promisor that the promisee would rely on the promise. Even if relief is granted under this theory, it "may be limited as justice requires" and it is likely that recovery will be limited to damages based on the reliance interest.

CHAPTER 4

Statute of Frauds

REVIEW OF THE STATUTE OF FRAUDS

R2d § 110, 116, 127, 130,
131, 132, 134, 139

Certain agreements must be in writing to be enforceable. When we speak of such an agreement, we say that the contract "falls within the statute of frauds." This does not mean that an agreement must be in writing to be legally binding. Oral agreements may be as binding as written ones. However, certain classes of agreements fall within the statute's requirement and must be in writing to be enforced by legal action. Typically, a defense based on the statute of frauds is raised at the beginning of litigation by a motion to dismiss or a motion for summary judgment. If the plaintiff overcomes the statute of frauds challenge, the case proceeds to a trial on the merits where she has the burden to establish a contract was formed, the defendant breached, and plaintiff has suffered damages.

The Restatement Second identifies the types of contracts required by the statute of frauds to be evidenced by a "written memorandum" as follows:[1]

1. Contracts of executors or administrators to answer for the duty of their decedents.

2. Contracts to answer for the duty of another (the suretyship provision).

    This provision refers to a suretyship agreement. Specifically, it is a promise made (1) by one who is not presently liable for the debt (2) to a creditor (3) in order to discharge the present or future obligations of a third person (the present debtor).

    For example, suppose Sam wants to borrow money from Dan but his credit history is poor and Dan does not want to rely solely on Sam's ability to repay the loan. Dan agrees to make the loan if Sam can find someone who will pay Dan if Sam defaults. Sam's law school study partner, Gina, agrees to do so. She enters into a separate agreement with Dan where she promises to pay Dan if Sam does not. This agreement must be in writing and signed by Gina to be enforceable.

    Note, however, that this does not apply if the underlying contract was between the promisor and the creditor. For example, if Sam orally tells Ben to "send the Contracts casebook to Dan and send the bill of $85 to me," the primary contract is between Sam and Ben and not between Sam and Dan. Dan is merely a third party beneficiary and the contract between Sam and Ben is enforceable even though it is not in writing.

    The exception to the suretyship provision is the "main purpose" rule.[2] This is where the guarantor's main purpose in making the promise is to benefit herself. Even where the promise is collateral ("I'll pay if X doesn't"), if it appears that the promisor's primary purpose in guaranteeing the obligation

---

1. Restatement (Second) of Contracts § 110 (1979).

2. Restatement (Second) of Contracts § 116 (1979).

of another was to secure an advance or pecuniary benefit for herself, her promise is enforceable even though it is not in writing.

3. Contract made upon consideration of marriage (the marriage provision).

    This provision does not apply to mutual promises to marry but covers prenuptial agreements or contracts entered into in anticipation of the marriage in which some property settlement or other financial arrangement is made in consideration of the upcoming marriage.

4. Contract for the sale of an interest in land (the land contract provision).

    This provision pertains to any agreement with a promise to create or transfer an interest in land. It covers transfers of legal and equitable interests and of present and future interests.[3] The provision does not cover a right to use land if it is characterized as a license as opposed to an easement or a lease.[4] The term "interest" refers to "any right, privilege, power or immunity, or combination thereof[.]"[5] While a contract to make a lease is one to transfer an interest in land, most states have statute of frauds exceptions for short-term leases for a year or less.[6]

5. Contracts that cannot be performed within one year from their making (the one-year provision).

    This provision refers to a contract, which by its terms, cannot be fully performed within one year from its making. The one-year period begins from the date the contract is made, not from when performance is promised. Therefore, the two critical reference points to consider when determining whether a

---

3. Restatement (Second) of Contracts § 127 cmt. a (1979).

4. E. Allan Farnsworth, *Contracts*, § 6.5 (4th ed. 2004).

5. Restatement (Second) of Contracts § 127.

6. Restatement (Second) of Contracts § 125 cmt. b. (1979).

writing is necessary are the time of the making of the contract (not the making of the offer) and the time when performance is to be completed. A writing is required only if the contract specifically precludes performance within one year—not just that performance appears to be impossible to complete.

6.   Contracts for the sale of goods for $500[7] or more.

While sales of goods were one of the categories covered in the original statute of frauds, they are now incorporated into Article 2 and covered by UCC 2–201. The Code has made some major changes to the common law. These changes make it easier to satisfy the statute and relate to the requirements for a memorandum, the possibility of satisfaction by an admission or by a confirmatory memorandum, the effect of part performance, and the exception for specially manufactured goods.

Satisfying The Statute

The requirements of the statute are cumulative: this means that if more than one requirement applies to a single contract, then all must be met. Also, the fact that a written agreement falls within the statute does not prevent its modification by a subsequent oral agreement. However, the modifying agreement may itself fall within the statute of frauds, in which case its requirements must be met to be enforceable. This is true regardless of whether the original agreement required a writing.

The statute of frauds has three requirements that must be satisfied to make the contract enforceable: a writing, a signature, and sufficient information in the writing to evidence the agreement. Although the statute requires the agreement to be memorialized in a writing, modern law recognizes advances in technology and accepts other forms of recording, including electronic recordings. As a result, the 2003 revision of Article 2 substitutes the word "record" for "writing," where "record" is

---

7.   U.C.C. § 2–201 (2004). The 2003 revision of UCC 2–201 changes this amount to $5000.

defined in revised UCC 2–103(1)(m) as "information that is inscribed on a tangible medium or that is stored in an electronic or
other medium and is retrievable in perceivable form."[8]

While the statute of frauds requires no particular form for a
writing, it must be signed by the party to be charged with its
enforcement and it must reflect the agreement with adequate
specificity. The writing need not be contained in one document but
can be pieced together from several related documents. Also, the
writing need not be signed by both parties, as long as the person
who is denying the contract ("the party to be charged") has signed
it. Here, too, there is considerable flexibility in what constitutes a
"signature": Restatement Second § 134 defines "signature" to
mean "any symbol made or adopted with an intention, actual or
apparent, to authenticate the writing as that of the signer."[9] Also,
UETA and E–SIGN give effect to signatures in electronic form.
Finally, the Restatement requires that the content of the writing be
sufficient to show a contract was made by stating "with reasonable
certainty the essential terms of the unperformed promises in the
contract."[10] UCC 2–201 is even more flexible in this regard and will
find the statute satisfied even if the writing "omits or incorrectly
states a term[.]"[11] Thus, the required writing need not contain all
the material terms of the contract and the ones stated need not
even be correctly stated. Further, it is permissible for the parties to
omit the price term in which case the Code's "gap filler" will
provide one. The only term the Code requires is the quantity
term.[12]

Exceptions

Part Performance

Generally, part performance does not make a contract that
otherwise falls within the statute enforceable. However, the party

---

8. U.C.C. § 2–103(1)(m) (Proposed Revision 2003).

9. Restatement (Second) of Contracts § 134
(1979).

10. Restatement (Second) of Contracts
§ 131(c) (1979).

11. U.C.C. § 2–201(1).

12. *Id.* § 2–201 cmt. 1.

may have a claim based on restitution or reliance. Although there is no exception for part performance of a contract within the one-year provision, most courts have held that a party who has fully performed such a contract can enforce it.[13]

The exception is limited and most commonly applied in contracts for the sale of land. For example, under the part performance rule, a court may grant specific performance of an oral agreement to transfer an interest in land if there has been "performance 'unequivocally referable' to the agreement, performance which alone and without the aid of words of promise is unintelligible or at least extraordinary unless as an incident of ownership[.]"[14]

Unilateral Contracts

Even though a promise under a unilateral contract may not be capable of performance within a year of its making, it does not fall within the statute of frauds. It would not make sense otherwise to apply the one-year provision in a jurisdiction where full performance within a year satisfies the statute—or even in jurisdictions that do not recognize the full performance exception. Think of it this way: in a unilateral contract, performance is the acceptance that creates the contract and so the contract is complete at the inception of the one-year period.

Promissory Estoppel

Generally, courts have found that promissory estoppel was not available where the statute of frauds was raised as a defense; the traditional view was that reliance on an oral promise did not make the promise enforceable.[15] Instead, reliance has become a basis for recovery through case law and the impact of a new section to the Restatement Second.[16] Under Restatement § 139, a promise is

---

13. Farnsworth, *Contracts*, at § 6.9. *See* Restatement (Second) of Contracts § 130 (1979).

14. *Burns v. McCormick*, 135 N.E. 273 (N.Y. 1922).

15. E. Allan Farnsworth, *Contracts*, § 6.12 (4th ed. 2004).

16. *Id.*

enforceable by virtue of action taken in reliance on a promise by the promisee or a third person when the reliance is foreseeable by the promisor, notwithstanding the statute of frauds, if enforcement is necessary to avoid injustice. This section identifies criteria for assessing whether injustice can be avoided. Even if the reliance was justified, the detriment suffered in reliance must be of a "definite and substantial character" to warrant enforcement of the promise.[17] The availability and adequacy of such other remedies as cancellation and restitution are considered as well.[18]

Some courts have refused to grant relief under promissory estoppel in cases involving the sale of goods. This is because UCC 2–201(3) lists the circumstances under which the writing requirement may be avoided and it does not include the estoppel principle. If estoppel is applicable at all, it enters via section 1–103 which states that principles of law and equity, including estoppel, are available to supplement the Code's specific provisions. But here it gets complicated because section 2–201 begins with the words, "Except as otherwise provided in this section" and these words have been read by courts to mean that estoppel is displaced by the specificity of section 2–201(3)(a).[19]

REVIEW OF THE STATUTE OF FRAUDS UNDER THE UCC

> UCC 1-103, 2-201

The general rule is set forth in UCC 2–201 and requires that there be "some writing sufficient to indicate that a contract for sale has been made between the parties and signed by the party against whom enforcement is sought[.]"[20] However, there are several notable exceptions where an oral contract is enforceable absent a writing. These include the following:

1. The contract calls for specially manufactured goods for the

---

17. *See* Restatement (Second) of Contracts § 130(2)(b) (1979).

18. Restatement (Second) of Contracts § 139(2)(a) (1979).

19. James J. White & Robert S. Summers, *Uniform Commercial Code*, § 2–6 n.9 (5th ed. 2000).

20. U.C.C. § 2–201(1).

buyer and the seller has made a substantial beginning in their manufacture. UCC 2–201(3)(a).

2. The contract is *between merchants* and within a reasonable time a written confirmation of the oral contract is sent by one of the parties and the party receiving it does not send a written objection within 10 days. UCC 2–201(2).

3. The contract is admitted in court pleadings or testimony by the party against whom enforcement is sought. UCC 2–201(3)(b).

4. Goods for which payment has been made and accepted or which have been received and accepted. UCC 2–201(3)(c).

 STATUTE OF FRAUDS CHECKLIST

With this review in mind, here is the checklist for analyzing problems presenting questions involving the statute of frauds:

A. **Type of Contract**—assuming a valid contract was formed, does it fall within the statute of frauds? Only certain categories of contracts are required to be in writing to be enforceable. To determine whether a writing is required, ask what type of contract it is:

- Is it a contract for a sale of an interest in land?

- Is it a contract for a sale of goods for $500 or more?

- Is it a contract that cannot be performed within a year of its making?

- Is it a contract to answer for the debt of another?

- Is it a contract made in consideration of marriage?

- Is it a contract by an executor or administrator to answer for the duty of their decedents?

1. **Yes.** If your answer is *"yes"* to any of the above, then the contract must be in writing. Further, the requirements of the statute apply separately so that if more than one requirement applies to a single contract, then all must be met. Proceed to Part B.

2. No. If not, then the contract does not need to be in writing to be enforceable and the analysis ends here.

B. Written Memorial—is there a writing or record sufficient to satisfy the requirements of the statute? Where a contract is required to be in writing, it must be in a permanent, written form, contain the essential terms, and be signed by the party to be charged. The requirements of the Code are similar and any differences will be addressed where applicable.

1. **Form of Writing/Record**—is there a written memorial of the parties' agreement? Is there some form of a writing even if it appears on a napkin, as an internal memorandum, a document written for some other purpose, a check, or a series of separate writings, which when considered together, provide evidence of the parties' agreement?

   a. **No.** If there is no evidence of a writing, then the statute is not satisfied. Proceed to Part C to determine whether an exception applies.

   b. **Yes.** As long as it is in a permanent, written form it does not have to be a fully integrated, formal contract. Proceed to the next question.

2. **Essential Terms**—does the writing/record contain the essential terms of the agreement? Ask: does it identify the subject matter of the contract, the parties to the contract, and state with reasonable certainty the essential terms of the unperformed promises?

   a. **No.** If the memo fails to identify the parties, the subject matter of the contract, and its essential terms, then the statute is not satisfied. There is an exception for the sale of goods where, with respect to the required terms, only the quantity term is required. Proceed to Part C.

   b. **Yes.** If so, then the general requirements of the memorandum are satisfied. Proceed to the next question.

3. **Signature**—is the writing signed by or on behalf of the party to be charged with its enforcement?

   a. **Yes.** If so, then this requirement is satisfied.

b. **No.** If not, then this requirement is not satisfied unless the following exception for the sale of goods applies. Ask: has a **merchant** sent a written confirmation to another **merchant** who has reason to know its contents and it is in a form sufficient to bind the sender?

    i. **Yes.** If so, then the requirement of a writing is satisfied and the other merchant is bound unless she gives written notice of objection within 10 days of receipt. UCC 2–201(2).[21]

    ii. **No.** If not, then the contract is not enforceable unless an exception applies. Proceed to Part C.

C. **Exceptions**—is there an exception that will allow enforcement of the contract despite the lack of a signed writing?

  1. **Part Performance**—has there been part performance of the contract?

    a. **Yes.** If so, then part performance of the oral agreement may provide reliable evidence that a contract was made. Ask the following:

      i. **Land Contract Provision?** Was there part performance of a contract falling within the land contract provision? For example, has the purchaser taken possession of the land and made substantial improvements which are not compensable in money and are such as to evidence a contract to sell as opposed to a landlord-tenant relationship?[22] If so, a court may grant specific performance of an oral agreement to transfer an interest in land.

      ii. **One-year Rule?** Was there part performance of a contract within the one-year provision? If so, then if the party has fully performed the contract, she can enforce it absent a writing.

      ii. **Sale of Goods?** Was it a contract for the sale of goods? If so, then a writing is not required "with respect to

---

21. This provision is the same in the 2003 revision.   **22.** Farnsworth, *Contracts*, § 6.9.

goods for which payment has been made and accepted or which have been received and accepted[.]" UCC 2–201(3)(c).[23]

b. **No.** If not, proceed to the next question to see if another exception may be applicable.

2. **Specially Manufactured Goods**—has the seller specially manufactured goods for the buyer or made a substantial beginning of their manufacture or commitments for their procurement? UCC 2–201(3)(a).

a. **Yes.** If so, and the goods are not suitable for sale to others in the ordinary course of the seller's business, then the contract is enforceable.

b. **No.** If not, then proceed to the next question.

3. **Admissions**—in a contract for the sale of goods, has "the party against whom enforcement is sought admit[ted] in his pleading, testimony, or otherwise in court that a contract for sale was made?"[24]

a. **Yes.** If so, the contract is enforceable but not beyond the quantity of goods admitted.

b. **No.** If not, proceed to the next question.

4. **Promissory Estoppel**—has the promisee relied to her detriment on a promise which the promisor could reasonably foresee would induce such reliance and injustice can only be avoided by enforcement of the promise?

a. **Yes**. If so, then the promise is enforceable.

b. **No.** If the reliance was not of a definite and substantial character or other remedies such as cancellation or restitution would be available and adequate, then the promise is not enforceable absent a writing.

ILLUSTRATIVE PROBLEMS

The following problems allow us to see how the checklist can be used to resolve issues regarding the statute of frauds.

---

23. U.C.C. §§ 2–20(3)(a) and (c) are the same in the current and revised Article 2.

24. The 2003 revision of U.C.C. § 2–

201(3)(b) substitutes the words "under oath" for "in court."

■ PROBLEM 4.1 ■

On September 1, Sam Picasso enters into an oral agreement to paint a mural of a scene from the novel, *The Great Gatsby*, in the lobby of the Gatsby Hotel for $1500. The parties agree that Sam would begin the project on November 1 and would complete it no later than December 31 of the following year, giving him almost 14 months to create the mural. The Gatsby Hotel agreed to pay Sam upon completion of the mural. On October 31, the Gatsby Hotel called Sam and told him not to paint the mural because it had decided to go with a completely different look in the lobby and would not need a mural. When Sam Picasso brings suit for breach of contract, the Gatsby Hotel claims the statute of frauds as its defense. What result?

Analysis

The first issue to determine is whether the contract falls within the Uniform Commercial Code or the common law. The agreement for Sam to paint a mural might be considered a hybrid transaction because painting the mural will require Sam to use paint, which is a "good" under the Code while his act of painting is the performance of services. In such cases where there is a combination of goods and services involved in the transaction, the Code applies the "predominant purpose" test and asks what is the predominant purpose of the contract. In this case, the question is whether the predominant purpose of the contract is the sale of paint or for Sam to use his artistic talents to paint a mural. It seems clear that the parties intended Sam to create a work of art which is a contract for his services, not the sale of paint. Consequently, the common law rules apply to this analysis.

The next question is whether it was the type of contract which was required to be in writing to be enforceable. Based on the facts, the statute of fraud's one-year rule is implicated. The one-year rule requires that contracts that cannot be completed within a year of their making must be in writing. Here, the Picasso–Gatsby contract was entered into on November 1. While the terms of the contract specified that Picasso was to complete the mural no later than December 31 of the following year, which would be 14 months after the making of the contract, it was possible for the contract to be completed before that time. The one-year rule is interpreted to mean that the contract, by its terms, clearly cannot be performed within a year of its making. In this case, since the mural could have been completed within a year and the contract terms only defined a final completion date, a writing was not required. The Gatsby Hotel will not be successful in its claim because the statute of frauds is not a bar to enforcement of the contract.

■ PROBLEM 4.2 ■

Meredith owns a chain of twenty children's furniture stores. She wanted to create a unique experience for the children who would come to the store with their parents so she decided to build two special play areas in each store, one with a Cinderella theme and one with a sports theme. Part of her plan was to include life-size figures of Cinderella and Derek Jeter, the Yankee baseball player. Meredith's friend, Lisa, manufactures mannequins for department stores so Meredith asked her about making the Cinderella and Jeter figures. Lisa thought it was a great idea. She had a mannequin mold she could use for Cinderella because she had created one for her daughter's fifth birthday party but she would have to create a special design and mannequin mold for Derek Jeter. Following negotiations, the parties reached an oral agreement on June 5 in which Lisa agreed to make 20 Cinderella figures and 20 Derek Jeter figures. Each figure would be life-size and fully bendable, just like a department-store mannequin. The Cinderella figure cost $300 each and each Derek Jeter figure cost $400. Lisa said that she would be able to deliver the figures by August 15. Meredith was thrilled because she wanted them in the stores by this date because many parents shopped for furniture when their children returned to school.

(1) On June 8, Meredith called and cancelled the order. She told Lisa that she decided on different themes for her stores after

finding "Hello Kitty" stuffed animals for $50 each and model cars for $100 at an auction. When Lisa said that Meredith could not cancel because they had a contract, Meredith said she never agreed to anything. Lisa has not started making the special design and mold for the Derek Jeter figure. Can Lisa enforce the oral agreement against Meredith?

(2) For the purposes of this question only, assume the following additional facts: on June 6, Lisa hired an artist to design the prototype mold for the Derek Jeter figure at a cost of $1000. She also called her supplier and ordered the necessary composite molds to make the 50 Cinderella and 100 Derek figures. When Meredith calls to cancel her order on June 8, can Lisa enforce the oral agreement?

(3) For the purposes of this question only, assume the following additional facts: on June 6, Lisa sent a memo to Meredith on her corporate letterhead with the company's mannequin logo on it confirming their contract. It contained all the terms of the agreement but Lisa did not sign it. When Meredith received the memo, she glanced at it and filed it away. On June 20, Meredith calls Lisa to cancel the contract. Can Lisa enforce the agreement?

Analysis

(1) As with all contracts problems, the threshold question is to determine whether the contract falls within the Uniform Commercial Code or the common law. Here it is a simple matter because the transaction involves the sale of figurines which would qualify as "goods" under the Uniform Commercial Code where goods are all things movable at the time of identification to the contract.

The next question is whether it was the type of contract which was required to be in writing to be enforceable. Contracts for the sale of goods for $500 or more ($5000 in revised 2–201(1)) are required to be in writing. Here the contract was well in excess of $500 since it was for $20,000 and therefore a writing would be required. However, there was no written agreement and unless there is an applicable exception, the agreement is unenforceable. Since the facts indicate that Lisa had not yet taken any steps in performing or beginning to perform the design or manufacture of the Cinderella or Derek Jeter figures, the part performance exception available under UCC 2–201(3)(a) would not be applicable. While Lisa might decide not to be friends with Meredith in the future, she has no legal basis on which to enforce the agreement.

(2)   Given the facts in this question, Lisa can invoke the part performance exception under UCC 2–201(3)(a) to survive a statute of frauds challenge. Under the Code, where a contract is valid in other respects but fails to satisfy the requirement of a writing, the contract is enforceable under the part performance exception if the goods are specially manufactured and not suitable for sale to others in the ordinary course of the seller's business. The seller would have to make either a substantial beginning of their manufacture or commitments for their procurement before the buyer repudiated.

Here, Lisa made a substantial beginning in the manufacture of the figures because she hired an artist on June 6 to design the prototype mold for the Derek Jeter figure for $1000. She also called her supplier and ordered the necessary composite molds to make the 50 Cinderella and 100 Derek Jeter figures. This was before Meredith called to cancel on June 8. However, Meredith could claim that Lisa's actions were insufficient to constitute a "substantial beginning" since it was just a design for the prototype for the Jeter mold and not the actual manufacture of the mannequins. Her argument with respect to Cinderella is similar— Lisa already had the Cinderella mold and was just ordering the composite necessary to make the mannequins. In this case, Meredith's argument is that there had been no actual manufacturing of the mannequins and they do not yet exist.

Alternatively, Lisa could claim that, at the very least, her actions represent "commitments for their procurement" because they are the essential prerequisites to manufacturing the mannequins. While Lisa will claim that her actions bring her within the statutory exception, Meredith has a strong argument that getting a design for a mold and ordering molds do not constitute the actions required by the statute.

The next question is whether the figures were suitable for sale to others in the ordinary course of Lisa's business even though they were to be specially manufactured for Meredith. Lisa's business is to manufacture mannequins for department stores and while it is possible that she might someday have an order for a princess or sports figure, it is highly unlikely that her ordinary business customers would be in the market to buy Cinderella and Derek Jeter mannequins for their stores.

However, no mannequins have yet been manufactured. Only a design for a Jeter mold and the composite molds have been ordered. The Jeter design would only be useful for a Jeter mannequin and the court might find that the contract with respect to this part of the agreement might be enforceable under the specially manufactured goods exception. The situation with respect to Cinderella is different: presumably the composite molds ordered to make the Cinderella mannequins could be used to manufacture any type of mannequin. In this case, the composite could be used for another order and would not satisfy the statutory exception.

(3)   Given these facts, Lisa can invoke the exception to the signature requirement where both parties to the contract for the sale of goods are merchants. Under 2–201(2), a confirmatory writing can be enforced against the party who did not sign it if the following requirements are met: both parties are merchants; the written confirmation is sent within a reasonable time following the oral agreement; the confirmation is signed by the sending party and fulfills all the statute's requirements for a writing; and, the recipient has reason to know its contents and does not object in writing within 10 days of receipt.

In this case, both Lisa and Meredith qualify as merchants: Lisa is a manufacturer of mannequins for department stores and Meredith owns a chain of furniture stores. Both of them would be considered persons who, by their occupations, have knowledge or skill peculiar to the practices or goods involved. Lisa sent a written memo to Meredith on June 6, the day following their conversation, so it was timely. The confirmation was on Lisa's corporate letter-head which identifies it as business correspondence. Since it contained all the essential terms of the parties agreement, it is in compliance with the general requirements for an enforceable writing. The fact that Lisa did not sign the memo is not fatal because the memo's letterhead with its corporate logo would be recognized as a signature. If Meredith had objections to the memo, she had a duty to do so in writing within 10 days of receipt. However, she did not do this but merely filed the memo. Conse-quently, when she called Lisa on June 20, she could not longer object to the contract and was bound.

POINTS TO REMEMBER

- As a general rule, oral agreements are binding even though it is always a good idea to record a contract in writing. However, certain kinds of contracts must be in writing to be enforceable and these contracts are said to "fall within the statute of frauds."

- Only the party who is to be charged with enforcement of the contract needs to have signed it, unless the "merchant excep-tion" is applicable.

- The statute of frauds does not require the entire contract to be written—there just has to be a memo which identifies the parties, the subject matter of the contract, and contains its essential terms.

- In applying the one-year rule, remember that the year starts to run from the making of the contract, not from when the performance under the contract is to begin. Only contracts which by their terms cannot be performed within a year of their execution must be in writing.

Formation ➡	Avoiding ➡ the Deal	Performance ➡	Third ➡ Parties	Remedies
Do we have a deal?	We have a deal, but	Who has to do what and when, or maybe not	Is there a third party to the deal?	Someone failed to perform when required, now what?
Mutual Assent + Consideration				

Excerpts of Contracts Time-line

AVOIDING THE DEAL
WE HAVE A DEAL, BUT

Statute of Frauds

Misunderstanding

Mistake

- Unilateral

- Mutual

Incapacity

Fraud/Misrepresentation

Duress

Undue Influence

Unconscionability

- Procedural

- Substantive

Illegality/Public policy

Close-up of Avoiding the Deal

CHAPTER 5

Defenses and Limits on Enforceability

Although parties may have satisfied all the requirements for an otherwise enforceable agreement—offer, acceptance, and consideration—there are still bases on which a court may refuse to enforce the contract. The focus in this chapter is on defenses which arise at the time of contract formation. These differ from defenses to performance which arise subsequent to formation and will be discussed in a later chapter. Generally, what is at issue is the question of assent: since a party's assent is critical to contract formation, if a court finds that there was no assent, it was induced by improper means, or a party was incapable of giving consent, then it may refuse to enforce the contract, in whole or in part.

The principles covered in this section share a common remedial theme even though each has its own specific requirements. In the case where there has been no assent, then naturally no contract has been formed. In other instances, the remedy is to allow the party to avoid the contract. A voidable contract is not the same as a void contract. A void contract is not a contract—it is a legal nullity. On the other hand, a voidable contract is one where the aggrieved party can choose to render the promised performance or rescind the agreement. The party entitled to avoid the contract may sue affirmatively or claim the right of avoidance if sued by the other party for non-performance.

REVIEW OF DEFENSES

For the purposes of our discussion, we will divide contract defenses or claims for avoidance into several categories. Of course this is not the only way to think about the material and it is very likely your professor will present it in another way. If so, then follow what your professor tells you. Just remember that legal principles do not fit neatly into categories so be prepared to be flexible in your thinking.

The first case is where no contract has been formed because of the problem of "misunderstanding." This is conceptually different from the following sets of circumstances where a contract has been formed but a court may refuse to enforce it:[1]

- Where the parties to the agreement are impermissible (incapacity)

- Where there are defects in the bargaining process (mistake, fraud and misrepresentation, duress, undue influence, unconscionability)

- Where there are impermissible terms in the agreement (unconscionability, illegality)

Misunderstanding

R2d § 20

In order for a contract to be formed, both parties must agree to the same deal. However, it may happen that although both parties think they are agreeing to the same terms, each has a different subjective belief about what the deal is. If this discrepancy in subjective belief is sufficiently material, it may prevent a contract from forming.

In cases of misunderstanding, the parties express assent to the same words or terms, but attach materially different meanings to

---

1. Edward J. Murphy, Richard E. Speidel, & Ian Ayres, *Studies in Contract Law*, 450 (6th ed. 2003).

what they have said. While each person may say the same thing, each means something completely different. Consequently, there is no mutual assent and hence, no contract is formed.

However, it is not always this simple since the meaning attributed to words depends on the context and surrounding circumstances. As a result, there is often a problem of interpretation in determining whether a contract has been formed as well as in determining the terms of the agreement.[2]

The classic case on this subject involves the ship Peerless, or more accurately, the two ships named Peerless. In *Raffles v. Wichelhaus*,[3] the plaintiff agreed to sell to the defendant, and the defendant agreed to buy, cotton at a stated price. The cotton was to arrive on the ship Peerless sailing from Bombay. However, when the ship arrived in Liverpool, the defendant refused to accept delivery and pay for the cotton. Apparently, there were two ships named Peerless leaving from Bombay—one sailing in October and the other in December—and the parties had different "Peerlesses" in mind when making the contract. The defendant refused to accept the cotton that arrived on the December Peerless, claiming that he had meant the earlier ship when he made the agreement. The plaintiff brought suit and the court held for the defendant, finding that there could be no contract if the defendant meant one ship while the plaintiff meant another. There was no *"consensus ad idem"*—no agreement on the same thing.[4] The general principle from this case is found in Restatement Second § 20 which states that where parties attach "materially different meanings" to their "manifestations" and neither party has reason to know of the meaning attached by the other, there is no "manifestation of mutual assent."[5]

---

2. Restatement (Second) of Contracts § 20 cmt. c (1979).

3. 159 Eng. Rep. 375 (1864).

4. *Id*. at 376.

5. Restatement (Second) of Contracts § 20(1).

Capacity to Contract

R2d § 12, 14, 15, 16

A person must have legal capacity to contract. The general rule is that a contract made by a party while under a legal incapacity is voidable. The public policy is to protect children and the mentally infirm from exploitation.

Infancy

One such incapacity is based on age where a person under the age of 18 has the capacity to incur only voidable contractual duties "until the beginning of the day before the person's eighteenth birthday."[6] A minor may avoid or "disaffirm" a contract or choose to perform. If a minor chooses to disaffirm, she may disaffirm at any time before reaching majority or within a reasonable time thereafter.[7] Even if the minor performed the contract during infancy, the right to disaffirm at attaining majority remains.

An infant may *disaffirm* a contract (the whole, not merely parts), by words or conduct, either before or after a reasonable time upon reaching majority. Failure to disaffirm within a reasonable time of attaining majority constitutes a "ratification" of the contract and the minor is bound, thus terminating the power to disaffirm. Ratification can be by words or conduct such as performance of the contractual obligation or accepting the other party's performance under the contract.

Upon disaffirmance, the minor is not required to make restitution; instead, the minor is required to return only what she

---

6. Restatement (Second) of Contracts § 14 (1979). Common law set the age of majority at twenty-one; however, in almost every state this rule has been changed by statute where the usual age is 18.

7. What constitutes a "reasonable time" is a question of fact, depending on the transaction and all the surrounding circumstances. *See Bobby Floars Toyota v. Smith*, 269 S.E.2d 320

(N.C. 1980) (finding eleven car payments with ten being made after the eighteenth birthday to be ratification of the contract). *Cf. Keser v. Chagnon*, 410 P.2d 637 (Colo. 1966) (the court did not find ratification for the purchase of a car by a minor sixty days after reaching the age of majority before disaffirming and returning the car ten days after that).

still has in possession. Moreover, there is no obligation to account for use, depreciation, or loss in value. Even where necessaries are involved, recovery is limited to unjust enrichment.[8]

The exception to the minor's ability to disaffirm is where the contract is for "necessaries." Theoretically, this exception is not based in contract but upon quasi-contract—a contract implied in law.[9] "Necessaries" is a elastic term and includes goods and services that are essential for maintaining the minor's existence. Whether goods are "necessaries" is a question of law and if found to be so, their quantity, quality, and reasonable value are matters of fact. Determining what are or are not necessaries takes into account what is reasonable and necessary for the "proper and suitable maintenance of the infant in view of his social position and situation in life, the customs of the social circle in which he moves or is likely to move, and the fortune possessed by him and by his parents."[10] Clearly, necessaries can go beyond what is essential for bare sustenance, provided the minor actually needs them at the time and must procure them for himself.

Mental Incapacity

Unlike an infant, an adult is presumed to have contractual capacity. However, this presumption is rebuttable and the party claiming incompetence has the burden of proving a lack of mental competency at the time of contracting.[11] As in the case of a minor, most courts treat incapacity as making the contract voidable, not void.

In assessing a claim for mental incompetency, the reasonable expectations of the other contracting party play a greater role than they do with infancy claims. A person who enters into a contract with a minor is on notice that the other party may lack capacity because of the party's youthful appearance. It is easy enough to ask

---

8. Murphy, *supra* note 1, at 457 n.7. *See also*, Steven Wolfe, *A Reevaluation of the Contractual Rights of Minors*, 57 UMKC L.Rev. 145 (1988).

9. *Webster St. P'ship, Ltd. v. Sheridan*, 368 N.W.2d 439 (Neb. 1985).

10. *Bowling v. Sperry*, 184 N.E.2d 901, 904 (Ind. Ct. App. 1962).

11. *Heights Realty, Ltd. v. Phillips*, 749 P.2d 77 (N.M. 1988).

for some form of identification. However, the same is not true with mental competency. It may not be evident from outward appearances whether a party lacks competency. Therefore, claims of mental incompetency consider both the condition of the party seeking to avoid the contract and what the other party had reason to know about the incompetent's background or by general observation during the transaction. Also, the fairness of the exchange is often an important factor in the court's decision.[12]

Mental illness is not the only form of mental incapacity to negate the assent required for contract formation. Alcohol and drug use may impair contractual competency as well. According to Restatement Second § 16 comment b, "the standard of competency in intoxication cases is the same as that in cases of mental illness. If the intoxication is so extreme as to prevent any manifestation of assent, there is no contract."[13] Drug use is treated in much the same manner.

Still, voluntary intoxication not accompanied by another disability has been considered less excusable than mental illness.[14] Therefore, the courts look carefully at what the other party had reason to know: "a contract made by an intoxicated person is enforceable by the other party even though entirely executory, unless the other person has reason to know that the intoxicated person lacks capacity. Elements of overreaching or other unfair advantage may be relevant on the issues of competency, of the other party's reason to know, and of the appropriate remedy."[15]

---

12. Restatement (Second) of Contracts § 15 cmt. b (1979) ("Where a person has some understanding of a particular transaction which is affected by mental illness or defect, the controlling consideration is whether the transaction in its result is one which a reasonably competent person might have made.").

13. Restatement (Second) of Contracts § 16 cmt. b (1979).

14. *Id.* § 16 cmt. a.

15. Restatement (Second) of Contracts § 15 cmt. a (1979).

Mistake

> R2d § 151, 152, 153, 154, 155

In cases of mistake, the parties have reached an agreement but one or both of the parties entered that agreement on an erroneous assumption about the facts that existed at the time of contracting. At some point after making the contract, it becomes clear that what was believed to be true was not in fact the case. Now the aggrieved party claims that she would not have entered into the contract if things were then as she now knows them to be. In some circumstances, the mistake doctrine will provide this party with the equitable relief of reformation or rescission.

While mistake is a well-established doctrine, the cases are not so easy to reconcile. Still, there are three main themes that permeate the decisions. First, the mistake must relate to a fact in existence at the time of contract. It cannot be an error in business judgment or an incorrect prediction about the future. Parties make inaccurate predictions all the time and the mistake doctrine will not provide a basis for avoidance in this case. Second, the mistake must be with respect to a material aspect of the contract and have a significant effect on the agreed exchange of performances. Third, the aggrieved party neither assumed the risk of the mistake nor would it be fair or appropriate to allocate it to her.

Mutual Mistake

A mistaken belief may be held by one party or shared by both. A mistake shared by both parties is a mutual mistake and we will begin our discussion here. A claim of mutual mistake allows avoidance of the contract by the adversely affected party if the mistaken belief relates to facts in existence at the time of contract, concerns a basic assumption on which the contract was made, has a material effect on the agreed exchange, and the aggrieved party did not bear the risk of the mistake.[16] In making its determination, the court will consider the effect of the mistake on both parties to the exchange.

---

16. *See* Restatement (Second) of Contracts §§ 152, 154 (1979).

According to Restatement Second § 154, a party bears the risk of a mistake under the following circumstances: when it is allocated to her by agreement of the parties; she is aware, at the time of contract, that she has only limited knowledge with respect to the facts to which the mistake relates, but treats her limited knowledge as sufficient; or it is allocated to her by a term supplied by the court on the ground that it is reasonable in the circumstances to do so.

Unilateral Mistake

The elements for a unilateral mistake are very similar to those for a mutual mistake, except that the mistake is not shared by both parties. The mistake must still be material and the risk must not be borne by the mistaken party. However, it is also required that the mistaken party show that enforcement of the contract would be unconscionable or that "the other party had reason to know of the mistake or his fault caused the mistake."[17] To establish unconscionability, the mistaken party "must ordinarily show not only the position he would have been in had the facts been as he believed them to be but also the position in which he finds himself as a result of [the] mistake."[18] The Restatement gives the example of a builder submitting a mistake in the price of a bid. Here the builder "must show the profit or loss that will result if he is required to perform, as well as the profit that he would have made had there been no mistake."[19]

Scrivener's Error

Another type of mistake occurs when there has been a error as to expression in recording the parties' agreement. This might be a clerical or "scrivener's" error resulting in a written agreement that fails to express the parties' agreement correctly. The appropriate remedy is reformation of the writing to properly reflect the agreement reached by the parties.

---

17. Restatement (Second) of Contract § 153(b) (1979).

18. *Id.* § 153 cmt. c.

19. *Id.*

Comparing Mutual Mistake To Impracticability

The doctrine of mistake deals with assumptions about facts that exist at the time of contract while the doctrines of impracticability and frustration "deal largely with assumptions concerning circumstances that are expected to exist, including events that are expected to occur, after the contract is made."[20] A party that relies on the ground of impracticability or frustration of purpose must show that it was impracticable for the party to perform or that the party's purpose in forming the contract was substantially frustrated. If this is shown, no duty to perform arises.

In contrast, a party that relies on the ground of mistake need show that the mistake had a material effect on the agreed exchange of performances. The mistake must be one as to an existing fact, not merely an erroneous prediction as to the future. It is more likely that a party will be regarded as having borne the risk in the case of mistake than in the case of impracticability or frustration.[21] If the criteria for mistake is met, the contract is voidable by the adversely affected party.

The advantage of seeking discharge of a contractual duty based on mistake is shown in cases in which a party that must achieve a technological breakthrough in order to perform claims to be excused on failing to achieve the breakthrough. This party has two grounds for excuse—mutual mistake and impracticability. To succeed on the ground of mistake, the party must convince the court that there was a mistake as to an existing fact (the "state of the art"), and not simply an erroneous prediction as to the future (that the breakthrough would be achieved).[22] The advantage in claiming mistake is that for the party to succeed, it need only show that the mistake as to the state of the art had a material effect on the agreed exchange of performances under Restatement Second § 152(1), not that performance was impracticable. In this case, the focus seems to be on an imbalance in the exchange caused by the mistake.

---

20. E. Allan Farnsworth, *Contracts*, § 9.1 (4th ed. 2004).

21. *Id.* § 9.8.

22. *Id.*

Misrepresentation

R2d § 159, 160, 161, 162, 164,
167, 168, 169

"A misrepresentation is an assertion that is not in accord with the facts."[23] It may be expressed in words or by conduct. Even if a statement is true, it may be a misrepresentation if it leaves a false impression, i.e., a half truth. If part of the truth is told, but another portion is not so as to create an overall misleading impression, this may constitute a misrepresentation.

Under Restatement Second § 164, a misrepresentation makes a contract voidable if it is either fraudulent or material. The following requirements must be met to void a contract on the basis of misrepresentation: first, there must have been a misrepresentation; second, the misrepresentation must have been either material or fraudulent; third, the misrepresentation must have induced the recipient to make the contract; and fourth, the recipient must have been justified in relying on the misrepresentation.

The Fraudulent/Material Aspect

As assertion is fraudulent if it is made with the knowledge that it is false (i.e., telling a lie) and with the intent to induce the other party's assent. If the misrepresentation is not a deliberate lie, it may have been made innocently, where the speaker reasonably believed the representation to be true, or it may have been made negligently, where the speaker unreasonably believed the representation to be true because she failed to check facts that she had a duty to verify. These distinctions with respect to the state of mind are important for a couple of reasons. First, if the misrepresentation is intentional, then the party does not have to show that it was material. Second, only those who have been the victims of intentional misrepresentations are entitled to relief in either the form of damages (such liability is imposed under tort law) or avoidance of the contract.

---

23. Restatement (Second) of Contracts § 159 (1979).

It is not necessary for a misrepresentation to be fraudulent in order to make the contract voidable. However, if the misrepresentation is not fraudulent, then it must be material. It is material if it would be likely to induce a reasonable person to assent or if the maker knows that for some special reason, it is likely to induce a particular person to give her assent.[24]

Opinion Vs. Fact

Generally, a misrepresentation, to be actionable, must be one of fact rather than opinion. Usually, statements of opinion are not to be taken seriously and a party is not justified in relying on them. However, there are exceptions where reliance on an assertion of opinion is justified. They are as follows:

1. where the recipient stands in a confidential relationship to the person whose opinion is asserted such that the recipient is reasonable in relying on it. It need not be a fiduciary relationship but may be one between family members or where one party has taken steps to induce the other to believe that he can rely on the first party's judgment.[25]

2. where the recipient reasonably believes the other person has special skill or judgment with respect to the subject matter.[26]

3. where the recipient is "for some other special reason particularly susceptible to a misrepresentation of the particular type involved."[27]

Non-Disclosure/Concealment

A party may be liable for misrepresentation by failing to disclose a material fact when there is a duty to do so. While a party making a contract is not expected to tell all that she knows to the other party, she is required to disclose facts where non-disclosure would be equivalent to a misrepresentation.

---

24. Restatement (Second) of Contracts § 162 cmt. c (1979).

25. Restatement (Second) of Contracts § 169(a) (1979).

26. *Id.* § 169(b).

27. *Id.* § 169(c).

According to Restatement Second § 161, non-disclosure may be a misrepresentation in the following instances: where a party knows that disclosing the fact is necessary to prevent a previous assertion from being a misrepresentation or from being fraudulent or material; where a party knows that disclosing the fact would correct a mistake of the other party as to a basic assumption on which the party is making the contract and if non-disclosure amounts to a failure to act in good faith; where a party knows that disclosing the fact would correct a mistake of the other party as to the contents or effect of a writing; and where the other party is entitled to know the fact because there is a relationship of trust between the parties.

Concealment is the act of knowingly or intending to prevent another from learning of a fact that she otherwise would have learned.[28] Such an action is equivalent to a misrepresentation.

Duress And Undue Influence

R2d § 174, 175, 176, 177

As we've discussed, the process of forming a contract requires the mutual assent of the parties. Such assent must be freely and voluntarily given and not obtained through coercive conduct. If one party improperly pressures the other party into giving assent, then the contract may be avoided. The defense of duress is available if the defendant can show that she was unfairly coerced into entering the contract or into modifying it. Duress is normally used as a defense to a suit for breach of contract or as a basis for recovering restitutionary relief. On the other hand, the defense of undue influence focuses on one party's taking advantage of the relationship with the other.

Duress is any wrongful act or threat by one contracting party which compels or induces the other party through fear to enter

---

28. Restatement (Second) of Contracts § 160 cmt. a. (1979).

into a transaction against her will. While the courts look only at whether the victim exercised free will in entering into or assenting to the transaction, factors such as age, emotional nature, surrounding circumstances, etc. are generally considered. Where duress is accomplished by physical compulsion, then there is no contract at all or a "void" contract. The more challenging issues arise when the coercion is by threat.

Originally, common law courts imposed a very narrow reading of what constituted a sufficient threat and limited it to threats involving a loss of life, mayhem, or imprisonment. These restrictions have been greatly relaxed and the modern view is to recognize a much broader range of threats as being improper, including those to cause economic harm. Here, the threatened harm is to the victim's economic interests and the court considers the fairness of the resulting exchange or whether the "assenting" party had reasonable alternatives in determining whether the threat was improper. This had led to the modern doctrine of "economic duress" or "business compulsion" as a basis to avoid a contract or contract modification.[29]

The requirements for showing duress by threat include: first, there must be a threat; second, the threat must be improper; third, the threat must induce the victim's assent to the agreement; and fourth, the threat must be such that it leaves the victim with no reasonable alternative.[30]

The defense of undue influence, like duress, makes a contract voidable and may be a defense or the basis for a claim in restitution. There are two elements required for a claim based on undue influence: first, that a special relationship existed between the parties; and, second, that the stronger party used unfair persuasion on the weaker party to gain that party's assent.

The claim of undue influence is effective only if the party is under the domination of the other or is justified, based on her

---

29. *Austin Instrument, Inc. v. Loral Corp.*, 272 N.E.2d 533 (N.Y. 1971).

30. Restatement (Second) of Contracts § 175 (1979).

relation with the other, in assuming that the other is acting is her best interest. Some relationships that would fall within this definition include those of parent and child, doctor and patient, clergy and parishioner, and husband and wife.[31] Where this relationship is shown, it must then be shown that the weaker party's assent was induced by unfair persuasion on the part of the stronger. The degree of persuasion depends on a variety of factors but the primary question is whether the result was obtained by "means that seriously impaired the free and competent exercise of judgment. A particularly important factor in showing unfairness in persuasion is imbalance in the resulting bargain."[32]

Unconscionability

| R2d § 208 |
| UCC 2 - 302 |

An unconscionable contract[33] is one that is manifestly unfair or oppressive–a contract which no one in her right senses and not under a delusion would make. The contract must be unconscionable at the time of its making. In determining whether a contract is unconscionable, the court looks to see whether it is procedurally and substantively unconscionable.

The procedural aspect is one characterized by an absence of meaningful choice so the court looks to the relationship between the parties to determine if there was unequal bargaining power, a lack of opportunity to study the contract and inquire about the terms, and whether the terms were non-negotiable. The substantive aspect is one which looks at the terms of the contract to see if they are unfairly one-sided. A one-sided agreement may be found where one party is deprived of all the benefits of the agreement or left without a remedy for the other party's breach or there is a large disparity between the prevailing market price and the contract price.

---

31. Restatement (Second) of Contracts § 177 cmt. a (1979).

32. Farnsworth, *Contracts*, at § 4.20.

33. U.C.C. § 2–302 (2004). There are no significant changes to UCC 2–302 in the 2003 revisions to the Code.

Illegality And Public Policy

R2d § 178, 179

What constitutes illegality with respect to contractual agreements? If either the consideration or the object of the contract is illegal, the bargain is treated as an illegal contract. Some contracts are illegal because they are expressly prohibited by statute (for example, gambling agreements or promises for usurious interest) whereas others are classified as illegal because they violate public policy (for example, contracts in restraint of trade or contracts to impair family relations[34]).

While it is easy to see why a contract that violates a rule of law is illegal and will not be enforced, it is not always so clear in cases where the contract is not illegal but rather offends public policy. Although such contracts may have been the result of a bargained-for exchange, notions of public policy would be seriously offended if such contracts were enforced by a court of law. Here the court must consider the competing interests of freedom of contract and the wider public interest. Consequently, courts take a cautious and measured approach so as not to overstep their bounds into the legislative domain.

In doubtful cases, where it is not clear that unenforceability is warranted because the agreement involves only a trivial contravention of policy, the court's decision must rest on a delicate balancing of factors for and against enforcement of the particular agreement. A court may consider the following factors in favoring enforcement of the contract: first, the public interest in protecting the justified expectations of the parties; second, any forfeiture that will result if enforcement is denied—a factor of significance because restitution is generally unavailable when enforcement is denied on grounds of public policy; and, any special public interest in enforcing that particular term.[35]

---

34. *See* Restatement (Second) of Contracts §§ 179(b)(I)—(ii) (1979).

35. Restatement (Second) of Contracts § 178(2) (1979).

In weighing a public policy against enforcement of a term, a court may consider the following: first, the strength of the public policy involved; second, the likelihood that refusal of enforcement will further that policy; third, the seriousness and deliberateness of any misconduct that has occurred; and fourth, the closeness of the connection between that misconduct and the agreement.[36]

DEFENSES CHECKLIST

Here is the checklist for analyzing problems presenting questions regarding contract defenses.

A. **Misunderstanding**—do the parties attach materially different meanings to their understanding of the terms of their exchange?

   1. **Neither Party Knows**—do the parties attach materially different meanings and neither party knows or has reason to know the meaning attached by the other? If so, then there is no manifestation of mutual assent.

   2. **Each Party Knows**—do the parties attach materially different meanings and each party knows or has reason to know the meaning attached by the other? If so, then there is no manifestation of mutual assent.

   3. **One Party Knows**—what does one party know about the meaning attached by the other?

      a. Does one party *not* know of any different meaning attached by the other *and* the other knows the meaning attached by the first party? If so, the agreement is on the terms attached by the first party.

      b. Does one party *have no reason to know* of any different meaning attached by the other *and* the other has reason to know the meaning attached by the first party? If so, the agreement is on the terms attached by the first party.

---

36. *Id.* § 178(3).

B. Bases for Avoidance—assuming a valid contract was formed, is there a basis for avoidance?

    1. Incapacity of the Parties—did a party lack capacity to enter a contract? A party must have capacity to incur contract liability.

        a. **Age?** Was the party an infant at the time of the transaction?

            i. **No.** If not, then incapacity based on age is not a basis to avoid the contract. Procccd to Part B.1.b.

            ii. **Yes.** If so, was it a contract for **"necessities"**? Although the issue of whether it is a necessity is a question of law, you still need to make an assessment on the exam and proceed. Ask:

                • Is it a contract for food, shelter, clothing or other such basic items typically found necessary for the maintenance of life? If so, proceed to the next question.

                • What is the quantity, quality and reasonable value of that necessity in light of the infant's social status and situation in life? In answering this question, ask, "what is reasonable and necessary for the suitable maintenance of this infant in view of her social position and situation in life, the customs of the social circle in which she moves, and her financial situation and that of her parents."

            iii. **Ratification?** Upon reaching the age of majority, has the infant engaged in conduct so as to ratify the agreement either by performing the contractual obligation or accepting the other party's performance under the contract?

                • **Yes.** If so, then the infant is bound.

                • **No.** If not, then proceed to the next question.

            iv. **Disaffirmance?** Has the infant taken any actions which can be construed as disaffirming the contract?

                • **Yes.** If the infant has taken steps to disaffirm the whole contract by words or conduct either before or after a reasonable time upon reaching majority, then she can avoid the contract. The infant is not required to make restitution but is required to return only what she still has in possession. There is no obligation to account for use, depreciation, or loss in value. Even where necessaries are involved, recovery is limited to unjust enrichment.

- **No.** If not, then failure to disaffirm within a reasonable time after attaining majority is a ratification of the contract and terminates the power to disaffirm.

b. **Mental Incapacity?** Was the party mentally ill or defective at the time of contract?

  i. **Understanding?** If by reason of mental illness or defect, was the party able to understand in a reasonable manner the nature and consequences of the transaction?

  - **No.** If not, then the party may have incurred only voidable contractual duties.

  - **Yes.** If so, then this is not a basis to avoid the contract. Proceed to Part B.1.c.

  ii. **Knowledge of Other Party?** If by reason of mental illness or defect, was the party unable to act in a reasonable manner in relation to the transaction *and* the other party had reason to know of her condition?

  - **Yes.** If so, then the party has incurred only voidable contractual duties.

  - **No.** If not, then this is not a basis to avoid the contract.

  iii. **Fair Terms and Other Party without Knowledge?** Was the contract made on fair terms *and* the other party was without knowledge of the mental illness or defect?

  - **Yes.** If so, the power of avoidance terminates to the extent the contract has been performed in whole or in part or circumstances have changed such that avoidance would be unjust. The court may grant relief as justice requires.

- **No.** If not, then this is not a basis to avoid the contract.

c. **Intoxication?** Did the other party have reason to know that by reason of the person's intoxication,

   i. she was unable to understand in a reasonable manner the nature and consequences of the transaction?

- **Yes.** If so, then the intoxicated person incurs only voidable contractual duties.

- **No.** If not, then this is not a basis to avoid the contract.

Or

   ii. she was unable to act in a reasonable manner in relation to the transaction?

- **Yes.** If so, then the intoxicated person incurs only voidable contractual duties.

- **No.** If not, then this is not a basis to avoid the contract.

2. ' **Mistake**—did one or both of the parties enter the agreement based on an erroneous assumption about the facts that existed at the time of contract?

a. **Mutual Mistake**—if the mistake was shared by both parties as to a basic assumption on which the contract was made, does it have a material effect on the agreed exchange of performances?

- **Yes.** If so, then the contract is voidable by the adversely affected party **unless** she bears the risk of the mistake. Ask the following to determine whether the party bears the risk:

  — **Allocated by Agreement?** Was the risk of a mistake allocated to her by agreement of the parties?

  — **"Conscious Ignorance"?** Was she aware at the time of contract that she had only limited knowledge with respect to the facts to which the mistake relates, but treated her limited knowledge as sufficient?

— **Risk Allocated by the Court?** Was the risk of mistake allocated by a term supplied by the court on the ground that it was reasonable under the circumstances to do so?

- **No.** If not, then this defense is not applicable. Proceed to the next question.

b. **Unilateral Mistake**—if the mistake was held by one party as to a basic assumption on which she made the contract, does it have a material effect on the agreed exchange of performances that is adverse to her?

- **Yes.** If so, the contract is voidable by her if she does not bear the risk of mistake under the tests identified above in Part B. 2.a. and either:

— the effect of the mistake is such that enforcement of the contract would be unconscionable or

— the other party had reason to know of the mistake or it was her fault that caused the mistake.

- **No.** If not, then this defense is not applicable. Proceed to the next question.

c. **Scrivener's Error**—has there been a mistake as to expression in recording the parties agreement? If a clerical or "scrivener's" error results in a written agreement that fails to express the parties' agreement correctly, then the appropriate remedy is reformation of the writing to reflect the agreement actually reached.

3. **Misrepresentation**—did a party make an assertion that was not in accord with the facts? All of the following four elements must be satisfied to avoid a contract based on misrepresentation:

a. **Assertion**—did a party make a false representation as to a fact? An assertion can be oral or written or can be inferred from conduct. To determine whether a statement is false, ask the following:

- **False Impression or Inference?** If part of the truth is told, but another portion is not so as to create an overall misleading impression, this may constitute a misrepresentation. Proceed to Part B.3.b. If not, proceed to the next question.

- **Concealment?** Did one party take an affirmative act to keep the other party from learning a fact? If so, such conduct may be a misrepresentation. Proceed to Part B.3.b. If not, proceed to the next question.

- **Non-disclosure?** Do one of the exceptions to the "no duty to disclose" rule apply? In certain situations, the failure to disclose a fact is seen as an assertion that the fact does not exist. Ask the following:

  — **Relation of Trust or Confidence?** Is there a relation of trust or confidence between the parties? The relationship need not be a fiduciary one but may be one between family members or between doctor and patient, among others. If so, then the one in whom the trust and confidence is placed is expected to disclose what she knows. Failure to disclose the fact is equivalent to an assertion that the fact does not exist. If so, proceed to Part B.3.b. If not, proceed to the next question.

  — **Need to Correct?** Is disclosure necessary to correct an earlier assertion? If a party who has made an assertion later learns something that bears on the prior assertion, then she is expected to speak up. Failure to disclose the fact is equivalent to an assertion that the fact does not exist. If so, proceed to Part B.3.b. If not, proceed to the next question.

  — **Mistake in Basic Assumption?** Would disclosure correct the other party's mistake as to a basic assumption on which the party is making the contract and non-disclosure of the fact amounts to a failure to act in good faith and in accordance with the standards of fair dealing? If so, then failure to disclose the fact is equivalent to an assertion that the fact does not exist. Proceed to Part B.3.b. If not, proceed to the next question.

— **Mistake as to Writing?** Would disclosure correct the other party's mistake as to the contents or effect of the writing? If so, then failure to disclose the fact is equivalent to an assertion that the fact does not exist. Proceed to Part B.3.b.

b. **Material or Fraudulent**—was the misrepresentation material or fraudulent? A misrepresentation need not be fraudulent to make the contract voidable but if it is not fraudulent, then it must be material. Ask the following:

- **Fraudulent?** Was the misrepresentation intended to induce a party to assent and the maker

  — knew or believed that the assertion was not in accord with the facts, or

  — did not have confidence that what she stated or implied was true, or

  — knew that she did not have the basis that she states or implied for the assertion?

  If the answer is *"no"* to all of the above, then the misrepresentation must be material to make the contract voidable. Proceed to the next question.

- **Material?** Was the misrepresentation likely to induce a reasonable person to assent or did the maker know that it was likely to induce the recipient to do so?

  — **Yes.** If so, then it was a material misrepresentation.

  — **No.** If not, and it was not fraudulent, then this element is not satisfied and the assertion is not a misrepresentation.

   c.   **Inducement**—did the misrepresentation induce the recipient to make the contract? This question is answered by asking, "did the misrepresentation substantially contribute to her decision to agree to the contract? If the answer is *"yes,"* then the misrepresentation contributed substantially to her decision to make the contract and it is immaterial that she may also have been influenced by other considerations.

   d.   **Justified reliance**—was the recipient justified in relying on the misrepresentation? Typically, the most significant and difficult application of this requirement occurs in connection with assertions of opinion because opinions are not facts. A party is not justified in relying on statements of opinion unless one of the following exceptions apply. If the answer is *"yes"* to any of the following, reliance is justified. Ask the following:

       •   **Confidential Relationship?** Does the recipient stand in a confidential relationship to the person whose opinion is asserted such that the recipient is reasonable in relying on it?

       •   **Special skill or Judgment?** Does the recipient reasonably believe that the other person has special skill or judgment with respect to the subject matter?

       •   **Susceptibility?** Is the recipient particularly susceptible to a misrepresentation of the particular type involved for some other special reason?

4.   **Duress**—was the party unfairly coerced into entering or modifying the contract?

   a.   **Physical Compulsion**—was the party physically compelled to assent when she otherwise would not have done so?

       •   **Yes.** If so, then the conduct is not effective to create a contract.

       •   **No.** If not, then proceed to the next question.

   b.   **Improper Threat**—was the party's assent induced by means of a threat? The following four elements must be satisfied:

- **Threat**—was there a manifestation of intent to inflict loss or harm on another?

- **Improper**—was the threat improper? If the answer is "*yes*" to any of the following, the threat is improper:

  — Was the threatened act a crime or a tort?

  — Was it a threat of criminal prosecution?

  — Was it a threat of civil proceedings made in bad faith?

  — Was it a threat where the resulting exchange would not be on fair terms such as would be considered "economic duress" or "business compulsion"?

  — Was it a threat because the party had no reasonable alternative?

- **Inducement**—did the improper threat actually induce the making of the contract?

- **Sufficiently Serious**—was the threat sufficiently grave to justify the victim in succumbing to it?

5. **Undue Influence**—did one party induce the assent of the other by improper persuasion? There are two elements required for a claim based on undue influence:

   a. **Special Relationship**—did a special relationship exist between the parties? Is one party highly susceptible to persuasion by the other? Examples include the relationships between parent and child, husband and wife, and doctor and patient.

   b. **Unfair Persuasion**—did the stronger party use unfair persuasion on the weaker party to gain that party's assent? One way to determine whether the dominant party exercised this type of persuasion is to ask:

      - Was there an imbalance in the resulting transaction?

      - Did the weaker party have the benefit of independent advice?

- Was there time for reflection?
- How susceptible was the weaker party?

6. **Unconscionability**—is the contract manifestly unfair or oppressive? In determining whether a contract is unconscionable, look for an overall imbalance based on the following considerations:

   a. **Procedural Unconscionability**—was the bargaining process characterized by any of the following:

      - an absence of meaningful choice?
      - unequal bargaining power?
      - a lack of opportunity to study the contract and inquire about the terms?
      - non-negotiable terms?

   b. **Substantive Unconscionability**—were the terms of the contract unfairly one-sided? To determine whether an agreement is one-sided, consider the following:

      - Is one party deprived of all the benefits of the agreement or left without a remedy for the other party's breach?
      - Is there a large disparity between the prevailing market price and the contract price?

7. **Illegality**—is the promise or other term of the agreement unenforceable on grounds of public policy? Ask the following:

   - **Legislation**—is there a statute that identifies specified kinds of promises or other terms as unenforceable?
   - **Balancing of Interests**—what is the purpose to be served in denying enforcement? In answering this question, consider the courts' traditional interests:
      — Upholding the intent of the parties.
      — Protecting the expectations of the parties.
      — An abhorrence for unjust enrichment.
      — The need to protect the public welfare as in policies against the restraint of trade, the impairment of family relations, and interference with other protected interests.

ILLUSTRATIVE PROBLEMS

Here are some problems that will show how the checklist can be used to resolve questions involving defenses.

■ PROBLEM 5.1 ■

Sophie, age 58, depended upon her daughters for her day-to-day care. She was quite wealthy and owned substantial assets which her daughters managed for her, although they were not her legal guardians. For many years, she had been mentally ill, coming in and out of periods of mental clarity. Even at her worst, Sophie appeared competent although her behavior was often odd. She would stand for hours in front of her mirror and arrange and rearrange her hair and makeup, believing she was Elizabeth Taylor, the famous movie star. In truth, Sophie had been a beautiful woman who greatly resembled Miss Taylor. Even now, Sophie was very attractive and people often mistook her for Elizabeth Taylor, especially when she dressed in her extravagant clothes and jewelry.

One day, she went into the Klinger Dance Studio and asked the studio manager, Ken, about taking dance lessons. She was elegantly dressed and perfectly groomed. She announced that she had decided to become the world's greatest dancer since her movie career had ended (she claimed there were no longer suitable roles for women her age) and she planned to compete in the television series, "Dancing with the Stars" as one of the celebrity contestants. Ken smiled to himself, winked at the dance instructors, and thought this must be his lucky day indeed. Every single dance plan he mentioned, Sophie agreed to immediately, while laughing loudly, dancing around with the dance instructors, and promising to send autographed photos when she won first prize on "Dancing with the Stars." By the time she left the studio, she had signed a contract to learn ballroom dancing, belly dancing, disco, and hip hop for a total of $75,000 in dance lessons, payable over the next five years. In the entire ten-year history of the dance studio, no one had ever signed up for so many different types of lessons for so much money at any one time.

When she failed to show up for her lessons or make any payments, Klinger Dance Studios called Sophie. She said that she had no memory of the day and had always hated dancing. When she refused to pay, the Klinger Dance Studio sued. Sophie's daughters are panicked. They think their mother should be able to avoid the deal. Please advise Sophie's daughters.

Analysis

I would advise Sophie's daughters that the question of whether their mother can avoid the contract for dancing lessons depends on whether she lacked mental capacity when she entered the dance contract. The general rule is that an adult is presumed to have contractual capacity. However, this presumption is rebuttable and the party claiming incompetence has the burden of proving a lack of mental competency at the time of contracting by clear and convincing evidence. Here, the burden would be on Sophie since she is the one claiming incompetence to avoid the contract with the dance studio.

Under the common law, evaluations of claims of mental incompetency consider the condition of the party seeking to avoid the contract—whether she is able to act in a reasonable manner in relation to the transaction—and what the other party had reason to know about her condition by observation during the transaction or from previous knowledge. Also, the fairness of the exchange is an important factor in the court's decision—i.e., would a reasonable person have entered into such a bargain.

Here, it would be reasonable for Ken, the manager of the dance studio, to expect that people who sign up for dance lessons take them and pay for them. Sophie showed up at the Klinger Dance Studio and was elegantly dressed and groomed, leading a reasonable person in Ken's position to believe that she could afford to take dance lessons and was genuinely interested in doing so. There was nothing unusual in her outward appearance to alert Ken to possible mental incapacity.

However, when she started to talk about starring in movies and competing on television in "Dancing with the Stars," Ken had reason to question her behavior. While people have all kinds of reasons for taking dancing lessons, it is not typical to claim that one needs lessons to compete on a television show. Even so, people can be eccentric and this does not rob them of their capacity to enter into binding agreements. Still, Ken had reason to suspect Sophie's competency when she readily agreed to every single dance plan he mentioned, including belly dancing, disco, and hip hop. These dances might be odd choices for a woman of Sophie's age.

Even if Sophie's dance choices were not suggestive of a possible mental imbalance, then her behavior should have signaled something to him because she was "laughing loudly, dancing around with the dance instructors, and promising to send them autographed photos." Any one of these actions by themselves might not be dispositive, but taken together they indicate that Sophie might not be quite certain of what she was doing, especially since she firmly believed herself to be the famous movie star, Elizabeth Taylor. Unless Ken honestly believed that Sophie was indeed a movie star, then he had reason to question her ability to enter the contract. While we do not know for certain what Ken was thinking, we know that he suspected something since the facts state "he smiled to himself, winked at the dance instructors, and thought this must be his lucky day." This might indicate that Ken considered her an "easy mark" to whom he could sell dance lessons. We do not know from the facts whether his thinking indicated that he thought she was gullible, which is not a basis on which to avoid a contract, or that she was suffering a mental incapacity, which is a valid basis for avoidance. Still, Ken had reason to question her understanding of what she was doing since in the "entire ten-year history of the dance studio, no one had ever signed up for so many different types of lessons for so much money at any one time."

The fairness of the exchange is hard to evaluate because the contract was for $75,000 which is a lot of dance lessons, but it was payable over five years. We would need to know the market price of dance lessons and whether it was normal business practice to sell dance lessons so far into the future. However, the contract terms might not have been fair because the facts indicate no one had ever entered into a similar contract for so much money in the dance studio's entire ten-year history.

If the contract were rescinded, there would be no harm to the dance studio because the contract is purely executory and the studio has not taken any actions in reliance or given Sophie any lessons. The parties would be left where they had been before Sophie signed the contract.

It is likely that Sophie would be able to meet the burden by clear and convincing evidence that she was under a mental incapacity at the time of contract, thereby avoiding it. Ken either knew or should have known by her behavior during the transaction that Sophie suffered from a mental disorder.

■ PROBLEM 5.2 ■

Michelle was the lead singer of her own band and wanted to be the next music sensation. During college, she earned tuition and expenses by playing at local clubs and events. She was in great demand at teen parties where she earned most of her money. Michelle never advertised for business but got these jobs by referral from friends and family. Michelle made all the arrangements for the band, including the transportation of the equipment, the set-up, the lighting, and the costumes. She also took care of the band's finances since she was the only band member to graduate college with a degree in finance. Michelle was responsible for writing checks to pay for the equipment, making bank deposits, and balancing the checkbook. She was also responsible for scheduling engagements and negotiating fees but this was very simple–the band had agreed on a set hourly rate of $200 per hour so all

Michelle had to do was arrange the number of hours for each performance. No negotiations were involved.

One night while Michelle's band was playing at a local club, Tina, a well-known talent agent, approached Michelle and invited her to have dinner to discuss her career. At dinner, Tina told Michelle that she could be the next Miley Cyrus, a hugely popular teenage music artist. She said that Michelle had the "look" and while she was older than Miley, she had an appeal for a different market. Tina offered to be Michelle's agent and handed her a closely-written, 20 page typewritten contract. When Michelle asked Tina if she could have some time to review the contract, Tina said that this was Michelle's "golden opportunity" and that if she didn't sign the contract then and there, it would be withdrawn. Michelle signed the contract immediately.

The next day, when Michelle was reviewing the contract with her mother, they realized that it gave Tina the exclusive right to represent Michelle for the next ten years, as well as 60% of all of Michelle's gross income from employment in the music field during that period. Shortly thereafter, Michelle learned that the standard percentage for a talent agent is 20% and the usual term of such a contract is three years. Michelle then promptly advised Tina that she would not comply with the terms of their contract. What result?

Analysis

Whether Michelle's contract is enforceable depends on whether the court will find the manner in which it was entered into and the terms of the agreement unconscionable.

Under the common law, an unconscionable contract is one that is manifestly unfair or oppressive–a contract which no one in her right senses and not under a delusion would make. The contract must be unconscionable at the time of its making. In determining whether a contract is unconscionable, the court looks to see whether it is procedurally and substantively unconscionable.

The procedural aspect is one characterized by an absence of meaningful choice so the court looks to the relationship between the parties to determine if there was unequal bargaining power, a lack of opportunity to study the contract and inquire about the terms, and whether the terms were non-negotiable. The substantive aspect is one which looks at the terms of the contract to see if they are unfairly one-sided. A one-sided agreement may be found where one party is deprived of all the benefits of the agreement or left without a remedy for the other party's breach or there is a large disparity between the prevailing market price and the contract price.

Here, the tactics Tina used to get Michelle to sign the contract were unfair. Tina was a well-known talent agent and used her knowledge and position to pressure Michelle, an amateur musician, into signing the contract on the spot. Tina said it was Michelle's "golden opportunity" and she could be a big music sensation like Miley Cyrus. These words would be quite flattering and enticing coming from a sophisticated professional like Tina. Further, Tina did not give Michelle time to read the 20 page typewritten document, insisting that she sign it then and there. Because she did she allow her to review it, Tina gave Michelle a "take it or leave it" deal and under the circumstances it left Michelle in no position to bargain over the terms.

Still, Michelle did not have to sign the contract and could have walked away. She had a finance degree and some business experience which should have made her wary of Tina's rush to get her to sign. Still, Michelle was not an experienced negotiator. Even though she made all her band's arrangements, managed its financial affairs, and booked the events, she was not a professional like Tina. Michelle simply booked jobs on a pre-arranged dollar amount so that she did not have to negotiate contracts. Therefore, it is likely that a court would find that the way the contract was formed was procedurally unconscionable.

With respect to the substantive terms of the contract, these too would likely be found unconscionable because the duration of the contract (10 years) and the percentage of Michelle's salary (60%)

that Tina would be entitled to were not the standard terms (3 years and 20%) in such a contract. While Tina could argue that she was assuming the risk of representing a newcomer to the business like Michelle and therefore was entitled to a greater percentage, she still would not be justified in charging three times the normal rate for three times the normal representation period. Furthermore, Michelle may have been new to the recording industry but she had some success on the local level so Tina's risk was not as great as representing a totally unknown entity. The fact that her terms varied so much from the industry standard would lead a court to find them substantively unconscionable.

Because it is possible to find procedural unconscionability in the bargaining process and substantive unconscionability in the terms of the agreement, it is likely that a court would find the contract to be unconscionable. In this case, the court may refuse to enforce the contract or may enforce the contract without the unconscionable terms or may reform the unconscionable terms as to avoid any unconscionable result.

■ PROBLEM 5.3 ■

Murray Inc., the largest single buyer of potatoes in the area, manufactures several varieties of potato-based products. Murray entered into a written contract with Shane the Farmer where Shane would supply Murray with Spud potatoes.

No specific amount was stated in the contract but Shane estimated that Murray would need approximately 30 tons based on what other manufacturers in this area and industry required with similar needs.

Murray Inc. presented its standard form contract to Shane. The contract stated in relevant part,

> *"Shane the Farmer agrees to supply Murray Inc. at the end of the growing season in August of this calendar year with all the Spud potatoes from his farm that Murray Inc. might require at*

a price of $100 per ton, delivery included."

The contract also contained a clause prohibiting Shane from selling any excess Spud potatoes to a third party without Murray's consent. Shane objected to the provision because he had other customers for his potatoes and planned to sell to them. Although Shane promised to supply all the potatoes that Murray might require, Shane had estimated the amount to be about half the capacity of his fields and he could supply other customers even after satisfying his contractual obligation to Murray. Murray orally assured him that although the provision was standard in all of Murray Inc.'s contracts with its growers, Murray had never attempted to enforce the provision. Actually, quite the opposite was true and Murray routinely sought to prevent growers from selling their surplus crop to third parties. Shane relied on what Murray told him and signed the contract.

Shane always took proper care of his property and regularly rotated his crops and sprayed pesticides in accordance with all agricultural, state, and federal regulations. Unknown to either party at the time the agreement was made, however, a pesticide-resistant form of insect was nesting under the north, east, and west pastures of Shane's farm. It was a mutant strain and all traditional pesticides were useless against it. Since the insects burrow deep under ground while in hibernation, they were not even detectable when Shane commenced his usual spring planting. He put in his potato crop without finding a single insect.

On August 20, Shane began to work the south pasture and harvested 10 tons without incident. Having depleted the yield of the south pasture, he moved on to the west pasture where he discovered the insects. He went to check the east and north pastures and found the same infestation. All of the potatoes were infested with the mutant insects.

Shane called Murray on August 22 and told him what happened. He said he would only be able to provide 10 tons of Spud potatoes because of the unforeseen insect infestation over three-quarters of his farm and asked to be released from the contract. Shane shipped the 10 tons the next day.

(1). Shane claims that the contract was voidable in whole or in part because he was defrauded when he entered the contract. What's the likelihood of success on this theory?

(2). Shane plans to argue that the contract is voidable based on mistake. What result?

Analysis

A threshold question is whether this was a contract for the sale of goods or services. This agreement involves a transaction for the sale of potatoes. Since Article 2 of the Uniform Commercial Code defines "goods" as all things moveable at the time of identification to the contract including growing crops, then potatoes are goods, and Article 2 is the applicable law. The Code is supplemented by common law principles where applicable.

(1). The issue is whether Murray misrepresented the facts when he said that the contract clause prohibiting sales to others without Murray's consent was never enforced. A misrepresentation is an assertion not in accord with the facts. To be successful on this claim, Shane must prove: (1) a misrepresentation existed; (2) it was material; (3) it induced him to execute the contract; and (4) and his reliance was justified.

Here, a misrepresentation existed because Murray said the provision was not enforced when he knew that it was enforced. Second, it was material because Shane had other customers and planned to sell to them. This clause would prevent such sales without permission which might not be granted. The result could be a significant loss in income for Shane. Third, the misrepresentation induced Shane to sign the contract because he only agreed to do so when Murray assured him that it was a routine clause and never actually enforced. Finally, Shane's reliance on the misrepresentation was justified because he had no reason to believe Murray was lying or would seek to enforce the provision in his case since he said he never had. Further, when Shane asked specifically about enforcement of the provision, Murray had a duty not to mislead Shane. Instead, Murray assured him that the contract provision had never been enforced when quite the opposite was true and Murray routinely sought to prevent growers from selling their surplus crop to third parties.

(2).   The issue is whether the contract is voidable based on mistake when neither party knew there were insects on Shane's farm. Where a mistake of both parties at the time a contract was made as to a basic assumption on which the contract was made has a material effect on the agreed exchange of performances, the contract is voidable by the adversely affected party unless he bears the risk of the mistake.

In this case, it was a basic assumption that the potatoes would not be destroyed by mutant insects. Neither Shane nor Murray had reason to know of the insects, although ordinarily a farmer would bear the risk of such pests on his property. However, Shane took proper care of his property and sprayed pesticides in compliance with all regulations. He would have no way to know of a pesticide-resistant strain that burrowed deep within the earth and was not detectable even when planting. It would not be fair to hold Shane liable when the potato crop was destroyed by a mutant strain of insects over which he had no control. Further, since it was anticipated that the potatoes would be supplied from Shane's farm, Shane has no duty to purchase potatoes from another source to satisfy the contract. Consequently, Shane should be able to avoid performance of the contract beyond the delivery of the unaffected potatoes, which he has performed.

POINTS TO REMEMBER

- Be careful to distinguish between defenses which arise at the time of contract and those which arise subsequently: it matters with respect to the types of relief which may be available. For example, it is very different to find that there was a misunderstanding such that no contract was ever formed from finding that a contract was formed but it was void or voidable.

- When considering a defense based on infancy, do not confuse concerns about the other party's loss in the event of a minor's disaffirmance. A minor may avoid a contract even after having received some or all of the other party's performance under the contract. In such cases, the minor may not have anything to return. The effect can be harsh. Look for exceptions: is there a statute which restricts the infant's power to disaffirm certain obligations? Is it a contract involving necessaries?

- A party may be liable for misrepresentation by failing to disclose a material fact when there is a duty to do so. While a party making a contract is not expected to tell all that she knows to the other party, she is required to disclose facts where non-disclosure would be equivalent to a misrepresentation.

- Here is where it is important to understand the differences between a "voidable" and a "void" contract. A voidable contract is one where a party can choose to render the promised performance or rescind the agreement—as in the case of a contract entered into by a minor. On the other hand, a void contract is a legal nullity since the law does not provide a remedy for its breach nor a duty for its performance.

- Remember that the doctrine of mistake deals with assumptions about facts that exist *at the time of contract* while the doctrines of impracticability and frustration deal with assumptions concerning circumstances that are expected to exist, including events that are expected to occur, *after the contract is made*.

- Do not forget that one set of facts may give rise to multiple defenses. For example, a party who claims excuse by reason of existing impracticability or frustration of purpose may also claim excuse on the basis of mistake. The differences go to what the party must show in making out the causes of action. A party making a claim in impracticability or frustration must show that it was impracticable to perform or that the party's purpose in performing was substantially frustrated. In contrast, a party claiming mistake, need show only that the mistake had a material effect on the agreed exchange of performances. This must be a mistake as to an existing fact and not simply an erroneous prediction as to the future. It is more likely, however, that a party will be held to have borne the risk in the case of mistake than in the case of impracticability or frustration.

CHAPTER 6

Parol Evidence and Interpretation

Up to this point, we have been concerned primarily with the enforceability of promises and the mechanics of assent. However, many disputes do not relate to the formation of the contract but rather to the extent and nature of the rights and duties that the parties created in their agreement. In this case, the question is not whether the parties formed an agreement, but what it was they agreed to do. The parol evidence rule helps determine the scope of the subject matter to be interpreted while the principles of interpretation provide the means for doing so.

REVIEW OF THE PAROL EVIDENCE RULE

R2d § 209, 210, 213, 214 - 217

An issue involving the parol evidence rule arises only when the parties' last expression is in writing and forms a valid contract. Before they got to this point, however, the parties most likely engaged in negotiations during which each side made promises and otherwise engaged in the usual pre-contractual give-and-take. Should litigation arise after the contract has been signed, one party may seek to introduce evidence of these earlier negotiations to show that the terms of the parties' agreement are other than what it states in the writing.[1] Here the party will confront the "parol evidence rule" which may bar the use of such extrinsic evidence to contradict or even to supplement the written agreement. In short, if the writing was intended to be a final expression of the parties' agreement, then the parol evidence rule protects it from evidence of prior agreements, whether oral or written, to contradict or vary its terms.

"Parol evidence" is any evidence other than the parties' written agreement that is offered by a party to prove contract terms that do not appear in the writing. Despite its name, the rule is not limited to oral evidence and it is helpful to think of it as applicable to the parties' prior negotiations in the form of letters, memoranda, and preliminary drafts of the document subsequently executed as the final written agreement. The purpose of the rule is to give legal effect to whatever intent the parties may have had to make their writing a final or "integrated" agreement. This is based on the assumption that when parties commit to a writing, they often intend that writing to reflect the final and complete version of their agreement, thus superseding terms and provisions they may have discussed and perhaps even agreed to in earlier negotiations.

Applying the Parol Evidence Rule

If the parties intended a writing to be a final and perhaps a complete expression of their agreement, the writing is said to be "integrated." A writing that is final is an *integration* of the terms contained within it. When it is final and complete, the writing is a *complete integration*. When it is final with respect to the terms it contains but does not express all of the parties' agreement, then the writing is a *partial integration*.

The question of "integration" is a pivotal one and resolved initially by the judge as a matter of law. There are several views for

---

1. The concept of a "writing" no longer means only written words but may include other forms of recording such as electronic means. The 2003 revision to Article 2 reflects this by substituting the word "recording" for "writing" throughout Article 2. A "record" is defined in U.C.C. § 2–103(m) (Proposed Revision 2003) to mean "information that is inscribed on a tangible medium or that is stored in an electronic or other medium and is retrievable in perceivable form."

determining integration. If the jurisdiction follows the prevailing view embodied in the Restatement Second, then the judge makes this determination by considering evidence of prior negotiations, including all the surrounding circumstances in which the writing was made.[2] The theory is that it cannot be known what the parties intended to cover in the writing until all that was intended to be covered is known.[3] Alternatively, if the jurisdiction follows the "four corners" test, then only the writing itself is considered and the sole question for the court is whether the writing appears on its face to be a complete and exclusive statement of the terms of the agreement.[4]

In applying the parol evidence rule, the court asks two questions: is the parties' writing an integration, and if so, is it a complete or a partial integration. The first question addresses whether the parties intended the writing to be a final embodiment of their agreement. If the parties had such an intention, the agreement is said to be "integrated," and the parol evidence rule bars evidence of prior negotiations for at least some purposes. If the parties had no such intent, the agreement is said to be "unintegrated," and the parol evidence rule does not apply.

If the agreement is integrated, the next question is whether it is completely or only partially integrated. If the writing is a final expression of the parties' agreement and complete with respect to all of its terms, then it is a complete integration and cannot be

---

2. Restatement (Second) of Contracts § 209 cmt. b (1979).

3. Restatement (Second) of Contracts § 210 cmt. b (1979) ("a writing cannot of itself prove its own completeness, and wide latitude must be allowed for inquiry into circumstances bearing on the intention of the parties."). Corbin's view is that account should be taken of all the evidence and circumstances to determine integration since "[t]he writing cannot prove its own completeness and accuracy." Arthur L. Corbin, *The Parol Evidence Rule*, 53 YALE L.J. 603, 630 (1944).

4. Under this rule, the contract must appear incomplete on its face to allow admission of parol evidence. To determine whether the agreement is completely integrated, "the writing will be looked at, and if it appears to be a contract complete within itself, . . . it is conclusively presumed that the whole engagement of the parties, and the extent and manner of their understanding, were reduced to writing." *Gianni v. R. Russel & Co.*, 126 A. 791, 792 (Pa. 1924).

contradicted by any type of evidence nor supplemented by consistent (non-contradictory) additional terms. On the other hand, if the writing is final as to the terms it contains but not complete as to all the terms, it is only a partial integration and may be supplemented by consistent additional terms, but cannot be contradicted. This means that although the judge has found parol evidence admissible to supplement or explain the writing, it is not admissible to contradict it. Even with a finding of partial integration, parol evidence is never admissible where it would be inconsistent with what has been written.

The court's next inquiry is whether the parol term is consistent or contradictory to the written agreement. The question of consistency, however, is not so easy to separate from that of integration. The concepts overlap and often blend together in their application. For example, if the court finds that the parol term is incompatible with the writing, this may influence its determination of whether the agreement is integrated. Confusion arises when the same test to find a partial integration can and often is applied to determine whether the parol term is consistent or contradictory to the writing. Specifically, the Restatement Second's "natural omission" test can be applied as much to a determination of consistency as to a determination of integration: "[a]n agreement is not completely integrated if the writing omits a consistent additional agreed term which is . . . such a term as in the circumstances might naturally be omitted from the writing."[5]

This conceptual issue is best illustrated by examining one of the best-known parol evidence cases, *Masterson v. Sine*.[6] In *Masterson*, the Mastersons conveyed their ranch to the Sines, Mr. Masterson's sister and brother-in-law. The conveyance deed contained an option to repurchase the property at any time within the next 10 years for an amount equal to the purchase price plus the cost of any improvements made by the Sines. Mr. Masterson was subsequently adjudged bankrupt and the trustee in bankruptcy sought to

---

5. Restatement (Second) of Contracts   6.   436 P.2d 561 (Cal. 1968).
§ 216(2)(b) (1979).

exercise the option to purchase the property. The Sines claimed that there was a prior oral agreement that the option to purchase was personal to the grantor. If this agreement in fact was made and proved, the option could not be exercised by the trustee.

The court held that evidence of the non-assignability restriction on the option was admissible despite the parol evidence rule.[7] While parol evidence would be inadmissible to vary the terms of a completely integrated agreement, the majority found that the non-assignability agreement was the type of agreement that "might naturally be made as a separate agreement" because of the formalized structure of a deed and the close relationship of the parties.[8] The court also found it persuasive that the limitation on assignability did not contradict an express term in the option because the deed was "silent on the question of assignability" and contained "no provisions forbidding its transfer[.]"[9] The dissent, on the other hand, viewed "such words of limitation to be added by parol . . . to contradict the absolute nature of the grant[.]" The dissent characterized the majority's holding as "permitting defendant optionors to limit, detract from and contradict the plain and unrestricted terms of the written option in clear violation of the parol evidence rule."[10]

What is important for you to understand is that courts do not approach the question of consistency in a uniform manner. Consequently, when you are asked to analyze a parol evidence problem and, more specifically, the narrow question of whether the proffered term is consistent or contradictory to the writing, you should think broadly and consider whether the parol term can be reconciled with the overall substance of the writing.

Collateral Agreement Rule

Although an agreement may be completely integrated, the parties are not prohibited from attempting to show that they formed an entirely separate and distinct agreement. Under the

7. *See, e.g., id.*

8. *Id.*, at 565.

9. *Id.*

10. *Id.*, at 568 (Burke, J. dissenting).

"collateral agreement rule," parties may show that they entered into a side agreement as long as it does not contradict the main agreement. Courts have not required side agreements to be supported by separate consideration although they must be "collateral" in form. It is sufficient if the collateral agreement is one that "in the circumstances might naturally be omitted from the writing."[11]

The leading collateral agreement case is *Mitchill v. Lath.*[12] In *Mitchill*, a buyer of real estate attempted to show that the seller had promised to remove an unsightly ice house from an adjacent parcel of land. The parties' signed written agreement was silent on this issue. The Court of Appeals held that the parol evidence rule precluded a showing of the promise to remove the ice house because "an inspection of this contract shows a full and complete agreement, setting forth in detail the obligations of each party. On reading it, one would conclude that the reciprocal obligations of the parties were fully detailed. . . . Were such an agreement made [about the ice house] it would seem most natural that the inquirer should find it in the contract."[13] The court reasoned that since the promise about the ice house was not contained in the parties' written agreement and it was the type of agreement one would expect to find there, the parol evidence barred its admission.

Merger Clauses

Written contracts often contain a merger or integration clause stating something to the effect that the writing "embodies the entire understanding between the parties, and there are no verbal agreements or representations in connection therewith."[14] In most cases, the presence of such a clause is the best evidence of an integrated agreement. While a merger clause is presumptive of an integration, it is not absolutely conclusive on this point. A court may consider the surrounding circumstances to determine whether the

---

11. *Id.*, § 216 (2)(b).

12. 160 N.E. 646 (N.Y. 1928).

13. *Id.*, at 647.

14. *Luther Williams, Jr., Inc. v. Johnson*, 229 A.2d 163, 165 (D.C. Cir. 1967).

integration clause does in fact express the genuine intent of the parties to make the written contract a complete statement of their agreement.[15]

Limits to the Parol Evidence Rule

The parol evidence rule applies *only* to evidence of prior or contemporaneous agreements. Consequently, it does not exclude evidence of subsequent agreements. Nor does the parol evidence rule exclude evidence to show that there was no agreement. Parol evidence is therefore admissible to show that the written agreement is to take effect only if a stated condition occurs. Further, evidence is admissible to show that the agreement is invalid due to a lack of consideration, mistake, fraud, misrepresentation, duress, or illegality.

Condition Precedent

An important exception is the admissibility of parol evidence to show that the contract was subject to a condition precedent. In some cases, parties will reach an agreement but subject either one or both of the parties' performances to the happening of a future uncertain event. For example, suppose that when Michelle and George were negotiating the purchase of George's piano, Michelle told George that she would only be able to buy the piano if she could move into a larger apartment so she would have room for it. She was waiting for approval from the condo board for a new apartment. Michelle and George signed the contract for the sale of the piano with the oral understanding that the sale was contingent on Michelle's condo application getting approved. Here, because Michelle's duty to perform the contract is subject to a condition precedent, evidence of the parties' oral agreement would not be barred by the parol evidence rule should there be a subsequent dispute. So if Michelle did not get the larger apartment and did not buy the piano, she would be permitted to testify about the oral agreement should George bring suit for breach of contract.

---

15. *See, e.g., ARB, Inc. v. E–Systems, Inc.*, 663 F.2d 189 (D.C. Cir. 1980).

REVIEW OF PAROL EVIDENCE UNDER THE UCC

UCC 2-202

Where the transaction involves the sale of goods, UCC 2–202 applies.[16] The UCC approach to parol evidence is very similar to the Restatement Second in that the first question to be asked is whether the parol evidence rule applies at all. For it to apply, the parties must have a writing "intended by the parties as a final expression of their agreement with respect to such terms as are included therein[.]"[17]

Like the common law, the judge makes the threshold determination of integration. However, here the test for integration differs somewhat from the common law rule. Comment 3 to UCC 2–202 provides that, if there is a written agreement, evidence of terms not included in the writing are not admissible "[i]f the additional terms are such that, if agreed upon, they would certainly have been included in the document in the view of the court[.]"[18] The main difference between the Code's test for integration and the common law test is that under the Code, the court must find that the parties "certainly," rather than "naturally" would have included the terms in their writing in order to find the writing integrated.

If the judge finds the writing is complete and exclusive, evidence even of consistent additional terms may not be admitted but the writing may be explained or supplemented by course of dealing, usage of trade, or course of performance.[19] If the judge

---

16. U.C.C. § 2–202 (2004) The 2003 revision of Article 2 makes no significant changes to this section except for substituting the word "record" for "writing." U.C.C. § 1–205, which deals with course of dealing and usage of trade, has been moved to U.C.C. § 1–303 in Amended Article 1. This section also now includes course of performance, which was formerly contained in U.C.C. § 2–208(1).

17. *Id.*

18. *Id.* § 2–202 cmt. 3.

19. *Id.* § 2–202 cmt. 2 (stating that such evidence is admissible "to explain or supplement the terms of any writing stating the agreement of the parties in order that the true understanding of the parties as to the agreement may be reached. Such writings are to be read on the assumption that the course of prior dealings between the parties and the usages of trade were taken for

finds that the writing is not a complete and exclusive statement of the parties' agreement, then evidence of "consistent additional terms" is admissible unless the court finds the alleged extrinsic term, if agreed upon, would certainly have been included in the writing.[20]

REVIEW OF INTERPRETATION DOCTRINE

> R2d § 202, 203, 212, 220 - 223
> UCC 1-205, 2-208

After a contract has been formed and the parties are engaged in its performance, they may find that they disagree over what they presumably agreed to do. Suddenly, the terms that seemed perfectly clear upon contract execution are no longer so. Or the parties may not have considered certain aspects of their relationship and neglected to specify terms necessary for its performance. If a dispute arises, a court may be called upon to interpret the agreement.

Interpretation is the process by which a court determines the meaning to give the language used by the parties in their contract to determine its legal effect.[21] This includes ascertaining the meaning of specific contract language as well as implying terms where the contract itself may be silent. This later task of supplying terms to fill gaps in the parties' agreement is referred to as contract "construction." As always, the court's concern is to discern and give meaning to the intent and expectations of the parties in forming the contract.[22] The general rule for admissibility of extrinsic

granted when the document was phrased. Unless carefully negated they have become an element of the meaning of the words used. Similarly, the course of actual performance by the parties is considered the best indication of what they intended the writing to mean.") *C.f. id.* § 2–202 cmt. 1(c), which does not require a finding of ambiguity before this evidence is admissible; the 2003 revision makes this a provision of the section itself. *See* U.C.C. § 2–202(2) (Proposed Revision 2003) (stating that "[t]erms in a record may be explained by evidence of course of performance, course of dealing, or usage of trade without a preliminary determination by the court that the language used is ambiguous.").

20. James J. White & Robert S. Summers, *Uniform Commercial Code*, § 2–10 (5th ed. 2000).

21. E. Allan Farnsworth, *Contracts*, § 7.17 (4th ed. 2004).

22. *Id.*

evidence to explain the meaning of a writing is whether the offered evidence is relevant to prove a meaning to which the language is "reasonably susceptible."[23] If so, extrinsic evidence is admissible to explain the meaning even if it would otherwise be barred by the parol evidence rule.

The intent of the parties is central in determining contract meaning; however, courts are not necessarily in agreement as to how this intent is to be found. Many courts follow the "plain meaning" rule and look only to the four-corners of the document itself to determine what the language means. The contract is read as a whole to determine its purpose and intent. If the contract language appears clear and unambiguous to the judge, then extrinsic evidence is inadmissible to contradict that interpretation. However, some plain-meaning jurisdictions allow evidence of surrounding circumstances to aid in interpretation. Even within plain-meaning jurisdictions, therefore, there is a split of authority with respect to whether extrinsic evidence is admissible to show whether a term in the writing is ambiguous.[24]

Other courts apply a "contextual" approach and consider all the proffered evidence before deciding whether the contract language is reasonably susceptible to the meaning claimed. This is the approach adopted by the Restatement Second. The theory is that it cannot be known what the contract language means until it is known what the parties intended it to mean. This requires the court to examine extrinsic evidence to determine what the language meant to the parties who used it.[25]

Rules in Aid of Interpretation

Assuming a court will consider extrinsic evidence to interpret the language of a contract, the next issue is understanding how the

---

23. *Pacific Gas & Elec. Co. v. G.W. Thomas Drayage & Rigging Co.*, 442 P.2d 641 (Cal. 1968).

24. James M. Perillo, *Calamari and Perillo on Contracts*, 152 n.13 (5th ed. 2003).

25. *Pacific Gas & Elec.*, 442 P.2d at 644 (Judge Traynor reasoned that a rule that would limit the court's inquiry to the document's four-corners "because it seems to the court to be clear and unambiguous, would either deny the relevance of the intention of the parties or presuppose a degree of verbal precision and stability our language has not attained.").

court goes about the interpretation process. It may be helpful to think of the process as the application of a hierarchical series of rules, working from the specific to the general.

The usual starting point is the actual language the parties used in their agreement. Thus, the court's inquiry begins with the express wording of the oral or written agreement and the usual inferences to be drawn from the language. The term in dispute is read in light of the agreement as a whole. Where no precise meaning can be gleaned from the agreement, the inquiry extends to the surrounding circumstances and extrinsic evidence is admissible. This includes the parties' discussions and conduct when they negotiated the contract, their conduct in performing the contract (course of performance), their conduct in any prior agreements with each other (course of dealing), and the custom and usage in the market or industry in which they operate (usage of trade).

If these sources are not helpful in ascertaining the meaning of the disputed terms, the court next looks to rules applicable to similar contracts and considers supplementary rules, both statutory and common-law, to fill the gap. A good way to summarize the process is to think of it as the movement from the specific to the general: the first interpretive source is the specific agreement, followed by the totality of the transactions between the parties, trade usage, rules applicable to similar contracts, general rules of contract law, and finally the general standards of reasonableness and good faith.

There is also a hierarchy of statutory interpretation the court follows when the question involves the sale of goods under the Uniform Commercial Code. When construing a statutory provision, the court looks first to the statutory language and definitions, followed by the Official Comments, judicial opinions, views of commentators and legal experts, and finally, legislative history. With respect to contract interpretation, while there is no comprehensive approach, subsection (a) of UCC 2–202 provides that the terms in an integrated writing may be explained or supplemented by "course of dealing, or usage of trade or by course of performance."[26]

Perhaps the interpretive process is best understood by seeing how it was applied in one of the most well-known cases on the subject, *Frigaliment Importing Co. v. B.N.S. International Sales Corp.*, where the court was faced with deciding the issue "what is chicken?"[27] Here, the buyer ordered a large quantity of chicken from the seller. The contract specified "US Fresh Frozen Chicken, Grade A, Government Inspected"[28] chicken of two different sizes. The prices for the two sizes were different with a lower price per pound for the larger chickens. When the chickens were delivered, the buyer claimed the larger chickens were stewing chickens and not the frying chickens required by the contract. The buyer said that "chicken" meant "young chicken." The seller said its shipment of stewing chickens was not a breach of contract because chicken as meant in the contract meant both frying and stewing chicken and that the difference in price made it clear that the cheaper chicken was stewing chicken. Here, the price term in the contract supported the seller's argument that two different types of chicken were contemplated by the parties because the price of the larger birds was below the market price for fryers.

In resolving the dispute, the court's task was to determine what the parties meant by the word "chicken." It looked high and low in its efforts to do so: it looked to U.S.D.A. regulations, it considered expert testimony from those in the poultry trade, and it considered the parties' course of performance. None of the evidence clearly supported the position of either party. Since the court was unable to establish what the parties' meant by the word "chicken" from the written agreement, the surrounding circumstances, or the usage of trade, it resolved the case on the basis of the

---

26. U.C.C. § 2–202(a). The 2003 revision to § 2–202(2) now provides: "[t]erms in a record may be explained by evidence of course of performance, course of dealing, or usage of trade without a preliminary determination by the court that the language used is ambiguous."

27. 190 F. Supp. 116 (S.D.N.Y.1960).

28. *Id.*

burden of proof. It found that the buyer failed to meet its burden of "showing that 'chicken' was used in the narrower rather than in the broader sense[.]"[29] The buyer lost the battle of the chicken because it failed to prove that "chicken" meant *only* frying chicken and not frying and stewing chicken.

PAROL EVIDENCE CHECKLIST

If one party seeks to introduce evidence of a prior or contemporaneous agreement to show that the terms of the parties' written agreement are other than as shown in the writing, then that party will be met with the bar of the parol evidence rule. To determine the admissibility of such extrinsic evidence, proceed as follows:

A. **Written Agreement**—have the parties memorialized their agreement in a writing?

   1. **No.** If there is no written agreement, then your inquiry ends here and the parol evidence rule does not apply.

   2. **Yes.** If so, then the parol evidence rule may be implicated. Proceed to the next question.

B. **Parol Evidence**—is one party seeking to introduce evidence of another agreement, either oral or written, to show that the terms of the written agreement are other than as shown in the writing?

   1. **Separate Agreement?** Is it a separate agreement for separate consideration? If so, then the parol evidence rule does not apply and the evidence is admissible.

   2. **Subsequent Agreement?** Is it a subsequent agreement, one entered into after the written agreement? If so, then the parol evidence rule does not apply.

   3. **Condition Precedent?** Is it evidence to show that the contract was subject to a condition precedent? If one of the parties

---

29. *Id.,* at 121.

conditioned its performance on the happening of a future uncertain event, then evidence of that condition is not barred by the parol evidence rule.

4. **Other Purposes?** Is the evidence being offered to show that the agreement is invalid due to a lack of consideration, mistake, fraud, misrepresentation, duress, or illegality? If so, then such evidence is admissible.

5. **Prior or Contemporaneous Agreement?** Is it evidence of a prior or contemporaneous oral or prior written agreement? If so, then the parol evidence rule applies. Proceed to Part C.

C. **Deciding the Integration Question**—whether a writing is an integrated agreement and, if so, whether the agreement is completely or partially integrated are preliminary questions decided by the judge. Courts follow different approaches in making these determinations. Ask: which type of jurisdiction is involved?

1. **Corbin jurisdiction?** If it is a Corbin jurisdiction (the Code and Restatement reflect this view), then it will consider all the circumstances, including evidence of the prior negotiations, to determine the question of integration.

2. **Williston jurisdiction?** If it is a Williston jurisdiction, then it will focus on the writing itself. A "four corners" approach looks to the writing and only if the contract appears on its face to be incomplete will parol evidence be admissible.

D. **Integrated or Unintegrated?** To determine whether the agreement is integrated or unintegrated ask the following about the writing:

1. **Prepared by One Party?** If the document is prepared by only one party, then it is likely to be unintegrated and parol evidence is admissible. Your inquiry ends here.

2. **Memo to File?** If it is a memo to file, then it is likely to be unintegrated and parol evidence is admissible. Your inquiry ends here.

3. **Final as to One Term?** If the writing is final as to at least one term, then the agreement is integrated and the parol evidence rule bars evidence of prior negotiations for at least some

purposes. Proceed to Part E to determine whether the agreement is completely or partially integrated.

E. **Degree of Integration**—if the agreement integrated, is it completely or partially integrated?

1. **Completely Integrated?** Is the writing a final and complete statement of the parties' agreement? If the judge finds the writing is completely integrated, evidence even of consistent additional terms may not be admitted but the writing may be explained or supplemented by course of dealing, usage of trade, or course of performance. Consider the following to determine whether the writing is a complete integration:

   a. **Merger Clause?** Is there a merger or integration clause in the agreement? The presence of such a clause is the best evidence of an integrated agreement. However, a merger clause is only presumptive of integration—it is not conclusive. Proceed to the next question.

   b. **Consistent Additional Terms?** An agreement is not completely integrated if the writing omits a consistent additional term which is agreed to for separate consideration or such a term as in the circumstances might naturally be omitted from the writing. R2d § 216.

2. **Partially Integrated?** Is the writing a partial integration such that it is final with respect to the terms it contains but it is not does not contain all the terms of the parties' agreement? If so, then the agreement is only partially integrated and evidence of additional terms is admissible as long as it does not contradict a term of the writing. Ask: is the offered term consistent or contradictory to the writing?

   a. **Consistent?** If the offered term is consistent with the writing, then it is admissible.

   b. **Contradictory?** If the evidence is contradictory, then it is barred by the parol evidence rule. Only additional, supplementary terms are admissible.

F. **Other Purposes?** Is the evidence being offered to show that the agreement is invalid due to a lack of consideration, mistake, fraud, misrepresentation, duress, or illegality?

1. **Yes.** If so, then the evidence is admissible.

2. **No.** If not, then the evidence is barred by the parol evidence rule.

 ## INTERPRETATION CHECKLIST

Although evidence may be barred by the parol evidence rule, it may be admissible to interpret the writing. The interpretation checklist will help you analyze whether such evidence is admissible and, if so, what form it may take.

A. **Contract Meaning?** Do the parties dispute the meaning of a term in their contract? If the parties disagree as to the meaning of language in their agreement, then the court may be called upon to interpret the agreement. If so, proceed to Part B.

B. **Extrinsic Evidence?** Will the court allow admission of extrinsic evidence to interpret the contract language?

1. **Sale of Goods?** If the contract is for a sale of goods, then the Code does not require a finding of ambiguity before evidence of the parties' course of performance, course of dealing, or usage of trade can be admitted. Proceed to Part D.

2. **Common Law?** If the contract is for services, then it falls within the common law. Proceed to the next question.

3. **Corbin jurisdiction?** Under Corbin's approach, all relevant extrinsic evidence is admissible on the issue of meaning. Restatement Second § 212 follows this approach and allows consideration of all credible evidence to prove the intent of the parties.

   - **Is the language "ambiguous"?** After considering the evidence, the question for the court then becomes whether the offered evidence is relevant to prove a meaning to which the language is "reasonably susceptible."[30] If so, proceed to Part C for contracts involving the common law and Part D for contracts involving the sale of goods.

4. **"Plain Meaning" jurisdiction?** If it is a "plain meaning" jurisdiction, then the contract meaning must be determined from the "four corners" of the document without resort to extrinsic evidence of any kind. If the contract, read as a whole to determine its purpose and intent, seems a clear expression of the parties' full agreement, then the court will not allow the introduction of extrinsic evidence.

C. **Hierarchy of Interpretation**—if the court allows the admission of extrinsic evidence to resolve the contractual ambiguity, it follows a hierarchical sequence to interpret the agreement as it moves from the express wording of the parties' agreement to the surrounding circumstances.

1. **Course of Performance?** Does the conduct of the parties in the course of performing the contract provide an answer? According to Restatement Second § 202(4), "[w]here an agreement involves repeated occasions for performance by either party with knowledge of the nature of the performance and opportunity for objection to it by the other, any course of performance accepted or acquiesced in without objection is given great weight in the interpretation of the agreement." Ask: have the parties begun performing the contract? If so, then their conduct in performing may provide evidence of what they intended by the ambiguous language.

2. **Course of Dealing?** Have the parties engaged in prior dealings which may help to interpret the term in dispute in the present transaction? R2d § 223.

3. **Trade Usage?** Is there an applicable usage of trade? A usage of trade in which the parties are engaged or one of which they know may be considered in giving meaning to their agreement. R2d § 222.

4. **Essential Omitted Terms?** Did the parties fail to include a term which has turned out to be essential to a determination of

---

30. *See Pacific Gas & Elec.*, 442 P.2d 641.

the rights and duties of the parties? If so, the court may supply a term which is reasonable in the circumstances and if it possible to do so "by logical deduction from agreed terms and the circumstances[.]" R2d § 204 cmt. c.

5. **General Standards of Reasonableness and Good Faith?** Every contact imposes upon each party a duty of good faith and fair dealing in the contract's performance and enforcement. R2d § 205. In resolving contractual ambiguity, the court may imply general standards of reasonableness and good faith.

6. **"General Rules of Construction"?** There are general rules of construction which provide guidance in drawing appropriate inferences where the language is subject to interpretation.

   a. Is there a way to interpret the ambiguous term which gives effect to all of the terms of the agreement?

   b. Can the term be interpreted according to an ordinary or lay meaning rather than a specialized or technical meaning?

   c. Is it a specific provision? If so, then it should be given greater weight than a general provision.

   d. *Ejusdem generis* (of the same kind)? Are general and specific words connected? If so, then the general word is limited by the specific one so that it means only things of the same kind.

   e. *Expressio unius, exclusio alterius* ("expression of one thing excludes another")? Is there a specific list of items without being followed by a general term? If so, then the implication is that all other things of the same kind are excluded.

D. **Hierarchy of Statutory Interpretation—** where the contract involves the sale of goods, the court follows the Code's hierarchy for interpreting agreements. First distinguish between the rules for construing the statute itself (statutory construction) from rules for interpreting agreements which fall within the statute. Here you would follow the guidelines for interpreting the parties' agreement:

1. **Express Contract Terms?** Can the intent of the parties be determined from the express terms of their agreement? If so, the express language controls.

2. **Parties' Course of Performance, Course of Dealing, or Usage of Trade?** Under the Code, course of performance prevails over both course of dealing and usage of trade and course of dealing prevails over usage when determining the meaning of the agreement. The express terms of the agreement prevail over all.

3. **Statutory Language and Definitions?** Does the language of the statute have a commonly accepted meaning?

   a. Is the language of the statute clear? If the language of the statute is clear, then other evidence is unnecessary and the "plain meaning" of the statute controls. To determine meaning, ask the following:

      i. Can the plain meaning be inferred using the rules of grammar, i.e., the order and relationship of words within a sentence, dictionary definitions, and common and technical usage?

      ii. Do the "canons of construction" provide guidance?

         • *Ejusdem generis* ("of the same genus or class")? Does the statute contain a specific enumeration followed by a general phase? In this case, the general words should be construed to mean only things of the same kind as the specific class.

         • *Expressio unius, exclusio alterius* ("expression of one thing excludes another")? Does the statute expressly mention what is intended to be within its coverage? If so, then the statute excludes all that is not mentioned.

   b. Is the statutory meaning ambiguous? If so, then extrinsic sources can be consulted. Proceed to Part D.5.

4. **Official Comments?** Does the Code commentary provide clarification of the term in question?

5. **Judicial Interpretation?** Is there case law to explain the language at issue? Once a court interprets a statute, then *stare decisis* applies and the court follows the interpretation it has adopted. Can the court's reasoning be applied by analogy to explain the ambiguous term?

6. **Commentators and Experts?** Is there expert commentary available to interpret the language?

7. **Legislative History?** Is there legislative history to assist in ascertaining the meaning given to the language at issue?

ILLUSTRATIVE PROBLEM

Here is a problem that will allow us to see how the checklist can be used to resolve parol evidence and interpretation questions:

■ PROBLEM 6.1 ■

Murray is the owner of Seven's, a sports restaurant named after the baseball legend, Mickey Mantle. Murray began leasing space for Seven's ten years ago. The lease agreement was with Barry Maris, the son of Roger Maris, another Yankee player and a good friend of Mantle's. Sadly, Barry died two years ago and bequeathed his estate to his daughter, Jessica, a young woman who is not the slightest bit interested in baseball. Needless to say, Murray and Jessica do not have much in common and they have a terrible relationship.

Their first disagreement began in January 2009, when Jessica suddenly stopped paying for Murray's electricity. Under the existing lease agreement, the lessor "will pay for electricity" and the lessee "will pay for gas or fuel used in the preparation of food." When Barry was alive, he had consistently paid the electrical bill for Seven's. Jessica, however, was refusing to pay, claiming that electricity is fuel. Indeed, Murray knows that in the restaurant industry "fuel" has been interpreted to include electricity. However, he also knows that when he and Barry signed the lease agreement, Barry intended to pay for electricity. The only provision on the subject, was that if Murray were to install a new electric range in Seven's, then he would also install a special electric meter and pay for the electricity used by the range. Jessica maintains that none of the other lessors she knows is paying the electric bills of their lessees.

Despite the difficulty that Murray is experiencing with Jessica over the electric bill, he decided that he still wants to continue to operate Seven's on the same premises. To do so, he must renew the lease.

Under the existing lease agreement, Murray agreed to pay $10,000 monthly, which was precisely what he had been doing for nearly ten years. The lease provided Murray with an option to renew for five more years so long as he invoked the option "in a writing sent by certified mail no later than April 1, 2009."

On March 28th, Murray called Jessica and said: "I want to renew my lease." Jessica replied in her usual, monotone voice, "We will see about that. Don't bother to send a written request to me." She then hung up the phone.

On May 5th, Murray visited Jessica's office to negotiate a new rental price. Jessica showed him the door and said, "I don't have to negotiate with you for a new lease because you failed to give me written notice as the agreement requires. You had better start packing."

Murray was in a state of shock. He has come to you for advice as his attorney. He has related these facts to you and tells you the following as well, "when I dealt with my friend, Barry Maris, Jessica's dad, everything was so easy. Right before we signed the written lease agreement, Barry told me, 'Murray, we don't really need to be so formal with each other. If there is anything related to our contract that we need to discuss, just pick up the phone and give me a call, including renewing the lease.'"

(1) What is the likelihood that the court will order Jessica to pay for Seven's use of electricity?

(2) Is evidence of the oral conversation that Murray had with Barry Maris before they executed the written lease agreement admissible to prove that Murray could exercise the option to renew by phone?

Analysis

(1)   The issue is whether the contract term regarding payment for electricity is subject to interpretation. Interpretation is the process by which a court determines the meaning to give the language used by the parties in their contract where the language is ambiguous. Language is ambiguous when it is reasonably susceptible to more than one meaning.

Here the ambiguity is whether electricity is fuel because the lease states the lessor will pay for "electricity"and it also states the lessee "will pay for gas or fuel used in the preparation of food." If electricity is "used in the preparation of food," then it would appear to be "fuel" and the lessee, not the lessor, must pay for it.

In support of her interpretation, Jessica will offer extrinsic evidence of trade usage because in the restaurant industry, "fuel" includes electricity. Indeed, even Murray is aware that in the restaurant industry "fuel" has been interpreted to include electricity.

First, Murray will point to the express terms of the lease. The lease provision expressly provides that if Murray were to install a new electric range, then he would pay for the electricity used by the range. The logical inference supported by the general rules of construction where the expression of one thing excludes another, is that in all other cases, Barry would pay for electricity.

Second, Murray will point to the parties' course of performance over the past ten years to give meaning to the term "electricity." Barry has paid Seven's electric bill for the entire lease period. This course of performance of the parties' lease gives meaning to the language that the lessor will pay for "electricity."

Given the parties' course of performance over the past ten years and the lease provision, it is likely that the court will order Jessica to pay for Seven's use of electricity.

(2)   The question is whether parol evidence bars evidence of Murray's discussions with Barry Maris before he signed the lease.

The purpose of the parol evidence rule is to give legal effect to the parties' intent to make their writing at least a final and perhaps also a complete expression of their agreement to the exclusion of all prior or contemporaneous negotiations, whether oral or written. If the parties has such an intention, the agreement is "integrated," and the parol evidence rule bars evidence of prior negotiations for some purposes. If the parties had no such intention, the agreement is "unintegrated," and the rule does not apply.

The first question is whether the parties' lease agreement was integrated or unintegrated: did the parties intend the writing to be a final embodiment of their agreement? Here, the parties intended an integration because the lease agreement was in writing and signed by the parties.

The next question is whether the lease was fully or partially integrated. If the writing is a final expression of the parties agreement and complete with respect to all of its terms, then it is a total integration and cannot be contradicted by any type of evidence nor supplemented by consistent (non-contradictory) additional terms. A partial integration is final as to the terms it contains but not complete as to all the terms so it may be supplemented by consistent additional terms, but cannot be contradicted.

Here, it could be argued that the lease was fully integrated because it was reduced to a writing with terms regarding the rent amount and an option to renew. On the other hand, it could be argued that it was only partially integrated because there was no mention that matters could be handled orally or any way other than in writing. It is likely that the lease was only partially integrated.

With a finding of partial integration, the next question is whether evidence of Murray and Barry's oral agreement is admissible. Evidence is admissible to supplement but never to contradict the written agreement. Here, Murray could argue that the parol evidence rule does not bar evidence of the oral agreement because it is just an additional term allowing Murray to give notice by a means other than in writing. It is an additional method of communication and does contradict but merely supplements the written lease agreement. Conversely, Jessica could argue that the oral agreement is barred by the parol evidence because it contradicts an express term of the writing: the lease contains a provision that notice of renewal must be written. Consequently, the oral agreement contradicts the writing and would be inadmissible. If the court finds that notice by another means is supplementary rather than contradictory, then evidence of the oral agreement would be admissible.

POINTS TO REMEMBER

- A parol evidence issue arises *only* when the parties' last expression is in writing and forms a valid contract.

- Although the word "parol" means "oral," the parol evidence rule is not limited to only "oral agreements." It also applies to written communications.

- The purpose of the rule is to give legal effect to whatever intent the parties had to make their writing a final or "integrated" agreement.

- Even if a contract is integrated, evidence of a collateral agreement is not barred by the parol evidence rule as long as it does not contradict the main agreement. It is sufficient if the collateral agreement is one that "in the circumstances might naturally be omitted from the writing."

- A writing that is final is an *integration* of the terms contained within it. When it is final and complete, the writing is a *complete integration*. When it is final with respect to the terms it contains but does not contain all the terms of the parties' agreement, then the writing is a *partial integration*.

- If a writing is final as to the terms it contains but not complete as to all the terms, it is only a partial integration and may be supplemented by consistent additional terms, but cannot be contradicted.

- If a writing is a final expression of the parties' agreement and complete with respect to all of its terms, then it is a complete integration and cannot be contradicted by any type of evidence nor supplemented by consistent (non-contradictory) additional terms.

- Although a merger clause is presumptive of an integration, it is not conclusive.

- The parol evidence rule applies *only* to evidence of prior or contemporaneous agreements and does not exclude evidence of subsequent agreements.

- The parol evidence rule does not exclude evidence to show that there was no agreement, i.e., evidence to show that the agreement is invalid due to a lack of consideration, mistake, fraud, misrepresentation, duress, or illegality.

- Evidence which is otherwise barred by the parol evidence rule may be admissible to interpret ambiguous language.

Formation ➤	Avoiding ➤ the Deal	Performance ➤	Third ➤ Parties	Remedies
Do we have a deal?	We have a deal, but	Who has to do what and when, or maybe not	Is there a third party to the deal?	Someone failed to perform when required, now what?
Mutual Assent + Consideration				

Excerpts of Contracts Time-line

PERFORMANCE/NONPERFORMANCE
WHO HAS TO DO WHAT AND WHEN, OR MAYBE NOT

Finding the Contract Terms
- Parol Evidence Rule
- Interpretation
- Ambiguity

Implied Terms
- Good Faith

Warranties

Conditions
- Express/Implied
- Constructive

Excuse/Waiver of Condition

Modification

Impossibility/Impracticability

Frustration of purpose

Anticipatory Repudiation & Adequate Assurances

Material Breach
- Substantial Performance
- UCC Perfect Tender Rule

Close-up on Performance

CHAPTER 7

Performance: Promises and Conditions

R2d § 224-228

In the preceding chapters, we were concerned with contract formation and determining whether the parties had made promises which the law would enforce. Assuming a valid contract was formed, we then considered whether there was a defense or limit to its enforceability based on incapacity, mistake, unconscionability, or illegality, to name but a few. Next, we explored the scope and meaning of the parties' agreement—what were the terms of the parties' agreement and what did the parties mean by the words that they used?

Now we are ready to consider the performance phase of the contract. Here the parties are carrying out their respective duties and obligations when one party claims that the other has breached by failing to perform when required to do so by the terms of the contract. However, some performances are due only if something happens, that is, the party's performance has been made conditional on some event. If the event does not occur, then the performance is not due and the party is not in breach.

Whether a breach has occurred and the consequences which flow from the breach are generally addressed under the topics of "conditions" and "promises." We begin with conditions.

REVIEW OF CONDITIONS

The terms in a contract may be promises or conditions or sometimes both. Parties use promises and conditions to structure their performance obligations under the contract. You are already quite familiar with the concept of promise while the nature and function of conditions is new. While new in this context, however, you have seen parties use conditions in the bargaining process to induce an exchange. For example, a promisor says, "if you promise to wait a month to collect the money that Sam owes you, then I will pay the debt in full." Now we will examine more fully how parties use such terms to structure and allocate the risk of their performances.

A good starting place is to define the basic terms. A promise is a commitment to act or refrain from acting in a specified way at some time in the future.[1] The present exchange of promises for their future performances is the essence of contract and a concept we have discussed in depth. For example, when Nathan and Julia make a contract for the sale of a horse, Nathan promises to convey ownership and possession of his horse, Hearsay, in exchange for Julia's promise to pay the price of $10,000.

On the other hand, a condition is "an event, not certain to occur, which must occur, unless its non-occurrence is excused, before performance under a contract becomes due."[2] Here the parties agree when making the contract that a promised performance will not become due unless and until a particular event occurs or the condition is excused. The event can be any incident of the parties' choosing except for the mere passage of time since that is certain to occur. If the event does not occur, the party's duty to perform never arises. In cases where the performance is a condition of the other party's performance, the nonfulfillment of the condition leads to termination of the contract as a whole.

Some terms are neither promises nor conditions but simply a means by which the parties set the time for their performance. For example, suppose Nathan and Julia's contract regarding the sale of Hearsay stated that Julia was to make a down payment of $5000 on the 15th of the month with the balance to be paid on the 30th.

---

1. Restatement (Second) of Contracts § 2 (1979). **2.** Restatement (Second) of Contracts § 224 (1979).

These dates fix the time when payment is due; they do not make Nathan's duty to convey Hearsay conditional on payment at either of these times although the parties could do so if they wished.

Typically, parties use conditions to allocate the risk of performance. For example, suppose Ben wants to purchase a parcel of land from Seth for $500,000 but knows he cannot afford it unless he gets a bonus at work. He wants the property but doesn't want to be bound if he doesn't have the money to pay for it because then he would be in breach and liable for damages. In this case, Ben would limit his promise by inserting a condition in the agreement as follows: "Ben's obligation to purchase the property is conditional upon Ben's getting a $200,000 bonus from his employer by June 30th." Whether Ben will get the bonus and get it by June 30th is a condition to his performance: it is not certain that Ben will get the bonus, but if he does, he is obligated to purchase the property. On the other hand, if he doesn't get the bonus, then his duty never arises and he walks away. Ben does not have to buy the property and Seth has no basis to sue because there has been no breach of contract.

Promises, Conditions, and Promissory Conditions

As we noted earlier, contract terms can be promises, conditions, or both. A promise is a commitment and gives rise to a duty, i.e., the promisor assumes an obligation upon making a promise. On the other hand, a condition does not contain a promise but simply sets an event that must occur before a duty of performance will arise. Some contract terms combine both and are known as "promissory conditions." A promissory condition is both a condition and a promise that the condition will occur. In this case, there is an event that must occur before performance becomes due and there is a promise by one party that the event will happen.

The distinction between a condition and a promise is critical: while failure to perform a promise, unless excused, is a breach, failure to comply with a condition is not a breach. If the condition fails, then the promisor is discharged from the contract without any obligation to compensate the promisee. This can result in a complete forfeiture for the promisee while the promisor might not have been prejudiced at all by the failure of the condition. Accordingly, where there is doubt about whether a term is a condition or a promise, Restatement Second § 227(2) prefers an interpretation that finds a promise to avoid the harsh result of a forfeiture.

It is often quite difficult to determine whether a term is a promise or condition. Typically, the controlling factor is the intent of the parties. Intent may be indicated by the parties' choice of language in the contract. Words such as "if" or "unless" usually indicate the existence of a condition, while phrases such as "stipulate to" or "I promise that" indicate the intent to make an event a promise rather than a condition. While the words used by the parties are important, they are only one consideration in determining intent. The court will also consider the situation of the parties and the subject matter of the contract.

The key to understanding promises, conditions, and promissory conditions lies in appreciating the consequences which flow from each with respect to the parties' future performances and the entitlement to damages. Consider the following summary:

If the contract term is only a condition and the condition does not occur, then the party whose performance was contingent on the condition is discharged but has no claim for breach and damages against the other party. In other words, where a party's duty to perform is made conditional on the occurrence of an event and that event does not occur, then the party's duty to perform never arises—it simply does not become due. This is why there is no basis for claiming breach of contract. We have already seen an example of a term that is purely a condition in the contract between Ben and Seth: the contract stated expressly that *"Ben's obligation to purchase the property is conditional upon Ben's getting a $200,000 bonus from his employer by June 30th."*

If a contract term is only a promise and the promise is not performed, then the failure to perform is a breach of contract. Here the injured party has a claim for damages but that party's own duty of further performance under the contract is not discharged unless the breach is "material" and the breaching party makes no le;3qeffort to cure the breach in a reasonable time. If the breaching party effects a timely cure, then the other party's duty to perform under the contract is due although it may still have a claim for damages caused by any delay in performance.

If a contract term is both a promise and a condition, then the non-occurrence of the condition both discharges the injured party from any future performance obligation under the contract and entitles that party to damages for any loss suffered as a consequence of the breach.

Let's consider an example. Suppose Ben structured his deal for the purchase of Seth's property a little differently. Instead of making the deal contingent on getting a bonus, the parties include a provision in the contract that the land would be suitable for raising horses. Ben is only interested in the property if he can board and train his two thoroughbred horses, Diego and Untraceable. If he can do this, then he is willing to pay $500,000 for the land. The payment and conveyance of the land are both promises and conditions. The two promises are easy to see—Ben promises to pay $500,000 and Seth promises to convey the property. The promise to pay and the promise to convey are also concurrent conditions of exchange since the parties intend to render their performances simultaneously, each for the other. As we will discuss shortly, Ben's promise to pay is also a condition precedent to Seth's conveyance of the land.

However, the term in the contract to convey land suitable for horse raising is also a promissory condition. Seth's promise to convey the land is both a promise and a condition because he promises to convey land that is suitable for raising horses, a condition that is within his control because he is the landowner. Ben's promise to purchase the property is subject to an express condition that it be suitable for horse raising. If it is not suitable, he has no duty to purchase the property and Seth cannot sue him for breach.

Classifying Promises

Promises can be classified as either independent or dependent. If the parties' promises are independent, then each party's duty to render the promised performance is separate from the other party's duty of performance. In essence, each party's promise is independently enforceable where the failure of one party to perform does not, in itself, justify the other in withholding his or her own performance. For example, if Spencer agreed to sell and Ben agreed to buy 500 pounds of gravel, Spencer could demand payment for the gravel from Ben without first tendering delivery of the gravel and could sue for breach if Ben failed to pay. The opposite is true as well: Ben could demand the gravel without tendering payment and sue for breach if Spencer refused to deliver the gravel.

The concept of independent promises may seem strange to you since the modern view is that promises to a bilateral contract are in almost all cases found to be "dependent"—that is, the parties intend performance by one to be conditioned upon performance by the other. But this was not the rule until Lord Mansfield decided the case of *Kingston v. Preston*[3] in 1773 and articulated the principle of constructive conditions of exchange. In holding for the defendant, Lord Mansfield believed that the "greatest injustice would result"[4] if the plaintiff were to be required to transfer ownership of his silk business without receiving the required security from the plaintiff in exchange. Lord Mansfield found that the parties must have intended that the plaintiff's giving of security was a condition precedent to the defendant's delivery of his stock and business.

In deciding the case, Lord Mansfield explained that there were two types of bilateral contracts—those which are mutual conditions to be performed at the same time and those which are conditions and dependent where the performance of one party is a condition precedent to performance by the other party. While the parties' agreement did not expressly contain these conditions, the court construed them in the interest of justice. Constructive conditions are discussed in more detail below.

---

3. 99 Eng. Rep. 437 (1773) (cited and discussed within *Jones v. Barkley*) (Lord Mansfield found that "it would be highly unreasonable to construe the agreement, so as to oblige the defendant to give up a beneficial business . . . and trust to the plaintiff's personal security, (who might, and, indeed, was admitted to be worth nothing,) for the performance of his part.").

4. *Id.* at 438.

CLASSIFYING CONDITIONS

Conditions can be classified in two ways: one is by the time in which the conditioning event is to occur and the other is by the manner in which the condition arises. When conditions are used to order the sequence of the parties' performance, they are classified as either conditions precedent, subsequent, or concurrent. When conditions are defined by the manner in which they arise—whether agreed to by the parties or created by law—they are divided into express conditions and constructive conditions.

Let's begin with conditions based on the timing of their performance.

Condition Precedent

A "condition precedent" refers to a condition which must occur before the promisor's duty to perform arises. We have already considered several examples, but here is another: suppose Ashley enters into a contract to buy a pair of boots which states, "Buyer's duty to pay $250 is conditional on the boots' arrival in the store before October 1." The arrival of the boots before October 1 is a condition precedent to Ashley's duty to pay for them.

In this example it was clear that the boots had to arrive first before Ashley had to perform. Sometimes the contract language is not so clear. If it cannot be determined by the explicit language of the parties' agreement, the default rule is that the party whose performance takes longer is required to go first. For example, if Emma hires Jon to paint her house for $1,000 and it will take Jon two weeks to complete the job, then unless the parties agree otherwise, Jon will have to paint the house first before Emma will have to pay him the $1,000. It is important to note that many promissory conditions are conditions precedent as well.

It should be noted that the term "condition" as used in this example refers to an event which must occur before a party is obligated to perform a promise made in an existing contract. This is distinguishable from a condition precedent to the formation of a contract where the contract itself does not arise unless the condition is fulfilled. Here, the contract as a whole is conditional and the duties of both parties are subject to the condition as opposed to the performance of an individual party. If the contract as a whole is conditional, then failure of the condition means that neither party is bound to the agreement nor has the right to demand performance from the other. Even if one of the parties wanted to waive the condition and hold the other party to the deal, it would not be possible. On the other hand, if the condition is intended to affect the performance of only one of the parties, then that party may waive the condition and hold the other party to the contract.

Concurrent Conditions

Where the parties are to render their performances simultaneously—each for the other—they are known as "concurrent conditions." Each party's performance is a condition of the other's and must be performed at the same time. For example, suppose Giuliana agrees to sell and Sasha agrees to buy Giuliana's horse, Diego, on Saturday for $10,000. Unless the parties agree otherwise, delivery of Diego and payment of $10,000 are concurrent conditions. This means that if Sasha fails to tender the $10,000 at the appointed time on Saturday, Giuliana must be ready, willing, and able to tender delivery of Diego or show that tender has been excused in order to put Sasha in breach. And the opposite is true as well: for Giuliana to be in default, Sasha must be ready and able to tender the $10,000 or show that tender has been excused. In summary, the promises made by Giuliana and Sasha are "dependent" in that each party regards performance by the other party as a condition of her own obligation to perform.

Condition Subsequent

A "condition subsequent" is an event which discharges or extinguishes a duty of performance that has arisen. Insurance policies are the most common example of such conditions. Suppose Myra buys homeowner's insurance under a policy which provides that no recovery can be had if suit is not brought on the policy within 12 months after a loss. Myra pays her monthly premiums. One day, while doing the laundry, the dryer catches fire and Myra suffers damage to the property covered by the insurance policy. If

Myra fails to bring her claim within the specified period, then the insurance company's duty to pay for her loss under the policy is discharged. Myra's failure to commence the action within the prescribed time is the condition subsequent which extinguishes the insurance company's duty to perform which became due when the loss was suffered.

The distinction between conditions precedent and subsequent is more a matter of procedure than substance because it determines who bears the burden of proof. The party who brings suit for breach has the burden of proving that the condition precedent to that promise arose. If it had not, there would be no basis for breach. Similarly, a party claiming a duty that has already arisen has been discharged has the burden of proof on that issue.

Now we are ready to consider the manner in which conditions arise.

Express Conditions

Express conditions are created by agreement of the parties and usually can be recognized by the use of such contract language as "if," "on condition that," "provided that," "in the event that," and "subject to." Even if the contract language is not explicit, conditions may be implied from the contract as a matter of interpretation. These conditions are referred as "implied-in-fact" because the court implies the condition by implication from the other terms in the parties' agreement. Thus, if an obligor's duty cannot be performed without some act by the obligee, such as giving notice to the obligor, the court will supply a term making that act a condition of the obligor's duty.[5] In terms of their effect on the parties' duties of performance, there is little difference between an express or an implied-in-fact condition: each requires strict compliance.

Constructive Conditions

Constructive conditions are conditions created by the court because they are not to be found either explicitly or implicitly in the

---

5. *See Wal–Noon Corp. v. Hill*, 119 Cal. Rptr.
646 (Cal. Ct. App. 1975).

parties' agreement. They are also referred to as conditions "implied-in-law." As opposed to express conditions, "constructed" conditions permit the party to render something less than full performance and still be entitled to performance from the other party. Substantial compliance is sufficient for performance of constructive conditions whereas nothing less than full performance is acceptable for an express condition. Substantial performance is acceptable for a constructive condition because the court created the condition as opposed to an express condition which is agreed upon by the parties.

Courts do not only supply "conditions" but may supply other terms to an agreement where the parties themselves have been silent or the terms are otherwise indefinite. Perhaps the most widely recognized is the implied obligation of good faith. Both the common law and the UCC impose upon each party to a contract the duty of good faith and fair dealing in its performance and enforcement.[6] Courts are not in agreement, however, as to whether the doctrine creates independent rights to provide a cause of action for a bad faith breach separate from a duty imposed by the contract itself.[7]

---

6. Restatement (Second) of Contracts § 205 (1979) (providing that "[e]very contract imposes upon each party a duty of good faith and fair dealing in its performance and its enforcement."). *See also* U.C.C. § 1–203 (2004) (stating "[e]very contract or duty within this Act imposes an obligation of good faith in its performance or enforcement.") (There are changes to the definition of good faith in the revised version of Articles 1 and 2. Under the current version, Article 1 defines good faith as subjective, requiring "honesty in fact." Where the party is a merchant, Article 2 requires both "honesty in fact," and the "observance of reasonable commercial standards of fair dealing in the trade." Revised Article 1 was changed to read "honesty in fact and observance of reasonable commercial standards of fair dealing" and the special definition for merchants was deleted from revised Article 2. The definition in

Article 1 now applies throughout the Code except for Article 5 which retains the old definition of Article 1 for letters of credit.).

7. E. Allan Farnsworth, *Contracts*, § 7.17 n.14 (4th ed. 2004). Courts reluctant to find a cause of action for a bad faith breach have found support in an addition to the Code commentary. Language added to the commentary on the good faith provision states that the section "does not support an independent cause of action for failure to perform or enforce in good faith" and seeks to make clear "that the doctrine of good faith merely directs a court towards interpreting contracts within the commercial context in which they are created, performed, and enforced, and does not create a separate duty of fairness and reasonableness which can be independently breached." U.C.C. § 1–304 cmt. 1.

Conditions of Satisfaction

Another type of condition is one of satisfaction. Such conditions often appear as "satisfaction clauses" in the parties' agreement requiring performance only upon the obligor's satisfaction. A couple of issues arise with respect to such clauses. One is the requirement of good faith. The other and more complex issue is whether the standard of satisfaction is subjective or objective.

Since the promisor's obligation to perform is conditioned on satisfaction with the other party's performance, the promisor must act in good faith in determining its satisfaction or its promise is illusory. It is easy to see why—suppose a promisor is dissatisfied with the overall bargain rather than the promisee's performance and seeks to escape the deal by claiming dissatisfaction. This would be an act of bad faith. Consider the following example: buyer agrees to buy 12 loads of potatoes at $4.25 per hundredweight. The contract requires the potatoes to chip to "buyer satisfaction." After accepting three loads without objection, the seller then rejects additional tendered loads claiming that they failed to "chip" satisfactorily. Testing from a crop expert shows that the potatoes chip satisfactorily. It seems that the market price of potatoes had dropped precipitously and the buyer could "buy potatoes all day for $2.00."[8] Since the buyer no longer wanted to pay the contract price, he claimed that the potatoes failed to meet the condition of satisfactory chipping.

Typically, a determination of whether the standard is objective or subjective satisfaction depends on the subject matter of the contract. If it is a commercial contract such as one involving manufacturing or construction, then objective satisfaction, which requires the satisfaction of a reasonable person, is required. On the other hand, if the contract involves personal services where the taste, fancy or judgment of the individual is involved, then subjective satisfaction is required. Still, even personal satisfaction must be exercised in good faith which means honesty in fact, i.e., the party

---

8. *Neumiller Farms, Inc. v. Cornett*, 368 So.2d
272, 274 (Ala. 1979).

must be honestly dissatisfied with the performance and not the bargain itself. Where the contract language is not clear whether the test is one of honest satisfaction or reasonable satisfaction, then the preference is for an objective standard of reasonableness to avoid the increased risk of forfeiture.[9]

REVIEW OF EXCUSE OF CONDITIONS

R2d § 84, 229, 230
UCC 2-209

As we've seen, the general rule is that express conditions are strictly enforced. However, this can lead to harsh results if the condition is not met, including a complete forfeiture for one party whereas the other party may have been damaged very little or not at all. Courts have developed several doctrines to avoid the effect of a condition when it would inappropriate or unjust to insist on strict performance. These doctrines include waiver, estoppel, and excuse.

Waiver can be defined as the "intentional relinquishment of a known right."[10] This definition is somewhat misleading since what is involved is not the giving up of a right but rather the excuse of the non-occurrence of a condition or a delay in its performance. In essence, the party that was to benefit from the condition voluntarily elects to dispense with the requirement that it be satisfied as a prerequisite to her own performance. In effect, she abandons the condition such that her duty to perform has become unconditional.

A waiver may be express or implied from words or conduct. For example, a building is sold subject to the buyer's condition that a feasibility report finds it suitable for development. If the buyer decides to forgo the feasibility report and purchase the building, the buyer is said to have expressly waived the condition of a satisfactory feasibility report. An implied waiver would arise if the

---

9. Restatement (Second) of Contracts § 228 cmt. b (1979).   **10.** *Clark v. West*, 86 N.E. 1, 5 (N.Y. 1908).

buyer goes ahead and applies for a mortgage and takes other steps to buy the building despite receiving a dissatisfactory feasibility report.

Parties may dispute whether the conduct at issue was a waiver of a condition or a modification of the contract. Unlike a modification, which is an agreement between the parties, a waiver is a unilateral act. By characterizing conduct as a "waiver" rather than as a "modification," the three requirements for an enforceable modification are avoided: mutual assent, a writing if the agreement falls within the statute of frauds, and consideration or detrimental reliance.

While wavier is a useful tool for mitigating the harsh effect of the requirement of strict compliance for express conditions, it is limited to conditions that are relatively minor, such as those which are procedural or technical in nature.[11] Conditions which relate to the time or manner of a return performance or provide for the giving of notice would be considered non-material conditions which may be waived.[12]

Even if a waiver is effective, it may be retracted. If a party, without consideration, waives a condition before the time for the occurrence of the condition has expired and the condition is within the control of the other party, it can retract the waiver and reinstate the condition unless the other party has materially changed position in reliance.[13]

Conduct that gives rise to a waiver is often the same as that which creates an estoppel. As a result, the two doctrines are often confused and rightly so. Restatement Second § 84 comment b provides a useful distinction: "[w]hen the waiver is reinforced by reliance, enforcement is often said to rest on 'estoppel.' "[14] To see how this works, let's revisit the example where the buyer went ahead and secured a mortgage to buy the building despite receiv-

---

11. Restatement (Second) of Contracts § 84(1) (1979).

12. *Id.* § 84 cmt d.

13. *Id.* § 84(2).

14. *Id.* § 84 cmt. b.

ing a dissatisfactory feasibility report. Suppose the buyer knew that the seller had knowledge of the negative report as well as the buyer's act of applying for a mortgage. Here the buyer should have realized that the seller would think that the buyer was ignoring the condition of a satisfactory report. And suppose further that the seller did indeed believe that the sale was going through and so when he received an offer to purchase the building from another buyer, he declined it. Here, if the condition of a satisfactory feasibility report was material to the parties' agreement, then the additional elements of the seller's justified reliance to his detriment would allow the condition to be excused on the basis of estoppel.

Finally, the doctrine of excuse rests on the court's discretionary powers to do justice. In some cases, a court may find circumstances where it would not be appropriate to insist on strict enforcement of a condition. Where the failure of a condition would cause disproportionate forfeiture, a court may excuse the non-occurrence of that condition unless it was a material part of the parties' agreement. Excusing a condition has the same effect as performance—the duty of the other party to perform arises despite the fact that the condition has not occurred.

According to the Restatement, this rule is flexible and exercised within the discretion of the court. The determination of whether the forfeiture is "disproportionate" depends on weighing "the extent of the forfeiture by the obligee against the importance to the obligor of the risk from which he sought to be protected and the degree to which that protection will be lost if the non-occurrence of the condition is excused to the extent required to prevent forfeiture."[15] As usual, it is a careful balancing test of the interests of the parties. The limitation on the court's ability to excuse a condition is that it must not have been a material part of the agreed exchange.

Waiver Under The UCC

Although the Code has displaced the common law requirement of consideration, it still requires mutual assent for a modifi-

---

15. Restatement (Second) of Contracts § 229 cmt. b (1979).

cation and if the terms of the modification fall within the Statute of Frauds, a writing may be required. One issue that typically arises under the UCC, therefore, is whether an attempt at modification can be construed as a waiver, thus avoiding a requirement that the modification be in writing. Another question is whether the UCC requires detrimental reliance for an effective waiver of a contract term.

Section 2–209(4) states that:

> Although an attempt at modification or rescission does not satisfy the requirements of subsection 2 [contract clauses requiring that modifications be in writing to be enforceable] or (3) [statute of frauds must be satisfied if contract as modified falls within its provisions] it can operate as a waiver.[16]

In *Wisconsin Knife Works v. National Metal Crafters*,[17] the Seventh Circuit addressed this question. In this case, the buyer contracted for the purchase of spade bit blanks to use in its manufacturing process. The buyer and seller agreed that "[n]o modification of this contract shall be binding upon Buyer . . . unless made in writing and signed by Buyer's authorized representative."[18] The seller failed to deliver pursuant to the contract deadlines and the buyer sued for breach. The seller claimed that the buyer's conduct manifested agreement to the new dates. The court addressed the question whether the seller could nullify the contract term requiring that modifications be in writing by labeling the buyer's conduct allegedly agreeing to new dates as a "waiver" rather than a "modification"—which would have been required to be in writing.

Judge Posner held that an attempted modification is effective as a waiver pursuant to UCC 2–209(4) only if there is reliance.

---

16. U.C.C. § 2–209(4) (2004). The 2003 revision of Article 2 makes no significant changes to section 2–209 except for a few minor language changes and the substitution of the word "record" for "writing."

17. 781 F.2d 1280 (7th Cir. 1986).

18. *Id.*, at 1283. *See also* Restatement (Second) of Contracts § 209 cmt. 2 (1979).

Under this approach, if the jury found on remand that the seller had reasonably relied on assurances from the buyer that late delivery would be acceptable, then the attempted modification by conduct could operate as a waiver. If the seller did not incur any reliance costs, then the waiver would be ineffective. While there is support for this approach in the language of 2–209(4) which states that an attempted modification "can operate as a waiver," it does not say that it *is* a waiver.[19]

Not all courts agree with Judge Posner's reading of a reliance requirement for a waiver under the UCC, relying instead on the plain language of the statute. For example, in *BMC Industries, Inc. v. Barth Industries, Inc.*,[20] the Eleventh Circuit held that a waiver does not require a showing of detrimental reliance. Judge Tjoflat explained that Judge Posner ignored a fundamental difference between modifications and waivers in his analysis in that "while a party that has agreed to a contract modification cannot cancel the modification without giving consideration for the cancellation, a party may unilaterally retract its waiver of a contract term provided it gives reasonable notice. The fact that waivers may unilaterally be retracted provides the difference between [2–209] subsections (2) and (4) that allows both to have meaning."[21]

PROMISES AND CONDITIONS CHECKLIST

With that background, here is the checklist for determining the timing and order of performances due under the contract. Begin by asking, "Is the event a promise or condition of the party's performance?"

A. **Promise**—is it a promise? Did the party make a commitment to act or refrain from acting in a specified way in the future so as to justify another in understanding that a commitment has been made? Has the party used such promissory language as "I promise" or "I will"?

---

19. *Id.*, at 1287.

20. 160 F.3d 1322 (11th Cir.1998).

21. *Id.*, at 1334.

1. **Independent Promise**—is it an independent promise where one party's performance is not dependant on the other party's performance? If the parties intend that performance by each is in no way conditioned upon performance by the other, then the promises are independent.

    a. **Yes.** If so, then a failure to perform an independent promise does not excuse non-performance on the part of the other party, but each is required to perform her promise, and, if one does not perform, she is liable to the other party for such non-performance.

    b. **No.** If not, then the promises may be dependent. Proceed to the next question.

2. **Dependent Promise**—is it a dependent promise where one party's performance is dependent on the other party's performance? If the parties intend performance by one party to be conditioned upon performance by the other, then they are mutually dependent promises.

    a. **Yes.** If so, then ask, "what type of dependent promise is it?"

        i. **Precedent?**—Is it a promise that is to be performed before a corresponding promise by the other party is to be performed? If so, then one party must render its performance before the other party's return promise is performed.

        ii. **Subsequent?**—Is it a promise that is not to be performed until the other party has performed a precedent promise?

        iii. **Concurrent?**—Are the promises to be performed simultaneously? If so, then if either party fails to tender the promised performance at the time required for exchange, then the other has the right to withhold the return performance and to treat the failure as a breach of contract. If the contract does not specify the order of performances and they are capable of being performed simultaneously, then they are due at the same time.

    b. **No.** If not, proceed to Part B.

3. **Performance of the Promise**—has the promise been performed?

    a. **Yes.** If so, then the promisor's duty under the contract has been discharged.

    b. **No.** If not, then the failure to perform or the rendering of a defective performance is a breach of contract. Here the injured party has a claim for damages but that party's own duty of further performance under the contract is not discharged unless the breach is **material** and the breaching party makes no effort to **cure** the breach in a reasonable time. If the breaching party effects a timely cure, then the other party's duty to perform under the contract is due although it may still have a claim for damages caused by any delay in performance. The question of whether the breach is material is examined in Chapter 11.

B. **Condition**—is it a condition? Is the party's performance under the contract subject to the occurrence of an uncertain event such that unless and until the event occurs, the promised performance is not due?

  1. **Timing of the Condition**—is there an order to the parties' performances?

    a. **Precedent?**—Is the condition one which must be satisfied before the performance subject to that condition becomes due?

        i. **Yes.** If so, then it is a **condition precedent** and it must occur before a contractual duty becomes due.

        ii. **No.** If not, then proceed to the next question.

    b. **Subsequent?**—Is the condition one which discharges a duty that is already in existence?

        i. **Yes.** If so, then it is a **condition subsequent**.

        ii. **No.** If not, then proceed to the next question.

    c. **Concurrent?**—Are the conditions dependent on each other such that one performance is a condition of the other?

        i. **Yes.** If so, then they are **concurrent conditions of exchange** and the performances are due at the same time. Because the performances are concurrent conditions of each other, both parties must show up ready, willing, and able to perform and if either party fails to tender the promised performance at the time required for exchange, then the other has the right to withhold the return performance and to treat the failure as a breach of contract.

    ii. **No.** However, where there is doubt as to the order of performances, an interpretation is preferred where the performances are to be performed simultaneously.

2. Manner in which the Condition Arises—was the condition agreed to by the parties or created by law?

    a. **Express Condition?**—Is the event one that the parties have agreed to make a condition of performance by using such language as "if," "on condition that," "provided that," "in the event that," or "subject to"?

        i. **Yes.** If so, then strict compliance with the condition is required before the other party's duty to perform under the contract will arise.

        ii. **No.** If not, proceed to the next question.

    b. **Implied Condition?**—Is there contextual evidence that the parties intended a performance to be conditional even if they did not use express language creating a condition?

        i. **Yes.** If so, then the condition is implied-in-fact and strict compliance is required.

        ii. **No.** If not, proceed to the next question.

    c. **Constructive Condition?**—Are the circumstances and nature of the contract such that a condition should exist because if the parties had considered the issue, they reasonably would have intended it to be part of their agreement?

        i. **Yes.** If so, then the court will construe a condition and strict compliance is not required: substantial performance rather than full performance is permissible.

        ii. **No.** If not, then the court will not supply a condition.

3. **Condition of Satisfaction**—has the party made its promised performance conditional on their personal satisfaction or that of a third party? Ask: is performance conditional on the party's subjective or objective satisfaction?

   a. **Subjective Standard?**—Is the contract one for personal services where the taste or judgment of the individual is involved?

      i. **Yes.** If so, then the standard is one of subjective satisfaction. However, even personal satisfaction must be exercised in good faith which means honesty in fact. The party must be honestly dissatisfied with the performance to avoid performance.

      ii. **No.** If not, proceed to the next question.

   b. **Objective Standard?**—Is it a commercial contract such as one involving manufacturing or construction where objective criteria is available?

      i. **Yes.** If so, then the standard is one of objective satisfaction which requires the satisfaction of a reasonable person.

      ii. **No.** In case of doubt, however, the Restatement expresses a preference for use of the objective standard of reasonableness to avoid forfeiture. R2d § 228.

4. **Performance of the Condition**—has there been strict or substantial compliance with the condition?

   a. **Strict Compliance?**—Did the party whose performance was subject to an express or implied condition satisfy it completely? If so, then the condition has been fulfilled and the other party's duty to perform arises. If the condition has not be satisfied, then the other party's duty to perform does not arise unless the condition has been **excused** or **waived**.

      i. **Excused?**—Was the condition excused?

         • **Yes.** If so, then the promisor may still be obligated to perform despite the non-occurrence of the condition. A condition may be excused if the promisor had a duty to facilitate the occurrence of the condition and hindered its fulfillment or failed to act in good faith by obstructing its fulfillment. A court may excuse a condition to avoid a disproportionate forfeiture unless the occurrence of the condition was a material part of the contract.

- **No.** If not, then the non-occurrence of the condition discharges the duty when the condition can no longer occur.

ii. **Waived?**—Was the condition waived? Has the promisor whose performance is conditional indicated by either words (express) or conduct (implied) that she will perform even if the condition does not occur? A party may waive a condition that solely benefits the party waiving it.

- **Yes.** If so, then the promisor is still obligated to perform despite the non-occurrence of the condition.

- **No.** If not, then the non-occurrence of the condition discharges the other party's duty to perform.

iii. **Waiver Retracted?**—Was the waiver retracted before the time for occurrence of the condition has expired?

- **Yes.** If so, the condition may be reinstated unless the other party has relied on the waiver such that retraction would be unjust.

- **No.** If not, then the condition remains waived.

b. **Substantial Compliance?**—Did the party whose performance was subject to a constructive condition provide substantial compliance? If the condition is not expressly stated but is construed by the court as a matter of interpretation, then there is room for flexibility and substantial compliance may be sufficient to satisfy the condition.

i. **Yes.** If so, then the party has satisfied the condition.

ii. **No.** If not, then the party has failed to meet the condition and the other party's duty to perform does not arise.

ILLUSTRATIVE PROBLEMS

Now here are some problems that will let us see how to apply the checklist to resolve questions involving promises and conditions:

■ PROBLEM 7.1 ■

In August, when Robyn learned that her daughter, Ashley, wanted an outdoor wedding the following June, Robyn decided it was time to create the beautiful garden she had always wanted. It would be the perfect setting for the wedding.

While she knew exactly what types of flowers she wanted, she could not plant them herself since she was highly allergic to flower bulbs, flower seeds, and soil. Robyn met with Len the landscaper about planting the garden. She told him she wanted to create a garden that would be the portrait of pink with flowers in every shade of pink, *and only pink*. It also had to have peonies, her daughter's favorite flower. Robyn told Len that she had her heart set on a particular type of peony—a double-flowered, medium-to-dark pink peony.

Since peonies take a long time to bloom, Len would need to plant 2–year old, bedded peony plants in the fall. This way they would bloom in time for the wedding. Once they were planted, Robyn would have them in her garden for a long time, since peonies can live for up to a hundred years. The rest of the flowers for the garden could be planted in the spring. Robyn and Len agreed separately on the flowers and price for this portion of the garden and landscaping job.

Len agreed to order the peony plants immediately and plant them in September. Robyn and Len signed the following written contract:

"Len to supply and plant 50 2–year old double-flowered medium-to-dark pink peony plants of a type known as "Sarah Bernhardt" in Robyn's garden in September for $1500. Robyn has paid $500 to Len at the signing of this contract and she will pay him $1000 when the peonies bloom in June."

Len consulted a well-known flower farm. There were over 140 types of peonies. He eliminated all colors but medium-to-dark pink and all single-petal flowers. He found what looked like what Robyn described. It was the right price and color. This flower nursery called it the "Rose Reverence." Believing that Len had found just the right peony, Len ordered the plants. He planted them in September.

In May, Len and his landscapers transformed Robyn's barren backyard into a heavenly garden. There were flowers in every possible shade of pink, just as Robyn requested. She was delighted. Finally, it was June and the wedding was only a week away. Robyn walked into the garden and burst into tears: the 50 peony plants were in full bloom. Her garden was alive with vivid, medium-to-dark pink blossoms but with very small touches of purple at the edges of the flowers. Furthermore, upon very close inspection, Robyn could see that the flowers were not full double-flowered peonies, but only semi-double. No one else could detect these subtle differences, but Robyn could see them.

Robyn called Len. She wanted every single peony plant removed and replaced with the right peonies and in time for the wedding. Len said that if he had to remove and replace the 50 peony plants, it would double the cost of the peonies and he would also have to rip out all the other flowers he had planted and plant all new plants since they couldn't be saved. In addition, this would require tremendous overtime and would quadruple the cost of the entire project. Robyn said that she didn't care—she wasn't paying a penny extra and would not pay the remaining $1000 for the peonies.

Len has brought an action to recover the $1000. What is the likelihood of his success? Limit your discussion to determining whether the type of peony in the parties' agreement was a promise or condition of Len's performance and the consequences that flow from this determination. Ignore any other issues.

Analysis

The question is whether the "Sarah Bernhardt" peony was a condition or a promise of Len's performance. A condition is an event, not certain to occur, but which must occur for the other party's duty to perform to arise. If a party's performance is treated as a condition to another's duty, non-performance completely discharges the latter from her obligation, even though the failure of the condition has damaged her little or not at all.

It may be argued that the contract language is one of express condition because it refers to a specific type of peony, the "Sarah Bernhardt." Robyn identified the particular type of peony and was very specific in that it had to be pink, only pink, and double-petaled. Such specificity would indicate an express condition.

If the type of peony is found to be an express condition, then Len did not satisfy the condition by planting another type of peony, the Rose Reverence. As a result, he would not be entitled to payment for the peonies because he failed to meet the condition. However, finding that the type of peony was an express condition of Robyn's duty to pay would be very harsh to Len because he would be penalized far beyond the amount by which Robyn is damaged by the slight deviation from the contract terms. Len would lose the $1000 balance remaining on the contract and would have to rip up the entire garden, not just the peonies, to meet Robyn's express condition of providing a pink-only garden. This would quadruple his cost, which would be exorbitant in relation to the cost of the overall project.

Conversely, if it were only a promise to provide pink peonies, then it could be argued that Len substantially performed his promise. A party who breaches a promise is only liable for the damages caused by the breach. If a party's performance deviates only slightly from that specified in a contract, then she is liable for only nominal damages. This result is far less harsh than if her performance were treated as a condition to the other party's performance, in which case the latter's duty is discharged completely.

Here, Len promised to get "pink" peonies for Robyn's garden of a type known as "Sarah Bernhardt." The name was used to describe a type of pink, double-flowered peony and did not mean that it expressly had to be "Sarah Bernhart" peonies. If the type of peony was a promise, then Len's failure to get exactly the right peony—the peonies he planted had a purple edge and were only semi-double blossoms—would be treated as a breach and his performance would be evaluated to determine whether it was substantial.

[The following analysis would be the appropriate next step but it requires knowledge of material we will not cover until Chapter 11. It is included here because it follows from the facts of the problem and it is typical of what you would be expected to discuss on an exam. You might want to come back to this question after you complete Chapter 11.]

In determining whether a party has substantially performed, a court considers several factors. First, it considers the extent to which the breaching party has already performed. Here, Len planted the entire garden, including all 50 peonies, and they were in full bloom in time for the wedding. Second, it considers whether the breach was wilful, negligent, or purely innocent. Len's breach was innocent because he used reasonable efforts to find the right peony by going to a well-known flower farm. Further, he searched through over 140 types of peonies until he found what looked like what Robyn asked for, eliminating those that did not fit her specifications in compliance with her request. He ordered what he believed was the right peony based on price and color, which are objective and reasonable criteria.

Third, the court considers the extent to which the injured party has obtained the substantial benefit for which she bargained. Robyn bargained for a garden full of pink flowers **and** pink peonies, not just peonies. She received exactly this—a beautiful, blooming garden of pink flowers in time for her daughter's wedding. On the other hand, there are touches of purple in the pink garden. Even if the peonies are predominantly pink, there is a slight bit of purple at the edges of the flowers. Moreover, the peonies are only semi-double petaled peonies and not the full double-petal peonies that Robyn requested. However, this slight deviation was noticeable only to Robyn upon close inspection. No one else could detect these subtle differences. Still, this was Robyn's dream garden and she should be able to get what she bargained for. She bargained for a particular type of peony and has not received it. And because peonies can live for up to 100 years, she will see them in her garden as long as she lives in the house and most likely as long as she lives.

Fourth, the court considers the extent the breaching party will suffer forfeiture. In this case, Len will lose $1000. This is not a huge amount. Since the entire fee for the peonies was $1500, Len stands to lose 2/3 of the amount which he is owed which is sizeable but not a total forfeiture. Because Robyn paid him $500 at the time the contract was signed for the peonies, it is possible that this covered his out-of-pocket expenses. Moreover, Len would have been paid separately for all the other flowers and landscaping required for the garden so his loss would be limited to this amount.

Fifth, the court considers the extent to which the nonbreaching party can be compensated for the defective performance. It would be impossible to measure the difference in value between a garden of only pink flowers and one with touches of purple. It would be equally impossible to measure the difference in value between a garden with semi-petaled peonies and one with double-petaled peonies. One could look to the difference in cost but the price of the peonies was substantially the same or Len would not have selected them. While only Robyn can see the differences in the peonies, a homeowner is allowed to be idiosyncratic when it comes to her own home.

In considering all of these factors, it is likely that a court would consider the type of peony to be an express condition of the contract and that Len failed to meet the condition. Consequently, he will not recover the $1000.

[Depending on the analysis, one could come to the opposite conclusion.]

■ PROBLEM 7.2 ■

Heidi was walking down the street when she passed a window with a sign in it: "Artist Wanted." Heidi walked in and found Hannah, the owner, in the middle of a restaurant being remodeled to give it a country western theme. Hannah told Heidi that she needed someone to reproduce the country western scenes from some postcards on the two long, side walls of the restaurant. The restaurant was to open on May 1. Hannah wanted the paintings completed by April 28. Hannah and Heidi entered into a written agreement which stated in relevant part,

"Hannah agrees to pay Heidi $2000. Paintings guaranteed to be fully satisfactory."

On April 10, Heidi showed up with her paints and brushes. She took the two postcards Hannah gave her and got to work. It was easy. All she had to do was copy the scenes on the postcards. Nothing artistic or difficult about copy work. Everyone who saw the paintings as she worked on them said they looked exactly like the postcards.

Heidi finished the paintings on April 28. When Hannah saw them, she said, "Heidi, I am disappointed. I expected something with more excitement—maybe some buffalo on the prairie." Heidi said, "I gave you exactly what you asked for and copied the postcards down to the last detail. If you wanted buffalo, you should have asked for buffalo." Everyone in the restaurant agreed that Heidi's work was an exact duplicate of the postcards—they were virtually identical.

Hannah refuses to pay Heidi because the work was not done to her satisfaction. What result for Heidi?

Analysis

Whether Hannah is entitled to payment depends on whether Heidi's duty to provide "fully satisfactory" paintings was conditioned on an objective or subjective standard of satisfaction and, if so, whether the condition was met. A condition is an event that must occur before performance of a contractual duty becomes due. A party whose duty is conditioned on an event is not required to perform unless the event has occurred. Parties can make their promised performances conditional on their personal satisfaction. Here, Heidi made her duty to pay Hannah subject to a satisfaction clause.

The question is whether the standard of satisfaction to be applied is one of subjective or objective satisfaction. Subjective satisfaction is applicable in contracts for personal services because individual taste or judgment is involved. An objective standard of reasonableness is applicable in commercial contracts because objective criteria is available to evaluate the performance. The general preference is for an objective standard of reasonableness to avoid forfeiture.

Here, paintings were the subject matter of the contract. Because paintings are works of art and art is something that is personal to the individual, the standard is one of personal satisfaction. The paintings were to be placed in Heidi's restaurant and would be highly visible where Heidi would see them all the time. If so, then it is likely that a subjective standard would be applied to determine Heidi's satisfaction.

However, these paintings might not be considered works of art because they were not really paintings but copies of postcards. All Hannah had to do was replicate the postcards. There was nothing artistic or original about copying scenes from the postcards onto the walls of the restaurant. Furthermore, the postcards provided an objective standard by which to measure Hannah's performance. Consequently, an objective standard of satisfaction would be applicable. In this case, Hannah's work met the criteria because everyone who saw the paintings said that they were an exact match to the postcards. Even Heidi did not say that the paintings were not like the postcards but that she wanted something more exciting with buffalo. However, she did not ask for buffalo but only to have the postcards copied on her restaurant's walls. This is exactly the performance she received. Hannah should be paid the $2000 she is owed because her performance satisfied the contract condition.

POINTS TO REMEMBER

- It is often difficult to distinguish between promises and conditions. The key is to use the principles involved in contract interpretation—examine the intent of the parties as expressed in the language of the contract, the surrounding circumstances, and the parties' reasonable expectations.

- Where there is a question as to whether the term is a condition or a promise, an interpretation is preferred that finds a promise.

- A party "breaches" a promise. A party cannot "breach" a condition—a condition is either satisfied or it is not. If the condition fails, then the promisor is discharged from the contract without any obligation to compensate the promisee. This can result in a complete forfeiture for the promisee while the promisor might not have been prejudiced at all by the failure of the condition.

- Parties use conditions to structure and allocate the risk of their performances.

- Conditions can be classified by the manner in which they arise—express, implied, or constructive—or according to the timing of their performance—precedent, subsequent, or concurrent.

- An express condition requires strict compliance whereas a constructive condition can be satisfied by substantial performance. An express condition must be performed before the other party's duty to perform will arise.

- Many promissory conditions are conditions precedent as well. For example, suppose a contract for the sale of a horse provides that the seller promises to deliver the horse to the buyer on Monday and the buyer promises to pay the agreed price of the horse the following Friday. The contract may go on to state that the buyer's obligation to pay on Friday is conditional on the seller's delivery of the horse on Monday. In this case, the delivery of the horse is not only a promise, but it has also expressly been made a condition precedent to the buyer's performance of payment.

- The effect of excusing a condition is the same as full performance—the other party's duty to perform will arise despite the non-occurrence of the condition.

CHAPTER 8

Warranties

> UCC 2-312, 2-313, 2-314,
> 2-315, 2-317

Warranties often provide a definition for the quality and character of the parties' performance obligations.[1] Where the parties' agreement is silent, the UCC provides several default warranties. UCC 2–312, 2–314, and 2–315[2] identify certain minimum warranties that a seller makes regarding title to the goods and their quality. The two implied warranties relating to the quality of the goods are the implied warranty of merchantability and the implied warranty of fitness for a particular purpose. After a review of the warranty of title, we will examine the implied warranties of merchantability and fitness and then consider how the parties may contract around them, first by creating their own express warranty or by expressly disclaiming the implied warranties.

It is important to note at the onset that warranties are cumulative: it is often possible on one set of facts for a buyer to claim that the goods failed to meet the requirements for more than one type of warranty.

---

1. *See* U.C.C. § 2–313 cmt. 4 (2004) ("the whole purpose of the law of warranty is to determine what it is that the seller has in essence agreed to sell[.]").

2. U.C.C. §§ 2–312, 2–314, 2–315 (2004). These sections of the Code are not significantly altered in the 2003 revision of Article 2.

REVIEW OF WARRANTY OF TITLE

In a contract for the sale of goods, the buyer has certain expectations about the goods being purchased. One very basic expectation is that the seller has title to the goods which the buyer will receive upon purchase. The buyer receives this protection under UCC 2–312 where the seller warrants that "the title conveyed shall be good, and its transfer rightful[.]"[3]

Suppose, for example, Georgette has a collection of very valuable crystal vases she keeps in her beach house. One day she discovers her favorite vase missing. It turns out that it was stolen by Sam who works for Georgette to check on her beach house during the winter months. Sam sells the vase to Emma, who has no reason to believe that Sam was not the true owner. Emma's friend Lisa admires the vase, noting that the colors would match her living room decor perfectly. Emma sells the vase to Lisa. It turns out that Georgette and Lisa are friends and on her next visit to Lisa's house, Georgette finds her vase on Lisa's coffee table. Since friendships are more valuable than vases, Lisa gives back the vase. Of course Georgette could get it back anyway—from anyone who had it. Since Sam stole the vase, he never had title to it and therefore had no title to convey to anyone. And so on down the line to Emma and Lisa.

But Lisa is not without recourse when she gives the vase back: she can sue Emma for breach of warranty. When Emma sold the vase to Lisa, she warranted good title. It does not matter whether Emma knew she could not give title. Warranty is sort of like strict liability—she did not give what she contracted to give. And Emma can bring a breach of warranty claim against Sam.

REVIEW OF IMPLIED WARRANTIES

Under the Code, there are two implied warranties of quality: the implied warranty of merchantability, which arises when a merchant sells goods to a buyer and the implied warranty of fitness for a particular purposes, which arises after a buyer tells the seller

---

3. U.C.C. § 2–312(1)(a).

of his or her particular needs for the goods and relies on the seller's skill and judgment to supply them.

Warranty of Merchantability

For the implied warranty of merchantability under UCC 2–314 to attach, there must be a contract for the sale of goods and the seller must be a merchant. A merchant is one "who deals in goods of the kind or otherwise by his occupation holds himself out as having knowledge or skill peculiar to the practices or goods involved in the transaction[.]"[4]

There is no need for the buyer to rely on the representations of the seller for the warranty of merchantability to arise. Absent an effective disclaimer or modification, the warranty attaches to the goods at the time of sale that they are "merchantable" and "fit for the ordinary purposes for which such goods are used[.]"[5]

In bringing a breach of warranty claim under this section, the plaintiff must prove that a merchant sold goods which were not merchantable at the time of sale, there was injury and damages to plaintiff or its property which was caused proximately and in fact by the defective nature of the goods.

Warranty of Fitness for a Particular Purpose

This warranty is narrower in scope and more specific than the warranty of merchantability. The following conditions must be present if a plaintiff is to recover under UCC 2–315 for a breach of the implied warranty of fitness for a particular purpose: first, the seller must have reason to know of the buyer's particular purpose for the goods; second, the seller must have reason to know that the buyer is relying on the seller's skill or judgment to furnish appropriate goods; and third, the buyer must, in fact, rely on the seller's skill or judgment in purchasing the goods.

As you can see from the requirements of UCC 2–315, goods may be merchantable and still not meet the implied warranty of

---

4. U.C.C. § 2–104(1) (2004).   **5.** U.C.C. § 2–314(2)(c).

fitness for a particular purpose. The implied warranty of merchant-ability concerns fitness for the *ordinary purpose* for which the goods are sold as opposed to the warranty of fitness for a *buyer's particular purpose* of which the seller has reason to know and upon whose expertise the buyer relied in selecting the goods.

REVIEW OF EXPRESS WARRANTIES

Often in the course of a sale, the seller will make an explicit oral or written representation to the buyer regarding the nature of the goods. Since the Code does not require the seller to use such language as "warrant" or "guarantee" to create an express warranty or even have the specific intent to do so,[6] it is critical to know if and when a seller has assumed this liability.

Under UCC 2–313,[7] an express warranty relating to the goods is created by a seller when the seller makes an "affirmation of fact or promise" which relates to the goods and becomes part of the "basis of the bargain." A warranty may also be formed on the basis of a sample, model, specifications, or blueprints. Express warranty cases raise distinct questions: one is whether the seller's statement was an "affirmation of fact or promise" or only the seller's opinion or "puffery"; another is whether the seller's promise or affirmation became part of the "basis of the bargain."

---

6. *See* U.C.C. § 2–313(2) ("It is not necessary to the creation of an express warranty that the seller use formal words such as 'warrant' or 'guarantee' or that he have a specific intention to make a warranty[.]").

7. The 2003 revision to U.C.C. § 2–313 expands its scope to include "remedial promises," which is defined as a "promise by the seller to repair or replace goods or to refund all or part of the price upon the happening of a specified event." U.C.C. § 2–103(1)(n) (Proposed Revision 2003). The proposed revision of U.C.C. § 2–313(4) provides "[a]ny remedial promise made by the seller to the immediate buyer creates an obligation that the promise will be performed upon the happening of the specified event." U.C.C. § 2–313(4) (Proposed Revision 2003).

The 2003 revision adds two new sections on express warranties, U.C.C. §§ 2–313A and U.C.C. 2–313B (Proposed Revision 2003). These sections make clear that where a manufacturer makes an express warranty to the public, either in a document passed through a dealer to a buyer or directly to potential buyers through advertisements, it may be liable in damages to the remote purchaser if the goods do not conform to the express warranty.

REVIEW OF EXCLUSION OF WARRANTIES

UCC 2-316, 2-719

As we've seen, the Code's warranties are only default rules. Warranty obligations are subject to the same negotiation by the parties as are the other terms in their agreement. Hence, buyers and sellers are free to contract around them. However, if they choose to disclaim or limit the remedies available to them, they must be careful to conform to the statutory limitations on exactly how, when, and in what manner they do so.

Sellers may disclaim warranties with some qualifications. To determine whether a seller can disclaim or modify a particular warranty, it is first necessary to know whether it is an express or implied warranty. And if it is an implied warranty, you must know whether it is an implied warranty of merchantability or an implied warranty of fitness for a particular purpose. It makes a difference.

Disclaimers of Express Warranties

If the seller has made an express warranty, UCC 2–316(1) makes it almost impossible to disclaim it. This makes sense: if a seller makes an express representation about the goods that become part of the basis of the bargain, how can she turn around and disclaim that representation in the very same agreement? Consequently, if it is found that a seller's statement constitutes a warranty, then language purportedly disclaiming it will be "inoperative" for such disclaiming language is inherently inconsistent.

To a limited extent, the seller is protected "against false allegations of oral warranties" because UCC 2–316(1) makes clear that it is subject to "the provisions of this Article on parol or extrinsic evidence[.]"[8] Here, the rules under UCC 2–202 on parol evidence apply.

---

8. U.C.C. § 2–316(1) (2004).

Disclaimers of Implied Warranties

Typically, sellers' disclaimers attempt to negate the implied warranties of merchantability and fitness for a particular purpose.[9] UCC 2–316(2) sets out specific requirements for modifying or excluding implied warranties. They are as follows:

- Any written disclaimer must be conspicuous.

- An exclusion or modification of the warranty of fitness for a particular purpose must be in writing and be conspicuous.

- Any exclusion or modification of the implied warranty of merchantability, whether written or oral, must specifically mention the word "merchantability."

- Notwithstanding the requirement of UCC 2–316(2) that the disclaimer mention "merchantability," under UCC 2–316(3)(a), implied warranties may be disclaimed or excluded by expressions like "as is" or "with all faults" or "other language which in common understanding calls the buyer's attention to the exclusion of warranties and makes plain there is no implied warranty[.]"[10]

- The implied warranty of fitness for a particular purpose may be excluded by "general language," but it must be in writing and conspicuous. Language is sufficient to exclude this implied warranty if it states that "[t]here are no warranties which extend beyond the description on the face hereof."[11]

- Disclaimers of implied warranties must be conspicuous. Language is conspicuous "when it is so written that a reasonable person against whom it is to operate ought to have noticed it."[12]

---

9. The 2003 revision of Article 2 adds language to U.C.C. § 2–316 that must be included in a disclaimer of either merchantability or fitness for a particular purpose in a consumer contract. A consumer contract is defined in the revised U.C.C. § 2–103(d) to be a contract between a merchant seller and a consumer. A consumer is defined in revised U.C.C. § 2–103(c) to mean an individual who buys goods primarily for personal, family, or household purposes. *See* U.C.C. § 2–103 (Proposed Revision 2003).

10. U.C.C. § 2–316(3)(a).

11. *Id.* § 2–316(2). *See also* § 2–316 cmt. 4.

12. U.C.C. § 1–201(10) (2004). U.C.C. § 1–201(10) is not renumbered in revised Article 1 but includes subsections (A) and (B)

For example, language in a form would be conspicuous if it is in a larger or contrasting font or color from the surrounding text.

Modification or Limitation of Remedies

In addition to a seller's attempt to disclaim or modify warranties, a seller may also try to limit the buyer's remedies in the event of a breach. UCC 2–719(1)(a) permits parties to provide for remedies "in addition to or in substitution for"[13] those normally available. However, this section is typically used to limit the buyer's remedies to "return of the goods and repayment of the price or to repair and replacement[.]"[14]

Even if a contract contains a clause which states the buyer's exclusive or limited remedy, the buyer can still resort to UCC 2–719(2) to avoid its effect. If the buyer can establish that the exclusive remedy provided in the contract "[f]ails of its essential purpose,"[15] the limitation is disregarded and ordinary Code remedies are available. An exclusive remedy fails of its essential purpose when it "operates to deprive either party of the substantial value of the bargain[.]"[16] However, before the buyer can invoke this provision, it must usually allow the seller a reasonable opportunity to carry out the exclusive or limited remedy before claiming there has been a failure of its essential purpose.[17]

Exclusive remedy clauses limiting the buyer's damages to repair or replacement or refund of the purchase price also tend to include clauses denying liability for consequential damages. In seeking to recover consequential damages, buyers rely on UCC 2–719(2) and Comment 1 to argue that failure of the essential purpose of the original remedy also cancels the restriction on

---

wherein the characteristics for what constitutes "conspicuous terms" with respect to font size, color, and type with respect to surrounding text are described.

13. U.C.C. § 2–719(1)(a) (2004). This section is not changed in the 2003 revision to Article 2.

14. *Id.*

15. *Id.* § 2–719(2).

16. *Id.* § 2–719 cmt. 1.

17. James J. White & Robert S. Summers, *Uniform Commercial Code*, § 12–6 (5th ed. 2000).

recovery of consequential damages. Finally, UCC 2–719(3) provides that a court may strike a clause limiting or modifying consequential damages if the "limitation or exclusion is unconscionable."[18] Here, the court may exercise its powers under UCC 2–302 to police against any clause it finds to be unconscionable by refusing to enforce it or by limiting its application.

 ## WARRANTIES CHECKLIST

With that review in mind, here is the checklist for analyzing problems presenting questions in the warranty area:

A. **Warranty of Title**—has the seller attempted to exclude or modify the implied warranty that its title is "good, and its transfer rightful" and that the goods shall be delivered free from any security interest . . . or encumbrance of which the buyer at the time of contracting has no knowledge?" UCC 2–312(1)(a) and (b).

   1. **Yes.** If so, the seller must use "specific language or by circumstances which give the buyer reason to know that the person selling does not claim title in himself or that he is purporting to sell only such right or title as he or a third party may have." UCC 2–312(2).

   2. **No.** If not, proceed to the next question.

B. **Warranties of Quality**—has the seller made a representation of quality to which the goods must conform at the time of delivery?

   1. **Express Warranty**—did the seller's statements or acts create an express warranty? Did it arise in one of the following ways?

      a. **"Affirmation of Fact or Promise"**—did the seller make some statement of fact about the goods which became part of the basis of the bargain?

         i.   **Yes.** If so, an express warranty has been created.

---

18. U.C.C. § 2–219(3).

ii. **No.** If the seller's words lack specificity or are equivocal, then an express warranty has not been created. Such words may be only an expression of the seller's opinion about the goods.

  b. **"Description of the Goods"**—did the seller provide a description of the goods which became part of the basis of the bargain?

   i. **Yes.** If so, an express warranty has been created

   ii. **No.** If not, the seller's words may be mere puffery and do not create an express warranty.

  c. **Sample or Model**—did the seller make reference to a sample or model of the goods which became part of the basis of the bargain such that the whole of the goods shall conform to the sample or model?

   i. **Yes.** If so, an express warranty has been created.

   ii. **No.** If not, then an express warranty has not been created.

  d. **Post–Sale Statements**—did the seller use post-sale language that could be considered to become part of the basis for the bargain?

   i. **Yes.** If so, such language could be a modification of the original sales agreement and become part of the basis of the bargain. An express warranty may have been created.

   ii. **No.** If not, then it was simply a sales promotion for the product and an express warranty was not created.

  Because warranties are cumulative, whether or not you find that an express warranty was created, proceed to the next question on implied warranties.

2. **Implied Warranty**—did one of the implied warranties of quality arise?

  a. **Warranty of Merchantability**—did the warranty arise that the goods would be fit for their ordinary purpose? This depends on whether a merchant sold the described goods to the buyer. Under UCC 2–104, a merchant is one "who deals in goods of the kind or otherwise by his occupation holds himself out as having knowledge or skill peculiar . . . to the goods." Ask: did a merchant sell the goods?

    i.   **No**. If the goods were not sold by a merchant, then the implied warranty of merchantability did not arise.

    ii.   **Yes**. If the seller is a merchant, then the implied warranty of merchantability arose. Proceed to the next question.

    b.   **Warranty of Fitness for a Particular Purpose**—did the warranty arise that the goods would be fit for a particular purpose? The answer to all of the following questions must be *"yes"* for the implied warranty of fitness for a particular purpose to arise:

        i.   Did the seller have reason to know of the buyer's particular purpose?

        ii.   Did the seller know or have reason to know that the buyer is relying on the seller's skill to furnish appropriate goods?

        iii.   Did the buyer rely on the seller's skill or judgment to select the goods?

C. **Exclusion or Modification of Warranty**—was there a disclaimer of an express or implied warranty?

    1.   **Express Warranty**—has the seller attempted to disclaim an express warranty?

        a.   **Yes**. If so, then this would be inherently inconsistent and is ruled out by UCC 2–316(1) where words or conduct creating an express warranty and words or conduct negating or limiting warranty are construed wherever reasonable as consistent with each other. If the seller did not want to create an express warranty, then she had only to be very careful to avoid doing so. However, where the words creating the warranty and those limiting or excluding it cannot be reconciled, the parol evidence rule may come into play.

        b.   **No**. If not, proceed to the next question.

2. **Implied Warranties**—has the seller disclaimed one of the implied warranties? Unlike the case with express warranties, UCC 2–316 neither prohibits nor limits the seller's ability to disclaim implied warranties. It just has to be done in conformity with UCC 2–316(2) and (3). Ask: is the disclaimer of warranty valid?

   a. **Warranty of Merchantability**—has the seller excluded or modified the implied warranty of merchantability by using language which mentions the word "merchantability" and, if the disclaimer is in writing, is it conspicuous?

      i. **Yes**. If so, then the disclaimer is valid. If the warranty is disclaimed orally, then it must mention the word "merchantability" to be valid.

      ii. **No**. If the word "merchantability" is not used in the disclaimer, then it is not valid.

   b. **Warranty of Fitness for a Particular Purpose**—has the seller excluded or modified the implied warranty of fitness for a particular purpose by doing so in a writing which is conspicuous?

      i. **Yes**. If it is in writing, no specific language is required. It is sufficient if it states that "There are no warranties which extend beyond the description on the face hereof." UCC 2–316(2).

      ii. **No**. If it is not in writing and conspicuous, then it is not a valid disclaimer of the implied warranty of fitness.

   c. **Common Situations**—are the circumstances surrounding the transaction sufficient to alert the buyer's attention to the fact that no implied warranties are made or that one is being excluded?

      i. **Language**—has the seller used such language as "with all faults" or "as is"? If so, then all implied warranties are excluded.

      ii. **Examination of the Goods**—has the buyer had an opportunity to examine the goods (sample or model) fully or has refused to do so? If so, then there is no implied warranty with respect to defects which an examination would have revealed.

   iii. **Course of Dealing, Course of Performance, Usage of Trade**—can an implied warranty be excluded or modified by the parties' course of dealing, course of performance, or a usage of trade?

C. Modification or Limitation of Remedy—is there a clause in the parties' agreement limiting the buyer's available remedies upon breach? Limited remedies raise several questions:

  1. Exclusive Remedy—was the limited remedy "expressly agreed to be exclusive?" UCC 2–719(1)(b).

    a. **Yes**. If so, it is "the sole remedy" unless it fails of its essential purpose. Proceed to the next question.

    b. **No**. If not, then resort to it by the buyer is optional.

  2. Essential Purpose—did the "circumstances cause an exclusive or limited remedy to fail of its essential purpose?" UCC 2–719(2). To determine whether an exclusive or limited remedy fails of its essential purpose, ask whether the seller is unwilling or unable to repair the defective goods within a reasonable time or the seller is willing and able to repair but repairs cannot be done, perhaps because the goods have been destroyed.

    a. **No**. If not, it is enforceable.

    b. **Yes**. If so, the buyer can turn to the remedies available under the Act.

  3. Consequential Damages—did the seller exclude consequential damages? If the failure of the exclusive remedy allows the buyer to pursue normal remedies for direct damages under UCC 2–714, what happens when there is a clause excluding consequential damages? Ask the following:

    a. Is the limitation of consequential damages for personal injury in the case of consumer goods? If so, it is *prima facie* unconscionable.

    b. Is the limitation or exclusion of consequential damages unconscionable?

i. **Yes.** If so, the court may refuse to enforce the provision.

ii. **No.** If not, then the provision is enforceable.

ILLUSTRATIVE PROBLEM

Here is a problem that will let us see how the checklist can be used to resolve warranty questions.

■ PROBLEM 8.1 ■

George went to a golf shop to buy golf clubs. George explained to Sam, the salesman, that he had never played golf before and knew nothing about the game but wanted to learn. Sam told him that he knew just the type of golf clubs he needed. He measured George's height and arm span. Sam selected the clubs and irons for George. As Sam wrote up the sales ticket, which George signed, Sam advised George, "I promise that you will love these clubs."

George picked up the golf bag. There was a warranty disclaimer on a tag hanging from the golf bag which stated in bold print:

"THERE ARE NO WARRANTIES WHICH EXTEND BEYOND THE DESCRIPTION ON THE FACE HEREOF. THERE ARE ABSOLUTELY NO REFUNDS OR REPLACEMENTS; REPAIRS ONLY."

The following week, George went on a golf outing with his law school study partners. He was very proud as he lifted his new golf clubs into the cart. George decided to watch the other golfers and do exactly what they did. When it was his turn, he picked out the same number iron. But when he picked up the club, he could see that it was way too long—it came up to his armpit. He went back to his golf bag and checked all the clubs. They were all very long and seemed to be made for a giant. Still, George had to play so he found the shortest one he could and proceeded to swing at the ball. As soon as he hit the ball, the club came apart and the handle went flying out of George's hands and hit the side of a golf cart, causing extensive damage.

The next day, George went back to the pro shop and demanded a full refund. He screamed at Sam, "Not only did you sell me clubs meant for the Jolly Green Giant, but the club fell apart when I hit the ball!" Sam replied, "you must not have known what you were doing. These clubs require someone who knows what he is doing." George was getting angrier by the minute, "You knew I was a beginner when you sold them to me. The clubs are of no use to me and you are going to replace them or give back my money." Sam refused to do either. Instead, he agreed to repair the one broken club but George insisted on a whole new set of clubs that would be right for him. Once again, Sam refused. George has contacted you for advice.

In advising George, consider only the warranty issues; do not discuss any possible parol evidence issues.

Analysis

The question is whether George can return the golf clubs when there was a disclaimer of warranty, and if so, what might he be entitled to recover. It should be noted that Article 2 of the Uniform Commercial Code applies to this problem because it concerns a transaction involving the sale of golf clubs which are goods (all things movable at the time of identification to the contract.) Moreover, Sam is a merchant since he is one who deals in goods of the kind—Sam is a seller of golf equipment in a golf shop.

The first question is whether Sam made an express warranty to George regarding the golf clubs. Under UCC 2–313, the seller creates an express warranty by an affirmation of fact or promise about the goods which becomes part of the basis of the bargain. Mere statements about the value of the goods or an opinion about them does not create an express warranty. Here, Sam's words that "I promise that you will love these clubs" is not a warranty but more likely his opinion or puffery. Even when he said he knew "just what George needed," Sam was just using typical sales talk and did not intend to create an express warranty. However, since Sam specifically selected the golf clubs for George and told him they were exactly the type he needed, it is possible this formed an express warranty that the clubs would be just the ones that George needed.

The next question is whether an implied warranty of fitness for a particular purpose arose when George told Sam he had never golfed and Sam selected the clubs for him. According to UCC 2-315, an implied warranty of fitness for a particular purpose arises when the seller has reason to know of the buyer's particular purpose, the seller knows that the buyer relies on the seller's skill to furnish the appropriate goods, and the buyer in fact relies on the seller's skill or judgment. Here, Sam knew George's purpose in buying the clubs because he told Sam he needed golf clubs to learn to play golf. Sam knew that George was relying on Sam's skill to provide the right kind of clubs because George told him that he had never played golf before. George relied on Sam's judgment because Sam told George that he "knew just the type of golf clubs he needed" and George purchased the clubs that Sam picked out for him. As a result, the implied warranty of fitness for a particular purpose arose when George purchased the golf clubs.

It would seem that this warranty was breached because the golf clubs were far too long for George to use them as they were intended to be used. The facts indicate that Sam took George's measurements and George relied on Sam to select the proper golf clubs. Since they were not suitable for a man of George's size, the warranty was breached.

The next question is whether an implied warranty of merchantability arose when Sam sold the golf clubs to George. According to UCC 2-314, a warranty that the goods shall be merchantable, which means fit for the ordinary purpose for which they are sold, is implied if the seller is a merchant with respect to the goods sold. Here, Sam is a merchant with respect to the goods because he sells golf clubs. The golf clubs are impliedly warranted that they could be used as golf clubs are normally used which means that

George could expect to have clubs that do not come apart as soon
as he hit the ball. Golf clubs are intended to hit golf balls and the
handle should not come apart and cause such damage as they did
here to a golf cart.

Whether the length of the clubs falls within the implied
warranty of merchantability is another issue. Size is a relative
matter. However, George could claim that golf clubs are only fit for
their ordinary purpose if they can be used by a person of ordinary
size, not the Jolly Green Giant.

Even if the implied warranties of merchantability and fitness
for a particular purpose are applicable, Sam may have disclaimed
them. According to UCC 2–316, a seller may exclude or modify the
implied warranty of merchantability by using language which
mentions the word "merchantability" and, if the disclaimer is in
writing, it is conspicuous. Here, there was a tag hanging from the
golf bag which seems to be a disclaimer of warranty. It was written
in bold print and was conspicuous since it was hanging in plain
view on the outside of the golf bag. But since it did not use the word
"merchantability," it is not a valid disclaimer for the implied
warranty of merchantability.

However, it appears to validly disclaim the warranty of fitness
for a particular purpose because it states the precise statutory
language of exclusion:"there are no warranties which extend
beyond the description on the face thereof." It also limits George's
remedy to repairs only with no option for a refund or replacement.
In this case, George would be entitled only to repair of the broken
golf club and not a whole new set of clubs.

The question is whether this limited remedy "fails of its
essential purpose" for George. When the exclusive remedy fails of
its essential purpose, the limitation is disregarded and ordinary
Code remedies are available. The exclusive remedy fails when the
cumulative effect of all the non-conformities substantially impairs
the value of the goods to the buyer.

Here, the exclusive remedy of "repairs only" means that
George can have the one broken club repaired. This remedy fails of

its essential purpose because George has a set of golf clubs he cannot use. Unless repair is interpreted to mean fixing all the clubs so that they fit him, then the clubs are of no use to him. Moreover, the only club he used fell apart and the handle went flying. Fixing the one broken club will not get him what he bargained for when he purchased a set of clubs to play golf. In this case, all the remedies under the Code are available to him which would include a new set of clubs or his money back.

Further, George may claim that the express warranty was not negated because it was inconsistent with the disclaimer. Warranties are construed as consistent; if they conflict, the intent of the parties determines which warranty controls. Here, the parties intended the sale and purchase of golf clubs to be used for golfing.

POINTS TO REMEMBER

- There are two kinds of warranties, express and implied.
- Warranties can overlap and the same set of facts can give rise to more than one warranty or warranties of more than one type.
- The warranty of merchantability is implied if the seller is a merchant.
- An exclusion or modification of the warranty of fitness for a particular purpose must be in writing and conspicuous.
- Any exclusion or modification of the implied warranty of merchantability, whether written or oral, must specifically mention the word "merchantability."
- Any written disclaimer of warranty must be conspicuous.

CHAPTER 9

Impracticability and Frustration of Purpose

C ontract liability is strict liability. This means that the duties imposed by contracts are absolute and one is liable in damages for breach even if she is without fault and even if circumstances have changed to make the contract more burdensome or less desirable than expected. The maxim, *pacta sunt servanda* ("agreements are to be observed"), is often used to express this concept.

Nonetheless, there are exceptions to this strict view and an obligor's performance may be discharged where some drastically changed circumstance has made the obligor's performance impracticable or where the purpose in performing the contract has been frustrated. In these cases, the court may decide justice requires a departure from the general rule and may either discharge the duty or adjust the required performances.

REVIEW OF IMPRACTICABILITY

> R2d § 261-264, 266-268, 270
> UCC 2-615

Many of you will read the famous English case on this topic, *Taylor v. Caldwell*.[1] In this case, plaintiff rented a music hall from defendant for four separate days during the summer months at a rental of £100 a day. Before the music hall could be used for the planned events, it burned down. Neither party was at fault for the fire. The court held that it was an implied term of the contract that the hall would still be in existence at the time performance was due. The court excused the owner's duty since his performance was made impossible by the fire and defeated a basic assumption on which the agreement was made—that the thing needed for performance, the music hall, would continue to be in existence.

Over the years, the doctrine has expanded considerably. Courts no longer require that performance be objectively impossible for it to be discharged—impracticability of performance based on a drastic change in circumstances may be sufficient. Still, for a court to grant relief requires a showing of extreme and unreasonable expense, difficulty, or loss. The party seeking discharge must show that actual performance of the contract would be so significantly different from what was originally expected as to defeat the party's legitimate expectations in entering the agreement.

Restatement Second § 261 sets forth the common law doctrine of impracticability while UCC 2-615[2] provides the equivalent rule for the sale of goods. Although there are some minor differences in language between the two provisions, they are essentially identical. This chapter focuses on general principles applicable to both.

In determining whether a contract has become impracticable, the critical issues are materiality and risk allocation. While neither

---

1. 122 Eng. Rep. 309 (1863).

2. U.C.C. § 2-615 (2004). The 2003 revi-

sion of Article 2 makes no significant changes to this section.

term is stated explicitly in the Restatement or the UCC, courts consider both in assessing the parties' agreement. Relief is granted only if the change in circumstances creates a severe and unexpected burden on the party seeking discharge and that party has neither assumed the risk nor is it appropriate to allocate the risk of the change on that party.

A party claiming that a supervening event or "contingency" has prevented and thus excused a promised performance must demonstrate the following: first, that an event has made the "performance as agreed" impracticable; second, that the nonoccurrence of the event (UCC refers to it as a "contingency") was a "basic assumption" on which the contract was made; third, that the impracticability resulted without the fault of the party seeking to be excused; and fourth, that the party has not assumed a greater obligation than the law imposes. It is important to note that while these elements are analyzed separately, they are in fact very closely related. You will find that they overlap and that the facts relevant to one are often relevant to another.

Sometimes a party may seek to be excused based on existing impracticability. Here the ground for impracticability existed at the time of contract as opposed to an event that occurred subsequent to formation. In order to be excused on the basis of existing impracticability, a party must meet the same four requirements as in the case of supervening impracticability. In addition, the party must show that it neither knew nor had reason to know at the time of contracting of the facts that made performance impracticable.

See Chapter 5 for a comparison of existing impracticability and mutual mistake.

REVIEW OF FRUSTRATION OF PURPOSE

R2d § 265-268

Another famous English case, *Krell v. Henry*,[3] is associated with the doctrine of frustration of purpose. In this case, Henry had arranged to let rooms from Krell to see the coronation procession of King Edward VII. Before this could occur, the King required an operation for appendicitis and the coronation was indefinitely postponed. Henry refused to pay the balance of the money due and Krell sued. The court held for Henry on the ground that his duty to pay had been discharged because "the coronation procession was the foundation of the contract, and . . . the object of the contract was frustrated by the non-happening of the coronation and its procession on the days proclaimed."[4]

The cancellation of the coronation did not make performance of the contract impracticable by either party: Krell could let Henry use his rooms and Henry could pay the money owed. Rather, the benefit that Henry was to derive from Krell's performance of the agreement—using the rooms to see the coronation—was virtually worthless to Henry once the coronation was canceled.

The doctrine of frustration of purpose is very similar to that of impracticability. The party claiming a supervening event frustrated its purpose must meet four requirements, only the first of which is different from those for impracticability. First, the event must have "substantially frustrated" that party's "principal purpose" in entering the contract. Second, it must have been a "basic assumption on which the contract was made" that the event would not occur. Third, the frustration must not have occurred through the fault of the party seeking to be excused. Fourth, that party must not have assumed a greater obligation than the law imposes.

---

3. 2 K.B. 740 (1903).   **4.** *Id.*, at 751, 754.

IMPRACTICABILITY CHECKLIST

With these principles in mind, here is the impracticability checklist. The party claiming this excuse must satisfy all four requirements:

A. Performance is Impracticable—was there an event that occurred that made "performance as agreed" impracticable?

1. **Existing or Supervening Impracticability**—did the event exist at the time the contract was formed or did it occur subsequently? If the event existed at the time of the agreement, then excuse may be based on **existing impracticability**. If so, a party must meet the same four requirements as in the case of **supervening impracticability** with one additional requirement: did the party know or have reason to know at the time of contracting of the facts making performance impracticable?

    a. **Yes.** If so, then the excuse of existing impracticability is not available.

    b. **No.** If not, then proceed to address the four requirements for supervening impracticability.

2. **Agreed Performance**—since it is the party's agreed performance that has become impracticable, the first step is to determine what is the agreed performance.

    a. **Alternatives**—was there a choice between alternative ways of performing?

        i. **Yes.** If so, then the fact that one alternative becomes impracticable will not excuse the party if another remains available. In this case, the agreed performance has not become impracticable.

        ii. **No.** If not, then there may be a basis for excuse. Proceed to the next question.

    b. **Additional Expense**—has the performance become more expensive because of a change in market conditions? According to Comment 1 to UCC 2–615, "[i]ncreased cost alone does not excuse performance unless the increase is due to some unforeseen contingency which alters the essential nature of the performance." Market fluctuations will not excuse performance since they are the types of risk for which parties make contracts. Additional expense in the cost of performance does not rise to the level of impracticability.

B. Basic Assumption—what was the basic assumption on which the contract was made? The nonoccurrence of the event must have been a basic assumption on which the contract was made. According to the Restatement Second, "determining whether the non-occurrence of a particular event was or was not a basic assumption involves a judgment as to which party assumed the risk of its occurrence."[5] The assumption may be implied but it must be shared by both parties. Courts have excused promisors in the following categories of assumptions:

1. **Government Act**—did the parties assume that the government would not directly intervene and prevent performance?

2. **Necessary Person**—did the parties assume that a person necessary for performance would neither die nor be deprived of capacity before the time of performance?

3. **Necessary Thing**—did the parties assume that a thing necessary for performance would remain in existence and in such condition that performance could occur?

C. Promisor not at Fault—did the impracticability result without the fault of the party seeking to be excused? The party seeking to be excused must not be the source or basis of the impracticability.

D. Greater Obligation not Assumed—has the party assumed a greater obligation than the law imposes? If a party expressly undertakes to perform even though performance becomes impracticable, impracticability will not be an excuse. To determine whether a party assumed the risk of impracticability, ask the following:

1. **Foreseeability**—was the event foreseeable? Foreseeability is a factor in assessing whether the promisor assumed the risk of its occurrence, but it is not determinative. Even if the parties

---

5. Restatement (Second) of Contracts, Chapter 11, Introductory Note (1979).

could have imagined the event occurring, it may not be one that they expected to happen. For example, it is always a possibility that a fire could occur and burn down a theater or concert hall. Still, most parties proceed on the assumption that while a possibility, it is not a probability that a fire will occur. Ask: did the parties consider the event to have a real likelihood of occurring?

2. **Risk Bearer**—was the risk within a party's control? If so, then that party should bear the risk of its occurrence because it could have shifted the risk to a third party by contract (i.e., protecting oneself by getting insurance). For example, if a wholesaler contracts to sell goods that it obtains from a particular supplier, then the wholesaler can contract with the supplier to secure its source of supply.[6]

3. **Risk Allocated**—was there a clause in the contract allocating risk for some events and not others? If a clause excuses a party from specified events, it is possible to imply that the party assumed the risks of other events.

4. **Assumed the Risk**—do the surrounding circumstances justify an inference that the party assumed the risk? An example is where a manufacturer undertakes to produce a product based on a technological breakthrough. The risk of the break-through occurring is on the promisor unless the contract provides otherwise.

5. **Unqualified Promised to Perform**—did the party make an unqualified promise to perform? If so, the party is obligated to perform despite the occurrence of an event making that performance impracticable. For example, were the contract-ing parties sophisticated and capable of negotiating termina-tion provisions?

---

6. U.C.C. § 2–615 cmt. 5 (stating when "a particular source of supply is exclusive . . . and fails through casualty," there is no excuse "unless the seller has employed all due mea-sures to assure himself that his source will not fail.").

FRUSTRATION OF PURPOSE
CHECKLIST

Here is the checklist for analyzing problems presenting the question of frustration of purpose. The party claiming this excuse must satisfy all four requirements:

A. **Supervening Event**—was there a **supervening event** that **substantially frustrated** the party's **principal purpose** in forming the contract? The supervening event must totally or nearly totally destroy the purpose of the contract. In determining whether a party's principal purpose has been substantially frustrated, ask the following questions:

1. **Remaining Benefit**—can the party still benefit from the contract even if the supervening event has prevented the party from benefitting in exactly the same way that was anticipated?

   a. **Yes.** If so, then the party still has a purpose for the contract and excuse is not available.

   b. **No.** If not, then excuse may be available. Proceed to the next question.

2. **Total or Nearly Total Frustration**—is the frustration nearly total? It is not enough that a profitable contract has turned out to be a losing one. One cannot claim frustration of purpose simply because a deal has turned out not to be profitable.

   a. **No.** If not, then excuse is not available.

   b. **Yes.** If so, then excuse may be available if the other criteria are met. Proceed to the next question.

3. **Shared Purpose**—was the purpose or object of the contract known and recognized by both parties at the time of contract? The purpose cannot be a secret purpose, known by only one party.

   a. **No.** If not, then excuse is not available.

   b. **Yes.** If so, then excuse may be available. Proceed to the next question.

B. **Basic Assumption**—was it a basic assumption on which the contract was made that the event would not occur? The nonoccurrence of the event must have been a basic assumption on which the contract was made.

1. **No.** If not, then excuse is not available.

2. **Yes.** If so, then excuse may be available if the other criteria are met. Proceed to the next question.

C. **Fault**—did the frustration result without the fault of the party seeking to be excused?

1. **No.** If not, then excuse is not available.

2. **Yes.** If so, then excuse may be available if the other criteria are met. Proceed to the next question.

D. **Assumed the Risk**—has the party assumed a greater obligation than the law imposes? Even if the contract's principal purpose has been frustrated, a court might not excuse performance if the party assumed the risk of the occurrence of the frustrating event. Consider the following:

1. **Foreseeability**—was the supervening act or event reasonably foreseeable at the time of contract? Did the parties consider the event to have a real likelihood of occurring? Even if the parties could have imagined the event occurring, it may not be one that they expected to happen.

2. **Allocation of Risk**—is it possible to determine how the risk was allocated based on the parties' objective in forming the contract?

3. **Usage of Trade**—is there an applicable usage of trade which allocates risk? If so, then it may be considered in allocating risk.

ILLUSTRATIVE PROBLEMS

Consider the following problems. Here is an opportunity to apply the checklist to resolve questions involving impracticability and frustration of purpose.

■ PROBLEM 9.1 ■

NASA requested bids on a gravity-free scooter, the Moon-walker, capable of navigating the moon's terrain for a trip to the moon scheduled for 2010. It awarded the contract worth $45 million in early 2008 to Vista Vehicles, a high technology company specializing in experimental space vehicles.

There was much celebration in the corporate offices of Vista Vehicle when they won the contract. It was their first contract with NASA. While the contract bid was based on only a prototype, Vista was certain it could produce the final product—if certain technological breakthroughs occurred as planned.

Unfortunately, things got off to a rocky start. Vista had trouble getting the power supply to function at the necessary levels. After much trial and error, it completely redesigned the power source which added enormously to the cost of production since it required a capacitor manufactured by only one company in the whole United States, Excelsior. Vista placed an order with Excelsior but did not enter into a contract to secure this source of supply, even though it knew it would need to order more capacitors to complete production of the Moonwalker. Soon thereafter, when Vista went to place another order, Excelsior said it could not accept the order. Apparently, after meeting its one commitment with Vista, Excelsior agreed to sell all its capacitors to a manufacturer of self-propelled vacuum cleaners.

Then Vista's lead engineer left to pursue a singing career after winning *An American Idol*. Vista was counting on her to design the anti-gravity torque to propel the scooter and to redesign the power source to use a different capacitor. Design engineers of her intelligence and creativity are difficult but not impossible to find. However, they don't come cheap and Vista would have to offer at least double her salary of $100,000 to attract qualified applicants away from their current employers.

In March 2009, Vista called NASA to inform it of these difficulties. The project was turning out to be much more difficult and expensive than anticipated. Vista asked NASA to be released from the contract, without damages, claiming it has become impracticable to perform without its engineer and capacitors. Vista would lose an anticipated profit of $5 million dollars on the $45 million project.

Assume you have been hired by NASA. What do you advise?

Analysis

The contract is for the sale of goods because a gravity-free scooter is a good according to Article 2 of the Uniform Commercial Code where goods are "all things moveable at the time of identification to a contract for sale." Therefore, Article 2 of the UCC is applicable. The issue is whether Vista's troubles in producing the final product of the gravity-free scooter constitute an impracticability so as to excuse Vista's performance under the contract.

A party claiming that a supervening event or contingency has prevented and thus excused a promised performance must demonstrate the following: first, that a supervening event made the "performance as agreed" impracticable; second, that the nonoccurrence of the "contingency" was a basic assumption on which the contract was made; third, the impracticability resulted without the fault of the party seeking to be excused; and fourth, that the party seeking excuse has not assumed a greater obligation than the law imposes.

Here, the agreed performance which formed the basis of the contract was Vista's development of the Moonwalker, a space vehicle, for $45 million. Vista is claiming two separate supervening events made its performance impracticable: first, the increased costs of production based on the need for a system redesign due to the loss of its source of supply for capacitors and, second, the loss of its lead engineer. It is necessary to examine each separately.

The next step is determining the "basic assumption" on which the contract was made. Vista would claim that its basic assumption was that production costs would not increase, thus ensuring the contract's profitability. However, this is not a valid assumption: Vista is a high technology company and knows that new designs do not always go as planned. As a manufacturer, it would be the one to know the costs involved in designing experimental craft. Moreover, since it only submitted a prototype for the contract bid, it had to know that there would be design changes in the course of the Moonwalker's development.

Vista also assumed that the personnel necessary to design the vehicle would be available. Ordinarily, if the existence of a particular person is necessary for performing the contract, then her death or incapacity discharges the obligor's duty under the contract. Here, Vista's engineer left to pursue a singing career. While she was the lead design engineer on the project, it would not be impossible to replace her with another engineer. Another engineer could be hired, even though it would be more expensive to do so.

The next question is whether the impracticability resulted without Vista's fault. It cannot be said that either of the above contingencies were Vista's fault. There is no evidence of negligence or misconduct on Vista's part.

Finally, there is the question of whether Vista assumed the risk of these supervening events. Clearly, Vista did not expect to lose its source of capacitors from Excelsior to a manufacturer of self-propelled vacuum cleaners. However, while it was a basic assumption of NASA and Vista that there would be a sufficient supply of capacitors to build the Moonwalker, Vista bears the risk because it was in a better position to ensure against such a loss. Vista knew Excelsior was the "only company in the whole United States" to manufacture this capacitor and yet it took no steps to secure this single source of supply. Vista had a duty to enter into a contract with Excelsior to secure its supply.

Similarly, Vista bore the risk that the contract would turn out to be less profitable than anticipated. Since most commercial contracts are made with the intent to make a profit, Vista's argument to have its performance excused based on a loss in profit would allow any company who fails to realize its expected profit to be released from its contractual obligations. Markets fluctuate and contracts are a means to allocate such risks. Just because Vista may lose an anticipated profit of $5 million on a project valued at $42 million is an insufficient basis for an excuse under impracticability. Further, Vista does not claim a loss on the entire project, just the profit. Failure to realize a profit is not a basis for excuse under impracticability.

Finally, Vista could claim that the loss of its lead engineer to pursue a singing career after winning *An American Idol* was totally unforeseeable. However, personnel changes are frequent in business. If Vista was so dependent on the continued employment of this particular engineer, it could have entered into a contract with her. This would not have prevented her from leaving, but then Vista would have been entitled to contract damages to offset the cost of the new hire. Also, the facts indicate that it is possible to find another engineer, although it will be more costly.

Since Vista has failed to satisfy all the requirements for impracticability, its performance will not be discharged.

■ PROBLEM 9.2 ■

Adam's birthday was January 1. This year he was going to be 25 and wanted to celebrate in a special way. He had passed the bar exam, gotten a job at a good law firm, and couldn't be happier. Then he heard on the radio that his absolute favorite performer, Barry Manilow, was going to be hosting the New Year's Eve Countdown in Times Square. Adam called the Marriott Marquis Hotel on August 15th and made reservations for the night of December 31. Adam asked for a room overlooking Times Square because, as he told the clerk, "it's my 25th birthday and I want to celebrate by watching the ball drop. Also, I can't wait to see Barry Manilow perform." Adam was assured that he would have a direct view of the ball dropping to signal in the new year. Ordinarily, a hotel room at the Marriott Marquis was $500 a night but because it was New Year's Eve, the charge would be $1500. Adam thought it would be worth it to be in New York City to celebrate his 25th birthday and see Barry Manilow perform. He gave the clerk his credit card number to make the required $500 deposit to hold his reservation.

On Christmas Day, Adam heard on the radio that Barry Manilow had been rushed to the hospital to have emergency surgery. Apparently, Mr. Manilow had been practicing his famous Copacabana dance routine on the stage set up in Times Square when he missed a step, fell off the stage, and dislocated his left hip. He would not be well in time for the New Year's Eve show but since "the show must go on," Harry Connick Jr., another well-known entertainer, agreed to fill in and host the festivities.

Adam was sorry for Barry, but sorrier for himself. His celebration was ruined. He called the hotel to cancel his reservation and get his deposit of $500 back. The hotel refused.

Now Adam is trying to decide whether to bring suit. How should he decide?

Analysis

The issue is whether Adam's principal purpose in making hotel reservations was frustrated when he learned that Barry Manilow would not be able to perform. Where the bargained-for performance is still possible, but the purpose of the contract has been totally or nearly totally destroyed by some supervening event, such frustration will excuse the party's duty to perform. The purpose that is frustrated must have been the principal purpose in making the contract. The object must be so completely the basis of the contract that without it, the transaction would make little sense.

The first question is whether there was a supervening act or event. Adam would argue that the injury to Barry Manilow which made it impossible for him to perform was the supervening event. The next question is whether this injury was reasonably foreseeable at the time Adam and the Hotel entered into the contract. It could be argued that the injury was not unforeseeable because injuries during practice sessions are known to happen. On the other hand, it might not be the type of injury one would expect to happen because Barry was an accomplished performer and was practicing an established dance routine. Even if the parties could have imagined such an injury occurring, it may not be one that they expected to happen since it was only one performance for New Year's Eve. It could be reasonably inferred that special precautions would be taken to ensure performance because of the importance of the event. Nonetheless, the Hotel could argue that this performance was similar to a Broadway show, where sometimes an understudy may have to take the place of the star performer because of illness. However, Adam could argue that this is distinguishable from a Broadway show because it is a special event taking place once a year and it would be reasonable to expect to see the star performer whereas a Broadway show may be performed seven nights a week, and it is realistic to assume that at some point the star might not be able to make a performance.

The next question would be whether the purpose of the contract was known by both Adam and the Hotel at the time they entered the contract. Here, the Hotel would argue that when Adam made the room reservation, he asked for a room "overlooking Times Square" and while he mentioned that he wanted to see the ball drop and watch Barry Manilow perform, the Hotel could not have known that he meant to watch these events from his hotel room. A room overlooking Times Square might not necessarily provide a view of the ball dropping. Still, Adam was assured that he would have a direct view of the ball dropping to signal in the new year so it would seem that the Hotel was aware of this purpose for the room. However, Adam would argue that his purpose for reserving the room was also to see Barry Manilow perform. A court would likely find that Adam's statements would not be sufficient to convey to the Hotel that the central purpose of the reservation was to see Barry Manilow himself.

The next question is whether Barry Manilow's failure to perform would totally or nearly totally frustrate the purpose of the contract. Adam would claim that his principal purpose for making the reservation was to see Barry Manilow perform. Adam would argue that Barry Manilow was his "absolute favorite performer" and it was only after hearing that he would be performing on New Year's Eve that Adam called to make the reservation. If Barry were not scheduled to perform, Adam might not have made the reservation. Alternatively, the Hotel would argue that Barry Manilow's performance was not Adam's only purpose in making the contract because when he made the reservation, he mentioned that it was his 25th birthday and he wanted to celebrate by watching the ball drop. The Hotel would argue that while Adam did mention that he could not "wait to see Barry Manilow perform," this was an additional benefit and not the primary purpose for the contract.

A court would likely find that Adam had more than one reason for booking the room. First, Adam wanted to celebrate his birthday by spending it in New York City and watching the New Year's Eve festivities from his hotel room. Second, watching Barry Manilow perform was another reason for Adam to have the room with a view because Adam unequivocally stated that he wished to see Barry Manilow perform. But this was not the sole reason of the contract. In this case, Adam's purpose in making the reservation would not be frustrated so as to allow him to avoid the performance on the contract. He can still use the room to celebrate his 25th birthday, enjoy New Year's Eve in New York City, and see the famous ball drop at midnight.

POINTS TO REMEMBER

- Excuse under the doctrine of impracticability requires the party to meet all four requirements: a supervening event or contingency has made "performance as agreed" impracticable; the nonoccurrence of the event (UCC refers to it as a "contingency") was a "basic assumption" on which the contract was made; the impracticability resulted without the fault of the party seeking to be excused; and the party has not assumed a greater obligation than the law imposes.

- A claim for excuse based on frustration of purpose is very similar to that of impracticability of performance where only the first element out of the four is different: the event must have "substantially frustrated" the party's principal purpose in contracting.

- In determining whether the promised performance has become impracticable, the focus is on the increased burden on the party who is to perform.

- Increased cost alone does not excuse performance "unless the rise in cost is due to some unforeseen contingency which alters the essential nature of the performance. Neither is a rise or a collapse in the market in itself a justification, for that is exactly the type of business risk which business contracts made at fixed prices are intended to cover." UCC 2–615 cmt. 4.

- Foreseeability is a factor to consider in determining the basic assumption(s) on which the contract was made.

CHAPTER 10

Anticipatory Repudiation

> R2d § 250, 251, 253, 256
> UCC 2-609, 2-610, 2-611

An anticipatory repudiation occurs when one party to a contract expresses the intent, either through words or conduct, that a promised performance will not be forthcoming. Since this occurs before the actual time set for performance, it is referred to as an "anticipatory breach" or a "prospective non-performance."

It is well accepted that an anticipatory repudiation allows the injured party to assume that her own obligations under the contract have been discharged. This means that she no longer has to hold herself ready, willing, and able to perform her part of the bargain but is able to make alternate arrangements.

However, not every expression of unwillingness to proceed with a contract amounts to a repudiation. A party must be relatively certain that the other party's performance will not be forthcoming before treating it as a repudiation or *she is the one* in danger of becoming the breaching party by wrongfully suspending her own performance.

REVIEW OF ANTICIPATORY REPUDIATION

The seminal case on this topic is *Hochster v. De La Tour*.[1] In April 1852, Hochster agreed to work for De La Tour by accompanying him on a tour through Europe for three months to begin on June 1, 1852. However, on May 11, 1852, De La Tour wrote to Hochster that he had changed his mind and would not be needing his services. Hochster brought suit for damages on May 22. Between the commencement of the action and June 1, Hochster found other employment on equal terms, but not starting until July 4.

The court's problem was finding a basis for a breach of contract action on May 22 when De La Tour's performance was not due until June 1. Classic contract doctrine allowed for breach only when the time for performance had passed. In addressing the problem, the court identified two issues: first, whether a repudiation gives rise immediately to a claim for total breach; and second, whether a repudiation by one party discharges the non-repudiating party's remaining duties under the contract. The court answered both questions in the affirmative: an anticipatory repudiation of a promise to perform constitutes a total breach and, as a result, the injured party has a claim for damages and may assume that her own obligations under the contract have been discharged.[2]

Modern courts follow the rule from *Hochster* and find that an unequivocal expression of intent not to perform contractual obligations allows the innocent party to proceed with suit without having to wait for the actual breach. However, it is still necessary for there to be a clear indication that the promised performance will not be forthcoming before a party may proceed with legal action.

---

1. 118 Eng. Rep. 922 (1853).

2. This two-part rule is generally followed by the courts and is adopted by the Restatement (Second) of Contracts. *See* Restatement (Second) of Contracts § 253 (1979) ("(1) Where an obligor repudiates a duty before he has committed a breach by non-performance and before he has received all of the agreed exchange for it, his repudiation alone gives rise to a claim for damages for total breach. (2) Where performances are to be exchanged under an exchange of promises, one party's repudiation of a duty to render performance discharges the other party's remaining duties to render performance.").

In *Hochster*, there was no question that there had been a repudiation of the contract because De La Tour wrote to Hochster telling him that his services would not be required. A problem arises, however, when the conduct or language is not quite so clear.

What Constitutes A Repudiation

According to the Restatement Second, a repudiation can be either through words or conduct.[3] Further, it can be either express or implied. Case law has interpreted an express repudiation to be a "clear, positive, unequivocal refusal to perform[.]"[4] This means that the statement must be sufficiently absolute and certain so as to be reasonably understood that a party will not or cannot perform. Mere expressions of doubt as to willingness or ability to perform are insufficient. A statement such as "I doubt I will be able to perform" is not sufficiently definite to be considered a repudiation, although it may give reasonable grounds for insecurity, a matter we will discuss shortly.

A repudiation may also occur through conduct. Here, the party voluntarily does something to put the promised performance out of her power to perform. For example, on September 1, Ben contracts to sell and Seth agrees to buy Ben's house with payment and delivery of the deed to occur on September 30. On September 15, Ben contracts to sell his house to Sam. Ben's making of the contract with Sam is a repudiation through conduct of his contract with Ben.

This scenario assumes a repudiation has occurred. However, since mere doubts or an expression of unwillingness to perform is insufficient to constitute a repudiation, what may a party do if there is uncertainty about the expected performance?

---

3. *See* Restatement (Second) of Contracts § 250 (1979) (stating a repudiation is "(a) a statement by the obligor to the obligee indicating that the obligor will commit a breach that would of itself give the obligee a claim for damages for total breach under § 243, or (b) a voluntary affirmative act which renders the obligor unable or apparently unable to perform without such a breach.").

4. *Taylor v. Johnston*, 539 P.2d 425, 430 (Cal. 1975).

Right to Assurances

The Uniform Commercial Code introduced the concept that where a party has reasonable grounds for insecurity regarding the other party's prospective performance, it may in writing demand "adequate assurance of due performance[.]"[5] When such assurances are not forthcoming, the non-breaching party may treat such a failure as a repudiation of the contract.[6] Although the Code does not define the terms "reasonable" grounds or "adequate" assurances," the Code comments indicate that they should be defined by commercial standards and in accord with commercial practice.[7] What constitutes "reasonable grounds" and "adequate assurances" are therefore questions of fact.

The UCC provisions apply only to contracts for the sales of goods. However, the Restatement Second has adopted a similar rule and applies it to all kinds of contracts. However, it differs from the Code provision in two respects: first, it does not require that the demand for assurances be made in writing; and second, it does not set a 30–day period in which to provide assurances.[8]

Retracting a Repudiation

Both the UCC and the common law provide that a party may retract its repudiation if it does so before the aggrieved party has

---

5. U.C.C. § 2–609(1) (2004) (providing in relevant part: "[w]hen reasonable grounds for insecurity arise with respect to the performance of either party the other may in writing demand adequate assurance of due performance and until he receives such assurance may if commercially reasonable suspend any performance for which he has not already received the agreed return.") The 2003 revision of Article 2 makes no significant changes to this section.

6. *Id.* § 2–609(4) (providing "[a]fter receipt of a justified demand failure to provide within a reasonable time not exceeding thirty days such assurance of due performance as is adequate under the circumstances of the particular case is a repudiation of the contract.").

7. *See id.* § 2–609 cmt. 3, 4.

8. Restatement (Second) of Contracts § 251 (1979) (providing "(1) Where reasonable grounds arise to believe that the obligor will commit a breach by non-performance that would of itself give the obligee a claim for damages for total breach under § 243, the obligee may demand adequate assurance of due performance and may, if reasonable, suspend any performance for which he has not already received the agreed exchange until he receives such assurance. (2) The obligee may treat as a repudiation the obligor's failure to provide within a reasonable time such assurance of due performance as is adequate in the circumstances of the particular case.").

acted in reliance upon the repudiation by materially changing its position.[9] Retraction may be by any means sufficient to provide clear and adequate notice to the innocent party that the repudiating party intends to perform.[10] An effective retraction restores the repudiating party's rights under the contract.[11]

Responding to an Anticipatory Repudiation

Upon repudiation, the aggrieved party has several options. It may either wait a reasonable time for performance or treat the repudiation as a present breach and resort to its remedies, even as it urges the repudiating party to perform. In either case, the aggrieved party may suspend its own performance—whether it chooses to treat the repudiation as a breach or wait a reasonable time before doing so.

When the aggrieved party brings suit, it must show that had there been no repudiation, it would have been ready, willing, and able to perform its end of the bargain. In determining damages, a court will consider any costs saved in not having to perform as well as any damages that could have been avoided by appropriate action.

The aggrieved party is bound by the duty to mitigate damages. However, when it must take such action is not so clear, especially when the aggrieved party has the option to urge the repudiating party to perform and can await performance. Under

---

9. U.C.C. § 2–611(1) (2004) (providing "[u]ntil the repudiating party's next performance is due he can retract the repudiation unless the aggrieved party has since the repudiation cancelled or materially changed his position or otherwise indicated that he considers the repudiation final."). *C.f.* Restatement (Second) of Contracts § 256 (1979) (entitled "Nullification of Repudiation or Basis for Repudiation" and uses the word "nullification" to refer to the repudiating party's act of retraction but the meaning is the same as that of the U.C.C.). The 2003 revision of Article 2 makes no significant changes to U.C.C. § 2–611.

10. U.C.C. § 2–611(2) ("Retraction may be by any method which clearly indicates to the aggrieved party that the repudiating party intends to perform, but must include any assurance justifiably demanded under the provisions of this Article (Section 2–609).").

11. *Id.* § 2–611(3) ("Retraction reinstates the repudiating party's rights under the contract with due excuse and allowance to the aggrieved party for any delay occasioned by the repudiation.").

UCC 2–610(a), the aggrieved party may wait "for a commercially reasonable time[.]"[12] Comment 1 adds a limitation in that "if he awaits performance beyond a commercially reasonable time he cannot recover resulting damages which he should have avoided."[13]

Exception to the Rule

It is a widely excepted limitation to the rule in *Hochster* that the doctrine of anticipatory breach does not apply where there is a repudiation of an executory contract for the payment of money only. In this case, the aggrieved party must await the time for performance to bring suit for damages. In short, the doctrine applies only where there are executory obligations on both sides of the contract: it does not apply if a party repudiates a unilateral promise to pay money in the future or in future installments[14] or there is a bilateral contract where the aggrieved party has fully performed its end of the bargain.

ANTICIPATORY REPUDIATION CHECKLIST

The following checklist will help you determine whether a party has repudiated a prospective performance and assess the options available to the non-repudiating party.

---

12. U.C.C. § 2–610 (2004). Unlike the current version of U.C.C. § 2–610 which does not define what constitutes a repudiation (leaving it to the common law), the 2003 revision to Article 2 adds a new subsection providing guidance on when a party can be treated as having repudiated. *See* U.C.C. § 2–610(2) (Proposed Revision 2003) (stating "[r]epudiation includes language that a reasonable person would interpret to mean that the other party will not or cannot make a performance still due under the contract or voluntary, affirmative conduct that would appear to a reasonable person to make future

performance by the other party impossible.").

13. *Id.* § 2–610 cmt. 1.

14. *See Greguhn v. Mutual of Omaha Ins. Co.,* 461 P.2d 285 (Utah 1969) (stating a party many not sue for an installment until only after that installment has become due—even when the other party has denied any liability to make future payments.). Despite criticism, the rule remains that future installments shall be paid as they fall due and the obligee in such a contract must await a default as to each installment before seeking a claim for damages.

A. Anticipatory Repudiation—has one party expressed an intent not to perform the contract before the time performance is due? If so, then the aggrieved party may treat it as a present breach according to the options outlined in Part D. However, it must first be determined whether there has been a repudiation according to the following analysis:

  1. Express Repudiation? Did the party express a clear, positive, unequivocal refusal to perform?

    a. **Yes**. In order to constitute a repudiation, the party's language must be sufficiently clear and positive to indicate that it cannot or will not render the promised performance. If so, then the other party has several options. Proceed to Part D.

    b. **No**. If the language is equivocal and merely expresses doubt concerning a prospective ability to perform, then it is not enough to constitute a repudiation. However, an ambiguous statement may give the other party reasonable grounds to believe a breach might occur and it has grounds to request assurances of performance. Proceed to Part B.

  2. Implied Repudiation? Has the party voluntarily done something which makes it actually or apparently impossible for her to perform?

    a. **Yes**. If so, then the party has repudiated the contract. Proceed to Part D.

    b. **No**. If the act falls short of these requirements, it may still give reasonable grounds for insecurity and the aggrieved party may seek assurances of performance under Part B.

B. Assurances of Performance—has a party's expectation of receiving due performance under the contract been impaired?[15] Where there is uncertainty, the aggrieved party is advised to seek assurances. A party must be relatively certain that the other party's performance will not be forthcoming before treating it as a

---

15. *See* U.C.C. § 2–609(1) (a contract "imposes an obligation on each party that the other's expectation of receiving due performance will not be impaired.").

repudiation or *she is the one* in danger of becoming the breaching party by wrongfully suspending her own performance.

1. **Expression of Doubt?** Does a party's language or conduct make it uncertain whether it will render the promised performance? If there is a reasonable belief that the promised performance will not be forthcoming, it presents grounds for insecurity and the party in doubt is entitled to seek assurances.

   a. **Sale of Goods?** Is it a contract for the sale of goods? If so, then UCC 2–609 applies. Whether a party has "reasonable grounds for insecurity" is a question of fact but the Code comment indicates that commercial standards of reasonableness are considered.

   b. **Common Law?** Is it an agreement governed by the common law? If so, then R2d § 251 (1) applies a similar, but not identical, rule to the UCC. The aggrieved party must have "reasonable grounds" to believe that the other party will breach.

2. **Demand for Assurances?** Has the aggrieved party demanded assurances?

   a. **Sale of Goods?** Under the UCC, a party may in writing demand adequate assurances of due performance. While awaiting assurances, it may suspend its own performance for which it has not already received the agreed return performance if commercially reasonable.

   b. **Common Law?** Under R2d § 251, the demand for assurances need not be in writing, although it is preferable to an oral one. The party who demands assurances must do so in accordance with the duty of good faith and fair dealing. Comment *d*.

3. **Provided Assurances?** Have adequate assurances been provided?

   a. **Sale of Goods?** Under the UCC, a party has a reasonable time, not exceeding thirty days, in which to provide adequate assurances after receiving a justified demand. Failure to provide such assurances is a repudiation of the contract.

b. **Common Law?** The common law follows the UCC in requiring assurances to be given within a "reasonable time" but it does not impose the thirty day requirement. Failure to provide such assurances allows the aggrieved party to treat it as a repudiation.

C. Retracting a Repudiation—has the repudiating party attempted to retract the repudiation? The retraction may be oral or written but the other party must have knowledge of it to be effective. A valid retraction restores the contract and the non-repudiating party has no damage claims except for any harm incurred by the repudiation. While it is possible to retract a repudiation, there are limits to when a retraction is possible.

    1. Reliance—has the aggrieved party acted upon the repudiation?

        a. **Yes**. If the aggrieved party has acted in reliance on the repudiation by materially changing its position or commencing an action, then it is too late for the repudiating party to retract.

        b. **No**. If the aggrieved party has not changed its position, then the repudiating party can nullify the repudiation by giving notice of retraction.

    2. Communicated—has the aggrieved party communicated to the repudiating party that it considers the repudiation final? If so, the power of retraction has been terminated.

D. Responding to a Repudiation—if a party has repudiated before the time for performance has arrived, what are the non-repudiating party's options?

    1. Treat as Terminated? Can the non-repudiating party treat the contract as terminated and bring an action for damages? R2d § 253(1).

        a. **Yes**. The injured party may treat its remaining duties under the contract as discharged and bring suit immediately for damages for total breach. When bringing suit, the injured party must show that it would have been ready, willing, and able to perform but for the repudiation. R2d § 253(2).

b. **No**, not if the party has repudiated either a unilateral contract or a bilateral contract that has been fully performed by the injured party. The injured party must await the time for performance to sue for damages. This is the exception to the general rule that a party may bring suit immediately for an anticipatory repudiation.

2. **Urge Retraction?** Can the non-repudiating party try to save the deal by insisting that the repudiating party perform and urge it to retract its repudiation? The non-repudiating party can insist on performance and urge retraction. If the repudiating party retracts, the contract remains in force. If the repudiating party fails to retract, the injured party can still treat the repudiation as a breach and seek damages.

3. **Ignore and Await Performance?** Can the non-repudiating party ignore the repudiation and await the time for performance? The non-repudiating party can ignore the repudiation but may run into the problem of failing to mitigate damages. The question is how soon must the non-repudiating act to mitigate damages? Under UCC2–610(a), the aggrieved party may "for a commercially reasonable time await performance[.]" Comment 1 adds: "but if he awaits performance beyond a commercially reasonable time he cannot recover resulting damages which he should have avoided."

ILLUSTRATIVE PROBLEM

Here is a problem that will let us use the checklist to resolve anticipatory repudiation questions:

■ PROBLEM 10.1 ■

Lisa and Lauren own and operate a successful chain of boutiques, L & L, Inc. In January, 2009, they decided to open a store in their home town of East Hampton, New York, located about two hours driving time from New York City. The store's grand opening was planned for 12:00 p.m. on June 1, 2009. Lisa and Lauren anticipated a large crowd and thought it would be a good idea to have food and music to entertain the shoppers.

On March 5, 2009, L & L contracted with Lobster, Inc., a local seafood vendor for delivery of assorted seafood platters on June 1, for a price of $5,000. The next day, Lisa and Lauren went to hear a local jazz group perform. Kool and Company were well-known in the community. Lisa and Lauren contracted with Aiden Kool to provide two solo performances and three hours of background music for $5,000. The contract provided that there would be continuous music from 12:00 p.m. until 3:00 p.m. Aiden would perform at 12:30 and then again at 2:00 and the rest of the time his jazz group would provide background music.

On April 15, Lobster, Inc. called L & L and explained that, due to problems with his lobster traps, he might not be able to fill their order. Apparently, L & L's order was so large that Lobster's traps were inadequate and he was having trouble getting the super large size he needed from the lobster trap manufacturer. He was planning on borrowing some traps from another lobster company and he was hoping that would be sufficient. L & L immediately faxed a letter to Lobster, Inc. asking whether he intended to deliver the seafood platters and urging him to do so.

The next day, Lisa and Lauren were working in the store when their friend, Dave, a reporter for the local newspaper, stopped by. Dave said that the newspaper had just received an announcement for its local community news section that Kool and Company had won an award from the National Endowment for the Humanities. They would be accepting the award and performing at a special evening concert in Washington, D.C. on June 1. Assume that this information is reliable.

Lisa and Lauren could not believe what they heard. They were counting on Aiden Kool to provide the entertainment for their store opening. Lisa and Lauren decided they had to find other entertainment for the grand opening or L & L would be ruined. Luckily, Lauren knew Billy Joel, the singer and pianist, because they had gone to school together. Billy said he'd be delighted to help an old friend. He would even have his own piano delivered to the store.

On May 20, still having heard nothing from Lobster, Inc., Lisa and Lauren decided they could not wait any longer and placed an order with another local fisherman, Shrimpman Inc., to be delivered on June 1. Shrimpman advised L & L that the price was $7,500, which was the current market price.

On May 29, Lobster, Inc. called L & L and told them he would deliver the seafood as promised on June 1. L & L told Lobster, Inc. that since they had not heard from him, they had placed an order with another fish supplier and L & L would not accept delivery from him.

Finally, it was June 1 and opening day. Billy Joel's piano was in the middle of the store. Shrimpman's seafood platters were set up on tables. At 11:00 a.m., as Lisa and Lauren were putting the finishing touches on the display cases, Aiden Kool came through the door with his group and their equipment. "Where do you want us to set up?" he asked.

Lauren said that they had not expected him since they thought he would be in Washington to accept his award. They were happy for him but since they needed entertainment, they had found someone else to perform and would not be needing Kool and Company. Aiden said, "How could you find someone else? I never said I would not be here. I don't have to be in Washington until later this evening. I have plenty of time to get there after I perform here. I fully expect you to pay me the $5000 you owe me!" Aiden left the store.

The store opening was a huge success. Lisa and Lauren had a great day and made lots of sales. However, the following week was not so good: Lobster, Inc. brought an action against L & L for breach of contract and Kool and Company did the same.

Lisa and Lauren have contacted you. They would like to know the likelihood of their success in these two contract actions. What would you advise? Explain fully.

Analysis

Lobster, Inc. v. L & L:

In determining whether L & L is liable to Lobster, Inc. for breach of contract, the first question is whether Lobster's phone call of April 15 to L & L was a repudiation of the contract. An anticipatory repudiation occurs when a party, in advance of the time set for performance, expresses the intent not to perform. An express repudiation requires a clear, positive, and unequivocal refusal to perform. The statement must be sufficiently absolute and certain so as to be reasonably understood that the party will not or cannot perform. Mere expressions of doubt as to willingness or ability to perform are insufficient.

Here, Lobster did not use clear and unequivocal language that he would not perform. Instead, he said that, "due to problems with his lobster traps, he might not be able to fill their order." This is an expression of doubt. While he said he was having trouble getting the traps he needed, he also said he was planning to borrow some from another lobster company and was hoping to perform. This would be sufficient to raise reasonable doubts about his prospective performance entitling Lisa and Lauren to seek assurances—which they promptly did by sending a fax asking whether he intended to deliver the seafood platters.

The next question is whether L & L was justified in considering Lobster's failure to respond to their fax as a breach of contract, allowing it to cover with another supplier. Article 2 of the Uniform Commercial Code applies in this case since the transaction involves seafood which is a "good" (items which are moveable at the time of identification to the contract). Under the Code, a party may seek adequate assurances of performance when reasonable grounds for insecurity arise. Failure to provide such assurances within a reasonable time not exceeding thirty days constitutes a repudiation of the contract.

Here, L & L would argue that Lobster's phone call of April 15 gave them reason to doubt that he would deliver the seafood. When Lobster failed to respond to their request for assurances by

May 20, which was over 30 days from when they faxed him, they could rightly treat it as a present breach and cover with a substitute purchase. L & L waited a commercially reasonable time—from April 15 until May 20—to place the order with Shrimpman because it was over 30 days and the store opening was less than two weeks away on June 1.

Still, it is possible for a party to retract its repudiation and this is what Lobster attempted to do by calling on May 29 and saying he would deliver the seafood. However, it was too late. A repudiating party may retract its repudiation at any time before the party's performance is due unless the aggrieved party has materially changed her position or otherwise indicated that she considers the repudiation final. Here, L & L placed an identical seafood order with Shrimpman, thus changing its position in reliance on Lobster's repudiation. Consequently, Lobster's attempt to retract its repudiation was too late to be effective.

> [The following analysis would be the appropriate next step but it requires knowledge of remedies, a topic we will not cover until Chapter 12. It is included here because it follows from the facts of the problem and it is typical of what you would be expected to discuss on an exam. You might want to come back to this question after you complete Chapter 12.]

L & L may recover $2,500—the difference between the contract price it had with Lobster for $5,000 for seafood platters and the $7,500 for the cost of cover it had to pay Shrimpman. After a breach, the buyer may cover by making a reasonable purchase in good faith of substitute goods and recover from the seller the difference between the cost of cover and the contract price.

Aiden Kool v. L & L

Unfortunately, L & L will not be successful in this suit. The issue is whether Aiden repudiated the contract when he was to be in Washington on the same day he promised to perform for L & L. If either party to a contract, in advance of the time set for performance manifests an intent not to render the promised performance, the other party may treat it as a present breach. Here, Aiden did not expressly repudiate the contract because he did not say anything to L & L about not being able to perform at the grand opening. However, if by his conduct, he puts performance out of his control, he might have impliedly repudiated. The question is whether Aiden's accepting the award in Washington D.C. on June 1 is an implied repudiation.

From the news L & L received, it seemed that Aiden might not be able to perform for them if he were in Washington on the very same day as their grand opening in New York. However, Washington D.C. is not that far from East Hampton—accessible by car or a very short plane ride. The contract with L & L only required him to perform until three p.m.; the fact that he was accepting an award in Washington on the same day would not make it impossible for him to do both.

L & L should have sought assurances from Aiden when they learned about the award ceremony. Since he cannot be in two places at once, it would be reasonable for L & L to doubt whether he would perform their contract and therefore they would be justified in seeking assurances. Although the information came from a reporter and a reporter might be considered a reliable source of information, L & L had a duty to check with Aiden before taking any action. If after being asked whether he would perform, Aiden failed to provide such assurances within a reasonable time, then L & L would have been within their rights to treat it as a present breach and seek another performer in his place.

Unfortunately, L & L failed to seek such assurances and are therefore themselves in breach for asking Billy Joel to perform. Aiden is entitled to payment under the contract since he arrived ready, willing, and able to perform.

POINTS TO REMEMBER

- An anticipatory repudiation is a prospective breach that occurs before the date due for the contract's performance.

- A repudiation must be a clear, unequivocal refusal to perform. Expressions of doubt are insufficient.

- Where a party has reasonable grounds for insecurity regarding the other party's prospective performance, it may demand assurances of performance.

- The repudiating party may retract its repudiation by giving notice of retraction if the aggrieved party has not acted in reliance on the repudiation by materially changing its position or commencing an action for breach.

CHAPTER 11

Material Breach and Substantial Performance

R2d § 235, 237, 238, 239, 240,
241, 242, 243

As we discussed in a previous chapter, if a condition does not occur (and is not excused), then the party whose performance due under the contract is contingent on the condition need not perform. In this case, the duty to perform has been discharged by the non-occurrence of the condition. We have also seen that if a promise is not performed, then the promisee has a claim for breach. Further, if a term is both a promise and a condition, then the non-occurrence of the condition both entitles the injured party to withhold its own performance and sue for breach. This is the usual result because most promises are found to be "dependent" where each party's performance is a condition of the other's and must be performed at the same time. In this case, the breach by one party of its promise to perform will be not only a breach of promise, but also the failure of a condition. A claim of breach raises critical questions:

How do courts determine whether there has been a breach?

Assuming there has been a breach, is it a material breach?

If there has been a material breach, what is the effect on the parties' remaining duties under the contract?

REVIEW OF BREACH

A promisor commits a breach when, without justification or excuse, she fails to tender a promised performance when performance is due or tenders a defective performance. However, not all breaches are "equal"—some are trivial and others are serious. This difference is important because it affects the promisee's duties and rights under the contract. Before we discuss the subject in detail, consider the following summary:

- If a promisor commits a **material** and **total** breach, then the promisee may withhold her own performance, terminate the contract, and bring a claim of damages for breach.

- If a promisor commits a **material** but **not total breach**, then the promisee may suspend her own performance, await the promisor's cure of the defect in performance, and seek damages for any loss suffered as a result.

- If a promisor commits a **non-material breach** (**substantially performs**), then the promisee must tender her own performance but can seek damages for any loss suffered as a consequence of the promisor's defective performance.

Material Breach

A "material" breach is one where the defect in the promised performance is so serious that the non-breaching party may suspend its own performance. Sometimes, the word "total" is used instead of "material" to describe such a breach. However, in keeping with the terminology of the Restatement Second, we will use "material" to refer to a breach that justifies suspension of performance and "total" to describe a breach that justifies termination of the contract.[1] In contrast, an "immaterial" breach is one where the defect in performance is not so great as to relieve the injured party of its own performance due under the contract but may allow a claim for partial breach. If the injured party suspends its own performance in response to an immaterial breach, then that party may itself be committing a breach.

---

1. Restatement (Second) of Contacts § 237 cmt. a (1979). (A "material" failure of performance justifies suspension whereas a "total" breach justifies termination of the contract. Circumstances to determine whether a failure is material are set forth in § 241; circumstances for determining when remaining duties are discharged if a material failure is not cured are set forth in § 242. When such circumstances exist as to discharge the injured party's remaining duties, there is a claim for "total breach" under § 243.).

Let's consider some examples. Suppose Nancy enters into a contract with Daniel to put a new roof on her house for $20,000 by June 1. Upon completing the job, Nancy sees that the shingles are so many different colors that it looks like a patched rather than a new roof. The passage of time and Daniel's attempts to replace the discolored shingles do nothing to lessen the effect. Nancy refuses to pay Daniel and suit follows. The court finds that the only way to repair Daniel's defective performance is to completely redo the roof. Consequently, Daniel's performance is so defective that it constitutes a total breach; Nancy has no duty to pay Daniel the $20,000 and is entitled to damages.[2]

Substantial Performance

Now let's change the facts. Suppose Daniel completes the roof and Nancy inspects the job. Everything looks good to her—there are no streaks or discolorations and it is a roof of uniform color. However, instead of installing a Roof Master roof as specified in the contract, Daniel installs a Grand Roofer roof. Daniel explains that the failure to install the Roof Master was unintentional and purely innocent. Further, the roof he installed was substantially equivalent in all respects to the one Nancy specified. He claims that the value of the addition to her home is unchanged by the error but Nancy objects. She says that unless Daniel rips off the entire roof and replaces it with a Roof Master roof, she will not pay the $20,000 she owes him. Daniel says that it would triple his costs if he has to remove the roof and replace it. Nancy remains insistent.

If the court finds that Daniel committed a material breach, then Nancy has no duty to pay him and he earns nothing for his work. But that would not be the end of it—he would be liable in damages to Nancy for the difference between the contract price of $20,000 and the cost to replace the roof. This would be a very harsh result causing Daniel to suffer a tremendous forfeiture while Nancy has been harmed little, if anything, by the defective performance.

---

2. *See O.W. Grun Roofing and Constr. Co. v. Cope*, 529 S.W.2d 258 (Tex. Ct. App. 1975) (holding that the contractor committed a material breach by installing a roof with so many different colors that the only way to provide a roof of uniform color was to install a completely new roof).

However, if Daniel's breach is not material, then Nancy cannot cancel the contract and refuse to pay for Daniel's work. This is the rule of substantial performance from the famous case of *Jacob & Youngs, Inc. v. Kent.*[3] In *Jacob and Youngs,* Judge Cardozo found that a builder's failure to install Reading pipe was a trivial and innocent breach and the builder substantially performed by installing another pipe which was equivalent in price and quality. The measure of damages was not the cost of replacement which would have been great, but rather the diminution in value between what was promised and what was received, which in this case, was nominal or nothing.

Substantial performance is the antithesis of material breach: the more one has performed, the less likely there has been a material breach. Alternatively, if there has been a material breach, then the party has not rendered a substantial performance.[4] The question of whether a party has performed substantially comes up when that party, despite its breach, claims that it is nonetheless entitled to the other party's return performance. The question of whether a party has committed a material breach arises when the injured party seeks to use that breach as a justification for its own refusal to perform.

Since only a material failure by the other party operates as the non-occurrence of a condition which justifies the injured party in suspending her own performance and ultimately treating her duties as discharged, the first question is whether the failure is material. Restatement Second § 241 identifies the following five circumstances to be considered in making this determination: first, the extent to which the injured party will be deprived of the benefit

---

3.   129 N.E. 889 (N.Y. 1921).

4.   *See* Restatement (Second) of Contracts § 237 (a material failure of performance operates as the non-occurrence of a condition. The non-occurrence of a condition has two effects: first, that of preventing performance of the duty from becoming due, at least temporarily; and second, that of discharging the duty when the condition can no longer occur. A material failure of performance has these effects on the other party's remaining duties of performance under the contract: it prevents performance of those duties from becoming due, at least temporarily, and it discharges those duties if they have not been cured during the time in which performance can occur.).

she reasonably expected; second, the extent to which the injured party can be adequately compensated for the loss of that benefit; third, the extent to which the breaching party will suffer forfeiture; fourth, the likelihood that the breaching party will cure her failure; and fifth, the extent to which the breaching party meets the standards of good faith and fair dealing.

The Concept of Cure

A party can avoid committing a total breach by "curing" a serious defect in performance before it gets to the point of becoming a total breach. It is not a total breach if performance is still not due under the contract and there is time to cure.

In our example, suppose Daniel realizes on May 15 that he used the wrong type of roof and is willing to remedy it. By the contract terms, Daniel has until June 1 to complete performance. If he offers to cure the breach, then Nancy may be required to let him do so. This means that she cannot sue for breach on May 15 and must wait until the contract date to see if Daniel corrects the defect.

Now suppose Daniel installs the correct roof but the job is not fully complete until June 10. Here the question is whether the contract's completion date was itself a material term of the contract. If June 1 was a material term, then Daniel's performance was due on that date and performance at a later time would be a material breach. However, if the completion date was not a material term, then Daniel may have a reasonable time to cure. Assuming that June 1 is not a material term, Daniel's completion of the correct roof by June 10 has turned a material breach into a substantial performance. It is still only a substantial performance because Daniel is late in meeting the contract date and is liable for any damages Nancy has suffered as a consequence of the delay in completion.

While the breaching party may have an opportunity to cure its defective performance, there is a time after which an uncured material failure discharges the other party's remaining duties under the contract.[5] Restatement Second § 242 identifies the circumstances to consider in determining whether there is still time to cure a particular failure or whether the other party's duties may be discharged. The criteria are similar to those for determining a material breach.

Assessing the importance of delay to the injured party depends on the following: the extent to which it will deprive her of the benefit which she reasonably expected and the extent to which she can be adequately compensated; the extent of the forfeiture by the party failing to perform or offering to perform; the likelihood that the injured party's withholding of performance will induce the other party to cure her failure; the reasonableness of the injured party's conduct in communicating her grievances; whether the contract calls for a single exchange or a series of performances so that a continuing relationship is contemplated, in which case the injured party may be expected to give more opportunity for cure; and finally, the nature of the behavior of the non-performing party.[6]

Divisible Contracts

Even if a party's performance falls short of that required by the doctrine of substantial performance, a court can avoid forfeiture and allow recovery on the contract if the contract is "divisible." A contract is divisible if the performances to be exchanged can be divided into "corresponding pairs of part performances so that the parts of each pair are properly regarded as agreed equivalents[.]"[7] The standard of determining whether performances can be considered "agreed equivalents" is flexible and similar to that of materiality under Restatement Second § 237.

While it is not likely that the parties themselves considered their contract divisible at the time of formation, a court may find it so based on considerations of fairness and the desire to avoid

---

5. Restatement (Second) of Contracts § 242 (1979).

6. *Id.* § 242 cmt. b.

7. Restatement (Second) of Contracts § 240 (1979).

forfeiture. Application of the doctrine, however, requires that the parties' performances can be apportioned into corresponding pairs of equivalent performances.[8] According to Restatement Second § 240 comment e, a finding of divisibility requires "that the parts of a pair be of roughly equivalent value to the injured party in terms of his expectation with respect to the total agreed exchange."[9]

For example, in *Lowy v. United Pacific Insurance Co.*,[10] a contractor agreed to perform specified work on the owner's property consisting of street excavation and grading of lots for $73,500 and street improvement work for $125,000 and provide separate performance bonds for each work phase. After the contractor performed 98% of the excavation and grading work, the parties had a dispute regarding payment for certain additional work and the contractor suspended performance. The owner promptly hired another contractor to perform the street improvement work and the contractor sued for breach of contract. The court found that the contract had two distinct parts and that the performances were severable where the fact that the contractor did not perform the second part did not prevent payment for the first. And even though the contractor did not entirely perform the first part, the doctrine of substantial performance was applicable since he had completed 98% of the required performance.

REVIEW OF BREACH UNDER THE UCC

UCC 2-508, 2-601, 2-612

In a contract for the sale of goods, a seller breaches when she repudiates, fails to deliver, or tenders non-conforming goods. A buyer breaches when she wrongfully rejects goods, wrongfully revokes acceptance of goods, fails to make a payment when due, or repudiates with respect to a part or the whole contract. It is well beyond the scope of this book to discuss all the rules under UCC

---

8. *Id.* § 240 cmt. d.
9. *Id.* § 240 cmt. e.

10. 429 P.2d 577 (Cal. 1967).

Article 2 regarding the tender, acceptance, and rejection of goods. By necessity, we will limit our discussion to substantial performance under UCC Article 2 by focusing on the perfect tender rule and the right to cure.

The Perfect Tender Rule

The doctrine of substantial performance does not apply to contracts for the sale of goods. Instead, the Code follows the perfect tender rule where a buyer is free to reject the goods unless the seller's tender conforms in every respect to the contract. In relevant part, UCC 2–601 states that "if the goods or the tender of the delivery fail in any respect to conform to the contract, the buyer may (a) reject the whole; or (b) accept the whole; or (c) accept any commercial unit or units and reject the rest."[11]

It is easy to see that the perfect tender rule can lead to some pretty harsh results, especially where the deviation is minor and curable. Still, the UCC provides some limitations on the perfect tender rule, one of which is the obligation of good faith. Here, the requirement of good faith may be invoked where the defect in performance is so trivial that the buyer is relying on the perfect tender rule as a pretext to avoid the contract. In addition to good faith, the two most important limitations on the perfect tender rule are the seller's right to cure and the substantial performance standard in installment contracts.

The Right to Cure

Under the common law, we saw that a breaching party may have the right to cure its defective performance and avoid a material failure. However, under Article 2, the right to cure assumes an even more critical role because the seller cannot seek a recovery for substantial performance.

---

11. U.C.C. § 2–601 (2004). There is no significant change to this section in the 2003 revision to Article 2.

UCC 2–508 provides for the seller's right to cure a non-conforming tender or delivery. Section 2–508(1)[12] applies if the non-conforming tender or delivery occurs before the contract's specified delivery date. In this situation, if the seller notifies the buyer of her intent to cure the non-conformity, the seller may deliver a conforming shipment within the contract time. On the other hand, section 2–508(2) applies where the seller seeks to cure a non-conforming shipment when the delivery date has passed. Here, the seller shipped non-conforming goods with reasonable grounds to believe that the buyer would accept them despite their non-conformity—perhaps because of a prior course of dealing, course of performance, usage of trade, or particular circumstances. In this case, the seller would have "a further reasonable time to substitute a conforming tender."[13]

Installment Contracts

UCC 2–612 defines an installment contract as one "which requires or authorizes the delivery of goods in separate lots to be separately accepted[.]"[14] Section 2–612(2)[15] allows the buyer to reject any non-conforming installment only if the non-conformity "substantially impairs the value of that installment and cannot be

---

12. U.C.C. § 2–508(1) (2004). There are several changes in the 2003 revision to section 2–508. First, it makes clear that if a seller's initial performance was non-conforming, it must have been made in good faith, the cure must be made at the seller's expense, the seller shall compensate the buyer for the buyer's reasonable expenses caused by the seller's breach, and the conforming tender must be made within the time for performance agreed to in the contract. Revised § 2–508(1) also makes clear that its cure provisions apply to installment contracts under Section 2–612. Section 2–508(2) no longer requires that the seller must have had reasonable grounds to believe that a non-conforming tender would have been acceptable to the buyer. Rather, the seller must have acted in good faith. In this case, cure is available upon seasonable notice to the buyer and at the seller's expense if the

cure is appropriate and timely under the circumstances. While revised § 2–508 abandons the "reasonable grounds to believe" test for when a non-conforming shipment would be acceptable to the buyer, Official Comment 3 to revised § 2–508 makes clear that the requirement of good faith prevents a seller from deliberately tendering non-conforming goods that it knows the buyer cannot use just to save the contract.

13. *Id.* § 2–508(2).

14. U.C.C. § 2–612(1) (2004).

15. U.C.C. § 2–612(2). The 2003 revision to Article 2 eliminates the language "and cannot be cured." Reading revised § 2–508 together with § 2–612(2), it is clear that the seller has the right to cure a nonconforming tender of an installment provided that it meets the requirements of § 2–508(2).

cured[.]"[16] With respect to installment contracts, therefore, Article 2 departs from the strict requirements of the perfect tender rule and allows for substantial performance.

Let's consider an example. Suppose Ben, the owner of a sports equipment store, buys 500 basketballs for delivery in five installments of equal lots of 100 each over a five month period. When Ben inspects the first shipment of basketballs, he finds that three out of the 100 are defective in that they are too soft. Under the perfect tender rule, Ben would have been able to reject the entire delivery, whereas under UCC 2–612(2), Ben must accept the installment if the seller gives adequate assurances that the non-conformity can be cured. Of course Ben is still entitled to any damages he has suffered as a consequence of the original non-conforming tender and, if the seller is unable to effect a cure, then the breach becomes material and Ben can reject the goods.

The other situation that arises with installment contracts is when a buyer receives a non-conforming installment and wants to use it as a basis to cancel the entire contract. Here, too, the UCC imposes the substantial performance rule in UCC 2–612(3) where the buyer can treat the breach of an installment as a breach of the whole if the "non-conformity or default with respect to one or more installments substantially impairs the value of the whole contract[.]"[17] Let's return to our example: suppose Ben's inspection of the first shipment of basketballs shows that they are all defective. Ben would most likely be able to claim that the value of the installment was substantially impaired by the non-conformity and reject it. However, Ben would not be able to use the non-conformity of this one installment as a basis to cancel the whole contract unless he can show that the defect in the single installment substantially impairs the value of the entire contract. For example, suppose Ben had purchased the basketballs for a contract he had with a sports camp. Assume that because he was unable to deliver the first shipment of basketballs, the camp had to get its basketballs elsewhere and cancelled its entire order with him. Because Ben lost his deal with

---

16. *Id.*   **17.** *Id.* § 2–612(3).

the camp, he no longer has any need for the basketballs. In this case, the breach of the installment "substantially impaired" the value of the whole contract for Ben.

Sometimes, it is the seller who has a basis for cancelling the entire contract based on the breach of a single installment. In some cases, non-payment for a delivered shipment may make it impossible or unreasonably burdensome from a financial point of view for the seller to continue to supply future installments as promised. Here, the buyer's failure to pay for one installment may create such a reasonable apprehension in the seller's mind concerning payment for future installments that the seller should not be required to take the risk involved in continuing deliveries.

MATERIAL BREACH AND SUBSTANTIAL PERFORMANCE CHECKLIST

I. Common Law

Here is a checklist for analyzing problems presenting questions regarding breach of contract under the common law:

A. Establishing a Breach—assuming there is a valid contract, has there been a breach?

   1. Failure to Perform—has there been a failure to perform when performance was due?

   a. **Yes.** If the party has failed to perform, without justification or excuse, when the promised performance was due, then she is in breach of contract and the aggrieved party is entitled to seek a remedy.

   b. **No.** If the party has rendered the full performance due under the contract, then its duty has been discharged and there is no breach.

   2. Defective Performance—has the party rendered a defective or improper performance when performance was due?

    a. **Yes.** If so, the next question is whether it is a material breach. Proceed to Part B.

    b. **No.** If not, then there has been no breach.

B. **Material Breach**—is the breach material? Is the defect in performance so serious that the non-breaching party may suspend its own performance? Since the standard for materiality is flexible and imprecise, the court considers a number of circumstances. As a result, the checklist works a bit differently here: there is no "yes" or "no" answer to any one of the factors but a weighing and consideration of them all which leads to a determination of whether the breach is material. To make this assessment, consider the following factors from Restatement Second § 241:

- **Deprivation of Expected Benefit**—what is the extent to which the injured party will be deprived of the expected benefit from the contract?

- **Adequate Compensation**—what is the extent to which the injured party can be adequately compensated for the loss of that benefit?

- **Unfair Forfeiture**—what is the extent to which the breaching party will suffer forfeiture? Where a breaching party's performance falls short of substantial performance, a court can avoid forfeiture and allow recovery on the contract if the contract is "divisible." Ask: is the contract divisible?

    i. **Yes.** If so, then the parties' performances can be apportioned into corresponding pairs of part performances and the doctrine of substantial performance can be applied to avoid forfeiture.

    ii. **No.** If not, the separation of tasks and payments were merely "progress payments" and the rule of substantial performance is not applicable.

- **Likelihood of Cure**—what is the likelihood that the breaching party will cure its failure?

- **Wilfulness of the Breach**—what is the extent to which the breaching party meets standards of good faith and fair dealing? Was the breach intentional or wilful?

1. **Material**—If, in considering the above factors, the breach is material, then the non-breaching party is justified in suspending her own performance. However, even if it is a material breach, it might not be a total breach. Proceed to Part C.

2. **Immaterial**—If, in considering the above factors, the breach is immaterial, then there has been substantial performance. In this case, the promisee must tender her own performance but can seek damages for any loss suffered because of the promisor's defective performance.

C. **Total Breach**—is the breach total? If there is still time to cure a material failure of performance, then it may not be a total breach. Ask: can the defective performance be cured?

1. **Yes.** If the time for performance under the contract is not yet due, the breaching party may offer to cure her performance. If so, then the other party may be required to allow her to do so but is still entitled to recover any damages suffered as a consequence.

2. **No.** If the time for performance has passed or the need for timely performance is so essential that any delay would result in a discharge of the contract, then there is no possibility for cure. In this case, the non-breaching party's remaining duties under the contract are discharged.

II. Sale of Goods

Here is a checklist for analyzing problems presenting questions regarding breach of a sales contract with respect to the perfect tender rule and the right to cure:

A. **Establishing a Breach**—assuming there is a valid contract, has there been a breach?

1. **Failure of Delivery**—has the seller, without justification, failed to deliver the goods when delivery was due?

a. **Yes.** If so, then the seller is in breach.

b. **No.** If not, then the seller may not be in breach. Proceed to the next question.

2. **Delivery of Non-conforming Goods**—has the seller tendered non-conforming goods? If the contract is an installment contract, proceed to Part A. 4.

a. **No.** If the goods are conforming, then the buyer must accept and pay for the goods. Failure to do so constitutes a breach on the part of the buyer.

b. **Yes.** If the goods or tender of delivery fail in any respect to conform to the contract, then a breach has occurred. According to the **perfect tender rule**, the buyer is entitled to reject the whole, accept the whole, or accept any part and reject the rest *unless* the time for performance has not yet expired. In exercising this right, the buyer's rejection must be made in good faith and not to avoid a bad deal. If it is a rightful rejection, then proceed to the next question.

3. **Right to Cure**—has the non-conforming tender or delivery occurred before the contract's specified delivery date such the seller may still cure the non-conformity?

a. **No.** If the time for performance has passed, then there is no possibility for cure and the seller is in breach unless the seller shipped non-conforming goods with reasonable grounds to believe that the buyer would accept them despite their non-conformity. If so, the seller would have a reasonable time to substitute a conforming tender. UCC 2–508(2).

b. **Yes.** If the non-conforming delivery occurred before the date performance was due, then "the seller may seasonably notify the buyer of his intention to cure and may then within the contract time make a conforming delivery." U.C.C. § 2–508(1).

4. **Installment Contract**—has there been a breach of an installment contract?

a. **Breach of an Installment**—has there been a breach of an installment such that the buyer may reject it? A buyer may reject an installment when it is non-conforming and the non-conformity substantially impairs the value of that installment and the seller cannot cure the non-conformity.

i. **No.** If the non-conformity does not impair the value of the whole contract, and the seller gives adequate assurance of its cure, the buyer must accept that installment.

ii. **Yes.** If so, then there has been a breach of the installment, but not necessarily a breach of the entire contract. Proceed to the next question.

  b. **Breach of the Whole**—has there been a breach of an installment such that it constitutes a breach of the whole contract because the non-conformity or defect in the installment "substantially impairs the value of the whole contract"? UCC 2–612(3).

    i. **Yes.** If so, then the breach of the installment may be treated as a breach of the whole.

    ii. **No.** If not, then there has not been a breach of the entire contract and performance of future installments is required.

ILLUSTRATIVE PROBLEMS

Here are some problems that will let us see how the checklist can be used to resolve questions involving breach:

■ PROBLEM 11.1 ■

While on vacation in the American Southwest, Kristle fell in love with western cooking, especially barbecues. She owns a restaurant and decided to remodel to give it a country western theme. The restaurant is to open on May 1.

The restaurant's kitchen required extensive renovation. All the appliances had to be super-sized to accommodate the huge quantities of beef to be served—especially the oven. Kristle researched the manufacturers before she decided on the oven model she wanted. She met with the contractor, Alex, and told him that the oven she wanted was the Grand Master. Its size and special copper heating element was necessary to reach the high temperatures (1500°F) required to cook Texas-style barbecue ribs. It was available in the fire-engine red color Kristle wanted to match the kitchen decor. Kristle also liked the Grand Master logo of a buffalo on the oven door which was an insignia of the Old West. Alex wrote the name of the oven, the heating element, and the color on his specification sheet and gave it to his project manager to purchase. The oven cost $100,000 and Kristle paid Alex $50,000 at the time of the order with the balance due upon installation.

On April 28, the kitchen was completed. Kristle was giving it a final inspection when she noticed that the buffalo insignia was missing from the oven door. Everything else looked right since the oven color matched all the other appliances. She asked to see the oven's warranty papers. Kristle learned that the oven was not the Grand Master but the Barbeque King. Kristle immediately called Alex and demanded that he remove the oven and replace it. Alex said that the failure to install the oven as specified was purely innocent and the oven he installed was substantially equivalent in all respects to the Grand Master. The Barbeque King was an industrial oven and capable of cooking at the required temperatures. He claimed that the value of the addition to kitchen was unchanged by the error but Kristle objected and refused to pay Alex the $50,000 for the oven. Kristle said, "it is not what I ordered and even if it cooks the same, it doesn't have the buffalo insignia." Alex said he could find a buffalo insignia for the oven and promptly did so. He also said that it would cost about $100,000 to remove and replace the oven because it would require ripping up and replacing the entire kitchen and moving the cabinetry. Kristle insisted that he do so or she would not pay the $50,000 balance due.

Kristle refuses to pay Alex because the oven was not the precise model she requested. What result for Alex?

Analysis

The issue is whether Kristle's refusal to pay Alex is a breach of contract. In turn, this depends on whether installing the Grand Master oven was a promise or express condition of Alex's performance.

A party who breaches a promise is only liable for whatever damage she causes by the breach. On the hand, if a party fails to meet a condition, then the other party's duty to perform under the contract never arises. Here, it is possible that installing the Grand Master was an express condition because Kristle was very specific and clearly identified the particular oven she wanted by model name. She could be specific and demanding in her restaurant and make the oven type—the Grand Master—a condition of her own duty to pay.

However, it is possible that it was only a promise to install the Grand Master oven and not an express condition of Alex's performance. Here, Kristle told Alex that she wanted the Grand Master oven in her kitchen. Although she specified the oven by name, this might only be an example of the type of oven she wanted and Alex then promised to supply an oven which met the specifications of the Grand Master. To treat it as an express condition would be unjust to the contractor since he would suffer a tremendous forfeiture of $50,000 and Kristle has been harmed very little, if at all, since the oven he installed, the Barbeque King, was substantially equivalent in all respects to the Grand Master. It was an industrial oven and capable of cooking at the required temperatures. It was even the same fire-engine red color as the Grand Master.

Assuming that it was a promise and not a condition to install the Grand Master, did Alex breach this promise? If a promisor is found to be under an absolute duty to perform, failure to render the promised performance at the time and place provided in the contract constitutes a breach. Alex committed a breach because he failed to install the precise oven model that Kristle ordered even though he installed one that was substantially equivalent. He breached the contract because he installed a Barbeque King and not a Grand Master oven.

The next question is whether this breach was material. In determining whether a breach is material, it is necessary to consider the following factors: first, the extent to which the breaching party has already performed; second, whether the breach was wilful, negligent, or purely innocent; third, the extent to which the injured party will be deprived of the actual benefit of the contract; fourth, the extent to which the breaching party will suffer forfeiture; fifth, the extent the injured party will or has obtained the substantial benefit for which she bargained; and sixth, the extent to which the injured party can be compensated for the defective performance by damages.

It is possible that installation of the Barbeque King instead of the Grand Master was a material breach of the parties' contract because the difference between the ovens was visible to Kristle: it did not have the buffalo insignia; the defect was visible to her unlike the hidden pipe in *Jacob & Youngs*; and, finally, it was not the oven she wanted and people have a right to get what they bargain for. Kristle was very clear in her request at the time of contract about the type of oven she wanted and went so far as to identify it by model number and provide all the specifications. The oven was a major appliance in her kitchen and she would see it whenever she walked into the room.

Alternatively, it could be argued that Alex substantially performed the contract and is entitled to payment of the $50,000 less any difference in value between the two ovens. He substantially performed because he completed the installation of the entire kitchen but for the different oven model. While it was missing the buffalo insignia, Alex said that he could get one and he promptly did so. Further, the mistake in the type of oven was "purely innocent," the value of the kitchen was "unchanged," and the oven was the right color red. The oven he installed was an industrial oven and capable of cooking at the required temperatures for western barbeque. Kristle could perform all the cooking functions she required with this oven and so she substantially received the benefit of the bargain. If Alex had to replace the oven, it would cost $100,000 because he would have to rip out the entire kitchen and remove the cabinetry. This would be a tremendous waste for Alex while Kristle has been injured very little since she received a substantially equivalent oven which cooks the same and has all the same specifications.

It is unlikely a court would require Alex to rip out the entire kitchen to replace the oven. Instead, it would order Kristle to pay the $50,000 due to Alex, less the difference in value between a kitchen with a Grand Master stove and one with a Barbeque King stove.

■ PROBLEM 11.2 ■

Seth agreed to build a house on Ben's land for $100,000. The parties agreed to the following payment schedule:

$10,000 to Seth upon signing the contract

$10,000 after the foundation is poured

$20,000 after framing is completed

$30,000 after the plumbing and electricity is installed

$30,000 upon final approval from the local housing inspector

Ben paid Seth $10,000 when the contract was signed and Seth began work on the house. He completed the foundation, framing, and plumbing in full compliance with the workplans and specifications. However, Seth's electrical work was so defective that it could not be made to work at all without starting over and Seth has refused to redo the necessary work, claiming it will take too long and he has to begin another job. Seth wants $60,000 for the work he has done. Ben does not want to pay Seth anything and has sought your advice. What would you advise?

Analysis

The question is what, if anything, Ben is obligated to pay Seth for his work when Seth is in breach of contract because he rendered a defective performance. While part of the work meets the contract's specifications, the electrical work does not. The issue is whether this defect in performance constitutes a material breach.

To determine whether a breach is material, we need to consider several factors. First, we need to determine the extent to which Ben will be deprived of the expected benefit from the contract. Ben expected to have a house built which would meet all required specifications so that it would pass inspection from the local housing inspector. Presently, this is not possible since the electrical work is defective. While it is possible to cure the defect, Seth has made it clear that he will not do so. In this case, it would be necessary for Ben to hire someone else to fix it. Second, we need to determine the extent to which Ben can be adequately compensated for this loss. While the electrical system is not working, it seems that it could be made to work but it would take time and money. Ben can be compensated for this loss by deducting this cost from what he would have paid Seth.

Another factor to consider is the extent to which the breaching party will suffer a forfeiture if he is not paid for his work. Here, Seth was paid $10,000 upon signing the contract. However, Seth did complete the foundation, framing, and plumbing. The facts indicate that only the electrical work was defective. In this case, it might be unfair not to pay Seth for the value of this performance since it would seem to be that, despite the breach, he performed a significant portion of the contract. Finally, there are no facts to indicate that Seth's breach was wilful or done in bad faith.

In some cases, a breaching party can avoid forfeiture if the contract was divisible or severable instead of entire. A contract is divisible if the performance to be exchanged can be divided into corresponding pairs of part performances in such a way that a court will treat the parts of each pair as if the parties had agreed that they were equivalents.

The question is whether the Seth–Ben contract was divisible. The contract may have been divisible because the tasks to be performed in building the house were identified individually and the payments were structured according to completion of different tasks. However, it is more likely the payments were merely progress payments because they were not structured to represent the value of each portion of the job since signing the contract would not be worth $10,000. Nor is likely that getting final approval from the housing inspector is worth $30,000. Consequently, this was most likely not a divisible contract and the dollar amounts assigned to the tasks cannot be used to determine the amount Ben owes Seth for his work.

I would advise Ben to hire another builder to complete the house to meet all required specifications and obtain final approval from the local housing inspector. Once he has paid the other builder for completing the house, he can deduct this amount from the $100,000 he expected to pay to build his house. This is the amount, less the $10,000 already paid, that he owes Seth for his work.

POINTS TO REMEMBER

- A breach analysis begins with determining the existence of a contract and its terms.

- A party breaches a contract by failing to render a promised performance when due or rendering a defective performance.

- Be sure to consider all the relevant factors in determining whether a party has committed a material breach. It is a fact-sensitive analysis and requires a weighing of the factors.

- Remember that substantial performance is the antithesis of material breach: the more one has performed, the less likely there has been a material breach.

- Realize that there is a gap between the time when a party commits a breach which justifies the non-breaching party in suspending its own performance, and when the breach is "total" so as to allow the non-breaching party to consider its remaining duties discharged. Further, only a material breach justifies the non-breaching party in suspending its own performance—if an injured party suspends its own performance in response to an immaterial breach, then that party may itself be in breach.

- Be careful to distinguish between contracts that are "divisible" and those where the division of tasks and payments are "progress payments" to be made during the course of the contract's performance.

- The common law doctrine of substantial performance does not apply to contracts for the sale of goods. Instead, the Code follows the perfect tender rule where a buyer is free to reject the goods unless the seller's tender conforms in every respect to the contract. Limits on the perfect tender rule include the buyer's duty to act in good faith and the seller's right to cure, where applicable.

Formation ➡	Avoiding ➡ the Deal	Performance ➡	Third ➡ Parties	Remedies
Do we have a deal?	We have a deal, but	Who has to do what and when, or maybe not	Is there a third party to the deal?	Someone failed to per-form when required, now what?
Mutual Assent + Consideration				

Excerpts of Contracts Time-line

REMEDIES
SOMEONE FAILED TO PERFORM
WHEN REQUIRED, NOW WHAT

Measuring money damages:
- Expectation interest
  - Loss in value
  - Cost of repair/completion
  - Diminution in value
- Reliance interest
- Restitution interest

Consequential damages

Incidental damages

Liquidation damages

Limitations on money damages
- Foreseeability
- Mitigation/avoidability
- Certainty

Equitable remedies
- Specific performance
- Injunctive relief

Close-up on Remedies

CHAPTER 12

Contract Remedies

> R2d § 344, 347, 348, 349,
> 350-53, 356, 371, 373, 374

This chapter begins with the premise that a valid and enforceable contract has been formed and one of the parties has committed a breach by failing to perform or rendering a defective performance. Therefore, it does not matter whether your contracts class considers damages at the beginning of the semester or the end—simply assume that the threshold question of a breach of a valid contract has been established and proceed with determining the appropriate remedy and damages.

Contract law is guided by the principle that an injured party has the right to seek relief in court by bringing a suit for damages. Remedies for breach of contract are categorized as either "legal" or "equitable," according to whether they were available from the common law courts or courts of equity before the courts of law and equity were finally merged. A legal remedy is an award of money damages; an equitable remedy is an order granting specific performance of the contract. As we will see, the equitable remedies of specific performance and injunctive relief are exceptional remedies and are not generally available.

REVIEW OF REMEDIES

The basic principle of contract remedies is simple: to make the injured party whole through compensation for the loss caused by the breach. However, our system of contract remedies does not seek to punish the breaching party but instead is concerned with compensating the non-breaching party for its loss—the goal is not compulsion of the promisor to perform the promise but compensation of the promisee for the loss resulting from the breach. Therefore, "willful" or "intentional" breaches are generally not distinguished from other breaches, punitive damages are not awarded,[1] and specific performance will not be granted where money damages are an adequate substitute for the injured party. However, since the concern is with economic loss, if a non-breaching party suffers no actual financial loss, there is no entitlement to damages beyond an award for nominal damages. This compensation principle is consistent with a market economy where freedom of contract is essential and only economic injury is recoverable. However, "along with the celebrated freedom to make contracts goes a considerable freedom to break them as well."[2]

According to Restatement Second § 344, the purpose of judicial remedies is to protect one or more of the promisee's three interests:

- The "expectation interest" represents what the injured party expected to receive if the contract had been fully performed and is often referred to as the "benefit of the bargain."

- The "reliance interest" represents the injured party's loss caused by reliance on the contract and seeks to put the plaintiff in as good a position as she would have been in had the contract not been made.

- The "restitution interest" represents the plaintiff's interest in having restored to her any benefit she has conferred on the other party.

---

1. Restatement (Second) of Contracts § 355 (1979). Since the purpose of awarding damages is to compensate the injured party, courts do not use damages to "punish" the breaching party or serve as a deterrent to future conduct. Punitive damages are not recoverable unless the conduct constituting the breach is also a tort for which punitive damages are recoverable.

2. E. Allan Farnsworth, *Contracts*, § 12.1 (4th ed. 2004).

Usually, a party will seek to recover expectation damages because they represent the greatest measure of recovery. They compensate the injured party for the benefit she would have received had the contract been fully performed, which would include lost profits. It is important to note, however, that there are several limitations on a party's ability to recover expectation damages. First, a party must show causation—that the breach of contract was the cause in fact of its loss. Second, a party's loss must be foreseeable and proved with reasonable certainty. Third, a party has a duty after the defendant's breach to make all reasonable efforts to avoid unnecessary damages. Finally, a party may not recover more than the contract terms would have provided.[3]

If a party is unable to meet the requirements for an expectancy claim, it may seek to recover under a reliance theory. Here, a party would seek any expenses incurred in reliance on the contract by preparing to perform or in performance. This type of recovery puts the party back in the position it would have been in had the contract not been made.

Finally, a party may seek to recover damages based on its restitution interest. The goal of restitution is not the enforcement of the promise but the prevention of unjust enrichment. If a party has changed position in reliance on the contract and has also conferred a benefit on the other party, the court may require the other party to disgorge the benefit received by returning it to the party who conferred it. The restitution interest is generally smaller than either the expectation or reliance interest because it includes neither the injured party's lost profit nor reliance expenditures that conferred no benefit on the other party.[4]

---

3. *Freund v. Washington Square Press, Inc.*, 314 N.E.2d 419, 420–21 (N.Y. 1974) (The New York Court of Appeals summed up the rule nicely: "so far as possible, the law attempts to secure to the injured party the benefit of his bargain, subject to the limitations that the injury—whether it be losses suffered or gains prevented—was foreseeable, and the amount of damages claimed be measurable with a reasonable degree of certainty and, of course, adequately proven. . . . But it is equally fundamental that the injured party should not recover more from the breach than he would have gained had the contract been fully performed.").

4. Restatement (Second) of Contracts § 344 cmt. a (1979).

The Efficient Breach

While it is not within the scope of this text to delve too deeply into theory, it is important to note the important role of economic theory in the law of contracts and specifically in the area of remedies. Your professor may spend some time on economic analysis and it might well take place in the context of the "efficient breach."

An efficient breach is one where the party in breach gains enough from the breach to have a net benefit, even after compensating the injured party for its loss. In other words, the defendant comes out ahead by breaching the contract and paying damages. Judge Richard Posner is a leading advocate of the concept: "Even if the breach is deliberate, it is not necessarily blameworthy. The promisor may simply have discovered that his performance is worth more to someone else. If so, efficiency is promoted by allowing him to break his promise, provided he makes good the promisee's actual losses." [5]

Calculating Expectation Damages

Some students seem to have the most difficulty with calculating damages—getting lost in "formulas" and making the process more complicated than it needs to be. Because the purpose of expectation damages is to approximate as closely as possible the plaintiff's position in the absence of breach, the key is to focus on comparing what the plaintiff expected to get from the contract and what she actually received. While it is true that the facts can get quite complicated, the basic concept is simple and if you keep it in mind, you will not get lost in the calculations: any measurement of the expectation interest must total up the losses caused by the breach and subtract any savings or gains realized as a result of not having to perform the contact.

Restatement Second § 347 provides a formula for measuring the injured party's damages based on her expectation interest:

---

5. *Patton v. Mid–Continent Systems, Inc.*, 841
F.2d 742, 750 (7th Cir. 1998).

Damages = The plaintiff's *loss in value* caused by the other party's failure to perform or the rendering of a defective performance (subtract the contract value of what the plaintiff received from what she was promised)

+ *Any other loss* (add in incidental or consequential damages)

− Any cost or other loss the plaintiff *avoided* by not having to perform the contract

Let's consider an example. Suppose Deb enters into a contract with Sarah in April where Deb agrees to tutor Sarah for the July bar exam. Deb is to meet with Sarah for two hours a week for seven weeks beginning the first week in June and continuing through July for an hourly fee of $200. In late May, Deb gets an offer to teach in a summer abroad program in London and notifies Sarah that she won't be able to tutor her. Sarah's "expectation" from the contract was to pay $2800 for bar tutoring services. Fortunately, Sarah is able to find another bar exam tutor but because it is right before bar review courses begin, this tutor charges $250 per hour for services comparable to Deb. Since Sarah planned to pay $2800 for the tutoring lessons and will now have to pay $3500, she has suffered a loss of $700. Sarah is entitled to an award of $700 to place her in the position she expected to be in by Deb's performance. On the other hand, if Sarah is able to find another tutor for the same price she was to pay Deb, then she has no claim for damages because she is in the same position as if Deb had performed.

The results are not very different if it were Sarah who breached the contract because the basic principle is the same. Suppose Deb is able to find another student to tutor but one who will only pay $100 per hour. Since Deb expected to earn $2800 from her contract with Sarah and will now earn only half that amount, she is entitled to $1400 in damages.

In these examples, Sarah and Deb chose to make substitute contracts and we measured their damages by comparing the difference between their original contracts and the substitute transactions. However, sometimes a party cannot make a substitute contract or chooses not to do so. In this case, the damages are measured by comparing the contract price with the current market value of a substitute performance. For example, even if Sarah chose not to hire another tutor when Deb breached, Sarah would be entitled to damages if the market price of the tutoring was higher than the contract price she had with Deb. The same principle applies for Deb: if she opts not to tutor another student when Sarah breaches, Deb is entitled to claim a loss based on the difference between the contract price and the market price she would have earned had she taken another student.

Sometimes, however, it is not possible for the non-breaching party to make a substitute contract. In these cases, the party's damages may be the full value of the bargained-for performance. For example, suppose that despite her best efforts, Deb could not find another job tutoring a student for the bar exam. In this case, she is entitled to the "benefit of her bargain" which would be $2800. She expected to tutor Sara for seven weeks for two hours per week at $200 per hour. This is her pure expectation interest.

For the purposes of using our "formula," however, assume that Deb would have incurred a couple of expenses in tutoring Sara: first, she would have transportation costs of $20 per week to Sara's house where she agreed to tutor her and she would have to spend $100 in making copies of practice bar exam questions. In this case, Deb would save $240 by not having to perform the contract. This amount represents the "cost avoided" by not having to perform and would be subtracted from the $2800 to leave a net amount of $2560.

It is important to note that only the costs that Deb avoided by not having to perform are deducted from her recovery. On the other hand, if there were fixed expenses that she would have to pay whether or not Sarah breached, these expenses would not be deducted. For example, Deb could not deduct her car payments because she had to pay them whether or not she tutored Sarah. This is often referred to as a "fixed cost" or "overhead" and would not be an expense saved by the breach.

Varying the Formula

As you know by now, there are quite possibly as many ways to breach a contract as there are types of contracts. As a result, it is impossible to provide a single formula that accounts for all possible damage calculations. Courts consider a multitude of factors in determining an award that places the non-breaching party in the position she would have been in had the contract been performed; we must be similarly flexible. Still, there are some common types of contract breaches that are helpful for organizing our analysis. We considered a few of them in the above example, but now we will look at them more closely.

Consider the following circumstances when measuring a party's expectation interest:

When Neither Party Has Performed

This is the situation where a party breaches by failing to perform and the aggrieved party withholds its own performance and brings suits seeking expectation damages. Here the court may use one of the measures we considered in the above example with Deb and Sarah to determine whether the defendant's performance would have had any economic value to the plaintiff: measuring damages based on a substitute performance or considering market value and comparing it to the terms of the contract. When neither of these formulations adequately compensate the plaintiff's loss, the court may decide that the plaintiff should receive the profit she would have earned on the contract.

A lost profits measure of damages is not always available to the plaintiff. It is only when the plaintiff would have earned the profit from two transactions absent the breach that she is considered to have "lost volume." For example, suppose that upon Sarah's breach, Deb was able immediately to find another student, Amy, to tutor for the same amount of money. In this case, the substitution measure would not provide any damages. However, suppose Deb would have found and tutored Amy even if Sarah had not breached the contract. Here, Amy was not a "substitute" performance and Sarah would have had two students to tutor and earned the profits from two contracts. On the other hand, if Deb would not have had the time or resources to tutor Amy unless Deb had breached, then the lost profits measure of damages would not be available. We will consider this measure of damages again in the context of the sale of goods when we consider the "lost volume seller."

When There Has Been Part Performance

Frequently, the breaching party renders a performance but it is either incomplete or defective. In this situation, measuring the value of the performance to the non-breaching party can be somewhat more complex. As we've seen in a previous chapter, a deficient performance may be a material breach or it may constitute substantial performance and be only a partial breach. A material breach excuses the non-breaching party from rendering her own performance due under the contract and she can then seek damages. On the other hand, if the breaching party has substantially performed, the non-breaching party cannot cancel her own performance and must perform her duties under the contract but may have a claim for damages. In assessing her damages, the court seeks to measure the difference in value, if any, between what she expected to receive and what she actually received under the contract. This is a frequent problem in construction contracts and courts consider a couple of ways to make this determination.

Diminution in Value

This formulation comes from the case of *Jacob & Youngs, Inc. v. Kent*,[6] where Judge Cardozo found that a builder's failure to install Reading pipe was a trivial and innocent breach and the builder substantially performed by installing another pipe equal in price and quality. The measure of damages was not the cost of replacement which would have been great, but rather the diminution in value between what was promised and what was received, which in this case, was nominal or nothing.

Sometimes you will see this referred to as a "difference in value" formulation where you look to the difference in market

---

6. 129 N.E. 889 (N.Y. 1921).

value between what was promised (the value of a house with Reading pipe) and what was received (the value of the house with the other pipe). This measurement is used where the cost of completion or repair would result in an unfair forfeiture or economic waste for the breaching party.

Cost of Completion or Repair

Alternatively, the court may consider the proper measure of damages to be the cost to complete or repair the defective performance. According to the Restatement, if a party's breach "results in defective or unfinished construction and the loss in value is not proved with reasonable certainty," then the owner is not limited to "the diminution in the market price of the property caused by the breach," but may recover damages based on "the reasonable cost of completing performance or of remedying the defects if that cost is not clearly disproportionate to the probable loss in value to him."[7]

Typically, in defective construction cases, it is easier for the injured party "to prove what it would cost to have the work completed by another contractor than to prove the difference between the values to him of the finished and the unfinished performance."[8] If the repair work has been completed, then damages will be based on the actual expenditures.

Difficulties arise, however, when the cost to remedy the defective performance involves the cost to "undo" what has been done such that the cost to remedy the defects will be disproportionate to the probable loss in value to the injured party. In this case, damages based on the cost to repair would result in a windfall and will not be made. This is referred to as "economic waste." If an award based on the cost to remedy the defect would be excessive and the injured party does not prove the actual loss in value to her, then damages will be based on the difference between the market

---

7. Restatement (Second) of Contracts   **8.** *Id.* § 348 cmt. c.
§ 348(2) (1979).

price that the property would have had without the defects and the market price of the property with the defects.[9]

Limitations on Recovery of Expectation Damages

The recovery of expectation damages is subject to certain limitations. First, the plaintiff must show causation, i.e., that her loss was caused by defendant's breach. Second, the plaintiff is entitled to recover only those damages which were reasonably contemplated by the parties at the time of contract. This is known as the foreseeability principle. Third, the plaintiff has a duty to act responsibly upon breach and cannot "run up" her damages. This is referred to as the "duty to mitigate," requiring the non-breaching party to take reasonable, appropriate action following the breach to avoid or minimize further losses. Finally, the plaintiff's damages cannot be speculative and must be "reasonably certain" of calculation. This is known as the "certainty" principle.

Foreseeability

The losses caused by the breach must have been reasonably foreseeable to the defendant at the time of contracting to be recoverable. This rule comes from the seminal case of *Hadley v. Baxendale*.[10] The facts in *Hadley* are simple: a crankshaft needed to operate the steam engine for Hadley's mill broke and was sent as a pattern to the manufacturer for a new one. When the carrier delayed in getting the crank shaft to the manufacturer, the reopening of the mill was delayed for several days. Hadley sued the carrier for damages equal to the income lost by the mill during the delay. While the jury awarded Hadley a verdict for lost profits, the court on appeal held that it was error for the jury to have considered lost profits at all.

According to the court, the mill owner did not communicate to the carrier at the time of contract that the item was a broken shaft for their mill. The court asked how the carrier was to know that the mill would lose profits by a delay in delivery of the shaft to some

---

9. *Id.*   **10.** 156 Eng. Rep. 145 (1854).

third party. It was true that the mill could not operate without the shaft and it had no other until its replacement was made; this was the only reason that profits were lost. However, under ordinary circumstances, such consequences would not have occurred. The mill owner might have had another shaft or the mill might have been defective in another way. In these cases, the carrier's delay would not have affected the mill's profits.

Two rules come from *Hadley*. The first rule is that the injured party may recover damages for loss that "may fairly and reasonably be considered [as] arising naturally, i.e., according to the usual course of things, from such breach of contract itself."[11] The second rule is the one for which *Hadley* is most frequently cited—that of "consequential damages." Damages for loss other than those "arising naturally" from the breach are not recoverable unless the loss was "such as may reasonably be supposed to have been in the contemplation of both parties, at the time they made the contract, as the probable result of the breach of it."[12] By introducing the requirement of "contemplation" for the recovery of consequential damages, the court imposed an important limitation on the scope of recovery.

The modern trend phrases the test in terms of foreseeability: "damages are not recoverable for loss that the party in breach did not have reason to foresee as a probable result of the breach when the contract was made."[13] In short, it is the foreseeability only by the party in breach that is determinative. Further, that loss may be foreseeable if it follows "in the ordinary course of events" or if it follows "as a result of special circumstances, beyond the ordinary course of events, that the party in breach had reason to know."[14]

Mitigation/Avoidability

The plaintiff has a duty after the defendant's breach to make all reasonable efforts to avoid unnecessary damages. This is re-

---

11. *Id.*, at 151.

12. *Id.*

13. Restatement (Second) § 351(1) (1979).

14. *Id.* § 351(2) (Section 351(2)(a) was taken by the Restatement from U.C.C. § 2–714(1) and § 351(2)(b) from U.C.C. §§ 2–715(2)(a)).

ferred to as the "duty to mitigate." The non-breaching party is not permitted to recover damages which she could have avoided through reasonable efforts. If the defendant, who has the burden of proof on this issue, can establish a failure to mitigate, then the plaintiff's ability to recover this loss may be denied.

Certainty

To be recoverable, plaintiff must establish the amount of the loss with "reasonable certainty."[15] This is necessary to establish plaintiff's loss as a result of the breach and to allow the factfinder to determine the amount of the award.

The main impact of this rule is felt with respect to lost profits. The difficulty of proving lost profits varies with the type of transaction but is most difficult in cases involving new businesses where there is no established history or basis for comparison. In these cases, the problem is that the projection of future profits are considered "too speculative."

Reliance and Restitution Damages

As we've just seen, expectation damages are not always recoverable. Sometimes damages cannot be established with reasonable certainty or they may not have been reasonably foreseeable. Or it may happen that the plaintiff has not actually been deprived of the economic gain caused by the breach because of a substitute transaction or because the contract itself would have been a losing one. If no loss can be shown, then the plaintiff has no basis for recourse against the defendant because there is no need for monetary compensation.

For example, suppose that Ben agrees to buy Seth's sailboat, the Hearsay, and then Seth breaches. If Ben is able to buy another sailboat for the same price, he has not suffered an injury to his expectation interest. However, suppose Ben paid $500 to have new sails made for the Hearsay which are not useable on any boat other

---

15.   *See* Restatement (Second) of Contracts
§ 352 (1979).

than the Hearsay. Suppose, also, that Ben paid Seth a $1000 deposit when they formed the contract. While these are not "expectation" damages, they may be recoverable.

Reliance damages are intended to restore any expenses or losses the plaintiff has expended in reliance on the contract, thus returning the plaintiff to the position she would have been in had no contract been made. Ben would not have paid $500 to make new sails for the Hearsay if he were not going to purchase it. This cost was incurred solely in reliance on the contract and would be recoverable as reliance damages.

At this point (if not earlier) you may recall reliance damages from our earlier discussion of promissory estoppel. In that situation, reliance damages were available to a party who relied to her detriment on a promise but it was unenforceable for some reason, i.e., a lack of consideration or a writing was needed to satisfy the Statute of Frauds. Here, we are considering a reliance recovery for a breach of contract action. It is appropriate where expectation damages are unavailable and the promisor has incurred expenses in reliance on the contract—just as Ben has done by ordering new sails for the Hearsay.

There is a limit to a party's recovery of reliance damages: they may not exceed the full contract price. This is a possibility in a losing contract—one where the non-breaching party would have suffered a loss rather than a profit and is actually saved from further loss by virtue of the breach. Here, the non-breaching party may recover reliance damages "less any loss that the party in breach can prove with reasonable certainty the injured party would have suffered had the contract been performed."[16]

Restitution damages, unlike expectancy and reliance damages, have as their objective the recovery of a benefit realized by the defendant and not compensation for the harm sustained by the plaintiff. Restitution is based on the prevention of unjust

---

16. Restatement (Second) of Contracts § 349 (1979).

enrichment. Such damages are intended to restore a benefit which one party has gained at the expense of another under circumstances which make it unfair for the recipient to retain the benefit without compensating the other party for it.

Restitution is both a remedy for a breach of contract and its own distinct body of substantive law. In fact, restitution is the subject of its own Restatement. It is important that you do not confuse restitution, which is a remedy, with unjust enrichment, which is the claim that gives rise to the remedy.

Unjust enrichment covers many situations. It can be a basis for liability in cases where the parties have not made an actual agreement or their agreement does not qualify as a contract, perhaps because of a failure during the formation process. Still, there was some interaction which resulted in one party gaining a benefit from the other. In such cases, a contract would be implied-in-law (quasi-contract) for the purposes of providing a remedy. Unjust enrichment also plays a role when there has been a breach of a valid contract. The contract may be an actual agreement or one implied-in-fact. One of the parties may have conferred a benefit on the other party before the breach occurred and restitution of that benefit might be a better option than any of the other contractual remedies.

Essentially, a claim for unjust enrichment has two elements: first, that one party obtained a benefit at the other party's expense; and second, that it would be unfair for the recipient to retain the benefit without compensating the other party for it.

The question is how to measure the party's restitution interest. The simplest case is where the benefit conferred on the party in breach is the payment of money, in part or in full, for a performance that is not forthcoming. In our example, Ben conferred a benefit on Seth when he gave him the $1000 deposit for the Hearsay. Seth would be required to "make restitution" of the $1000 deposit by returning it to Ben. Here, restitution is made by returning the money but in some cases restitution might require the restoring of a specific thing. This usually arises in connection with contracts to transfer land.[17]

Restitution may be granted when the benefit conferred is something other than money, such as a performance, although the court will measure the value of that benefit in money. One way to measure the value of a benefit is to look to its market value: what would the breaching party have to pay in the marketplace to receive that benefit? When a party seeks a recovery for the value of her labor, it is referred to as *quantum meruit* ("as much as deserved"). As always, the contract price is an indication of value but it is not dispositive. It is possible for a recovery in restitution to exceed the contract price.[18]

Although restitutionary relief may be sought in a wide variety of settings, Restatement Second identifies the following five situations that arise in connection with contracts:[19]

- The other party is in breach and the party seeking restitution has chosen it as an alternative to the enforcement of the contract.

- The party seeking restitution claims the benefit that she has conferred under the contract because she is precluded by her own breach from enforcing the contract.

- The party seeking restitution claims the benefit that she has conferred under the contract because she is precluded from enforcing it against the other party because of the Statute of Frauds.

- The party claims restitution upon avoidance of a contract on the grounds of mistake, misrepresentation, or duress.

- The party claims restitution on the ground that her duty of performance did not arise or was discharged as a result of

---

17. Restatement (Second) of Contracts § 372 cmt. b (1979).

18. *See* Farnsworth, *Contracts*, at § 12.20.

19. Restatement (Second) of Contracts, Chapter 16, Topic 4 Introductory Note (1979).

impracticability, frustration of purpose, non-occurrence of a condition, or disclaimer by a beneficiary.

Where the Breaching Party Seeks Restitution

While a breaching party is liable for the loss caused by her breach, she may nonetheless be entitled to recover if she has conferred a benefit on the non-breaching party in excess of that loss. At first, it might seem strange that a breaching party can assert a claim, but it would be unjust to allow the injured party to retain the entire benefit of the breaching party's part performance without paying something in return.

Once again, if the breaching party seeks restitution of money paid, it is easy to measure the benefit conferred on the other party. The difficulty is when the party in breach seeks a monetary recovery that represents the benefit of services rendered to the other party. Since the party seeking restitution in this case is also the breaching party, any doubts about the valuations of enhanced wealth will be resolved against her.[20] Here, too, the contract price is evidence of the benefit, but not conclusive. According to the Restatement, "in no case will the party in breach be allowed to recover more than a ratable portion of the total contract price where such a portion can be determined."[21]

Agreed Remedies

As we have seen throughout our discussion of contract law, parties have tremendous freedom in shaping their agreement, subject only to certain "immutable" principles and public policies. In contrast, their power to bargain over their remedial rights is limited. The most important restriction is the one that limits the setting of a sum of money payable as damages that is so large that it could be seen as a "penalty." Here, the remedial goal of contract law to provide compensation to the aggrieved party but not punish the breaching party supersedes the general freedom to contract. Still, parties have several options in fashioning their own remedies should there be a breach.

---

20. Restatement (Second) of Contracts   **21.** *Id.*
§ 374 cmt. b (1979).

Liquidated Damages

A liquidated damages provision is a term in a contract where the parties agree what the damages will be in the event of a breach by one of them. The parties may set an amount or identify a formula to calculate the damages. There are compelling reasons for contracting parties to "liquidate" (make certain) damages as part of their overall agreement: they eliminate the need for proof in the event of breach, provide compensation for loss which would otherwise be unavailable because incapable of proof with reasonable certainty, limit damages to the sum stated, and save the time and expense of litigation.

On the other hand, damage provisions that set the amount too high in relation to the actual loss have the opposite effect, which is that of penalizing a party for breach. Consequently, where the agreed-to amount is significantly larger than necessary to compensate the injured party for its loss, a court will consider the provision to be punitive in nature and not enforce it. Under the Restatement, the amount fixed by the parties must be "reasonable in the light of the anticipated or actual loss caused by the breach and the difficulties of proof of loss."[22] The Code follows a similar approach in recognizing liquidated damages "only at an amount which is reasonable in the light of the anticipated or actual harm caused by the breach[.]"[23]

Limiting Remedies

Parties may decide to limit the remedies available in the event of breach. They may put a cap on damages, specify categories of damages for which the breaching party will not be responsible, and limit the recovery of consequential damages.

It is also possible to limit the types of remedies. For example, a seller may restrict a buyer's sole remedy to "repair or replace-

---

22. Restatement (Second) of Contracts § 356(1) (1979).

23. U.C.C.§ 2–718(1) (2004). The 2003 revision to Article 2 limits the requirement that the anticipated or actual harm be difficult to prove or that an adequate remedy might not otherwise be available to cases of consumer contracts. Under revised § 2–718, the only question in a non-consumer contract is whether the pre-agreed amount was reasonable in view of the anticipated loss.

ment" of defective parts rather than the payment of money damages. Parties may also define the procedures to be followed in the event of a dispute such as resolving controversies through arbitration or other alternative dispute resolution methods as opposed to litigation.

The UCC provides special provisions regarding the limitations of remedies and we will discuss them in the section on Code remedies.

REVIEW OF EQUITABLE REMEDIES

> R2d § 357, 359
> UCC 2-716

Sometimes the award of money damages will not compensate the aggrieved party for its loss. In such cases, the court has discretion to fashion an award of specific performance or order injunctive relief.

Specific Performance

Where money will not make the plaintiff whole, either due to the difficulty of obtaining a suitable substitute performance or the uniqueness of the item or promised performance, the court may order specific performance. In such cases, the "order of specific performance is intended to produce as nearly as is practicable the same effect that the performance due under a contract would have produced."[24] Typically, this means an order to the breaching party to render the promised performance. However, a court will not grant an order requiring specific performance to provide a service that is personal in nature. There are several reasons for this refusal: personal performances are difficult for courts to enforce, supervise, or evaluate. It is also undesirable to require a continuing relationship where there has been such a serious dispute as to require court

---

24. Restatement (Second) of Contracts § 357 cmt. a (1979).

intervention. Further, compelling performance might be considered a form of involuntary servitude.

Orders awarding specific performance are typical in a breach of a contract for the sale of real property. Since land is unique, it is easy to see why money damages might be inadequate in the event of breach and a court would order the conveyance of the property. Specific performance is available in other cases as well where the court concludes that the payment of money damages would be insufficient to protect the injured party's expectation interest.[25]

The remedy of specific performance is also available under the Uniform Commercial Code where goods are "unique or in other proper circumstances."[26] Unique, one-of-a-kind goods are those that cannot be duplicated in the marketplace. Other circumstances where specific performance might be appropriate would be where damages are difficult to estimate, for example, as in the case of output contracts for a long term, or where an equivalent substitute performance is either unavailable or can be procured only with great inconvenience or hardship.

Injunctions

An injunction is a court order directing a party to perform a certain act—a mandatory injunction—or to refrain from doing a certain act—a prohibitory or negative injunction. In a sense, an order of specific performance is really just a form of a mandatory injunction. A prohibitory injunction, on the other hand, is an order directing the breaching party not to take a certain action that violates the terms of the contract.

---

25. Restatement (Second) of Contracts § 359(1) (1979).

26. U.C.C. § 2–716(1) (2002). The 2003 revision to Article 3 includes several changes to this provision. First, specific performance is no longer designated as a buyer's remedy only. The section heading has been changed from "Buyer's Right to Specific Performance or Replevin" so that it refers to specific performance generally. Official Comment 1(a) to revised § 2–716 states that the change is intended to make it clear that either a buyer or a seller is entitled to specific performance in the proper case and also allows for specific performance in a non-consumer contract where the parties have agreed to that remedy.

The classic case of a negative injunction is *Lumley v. Wagner* [27]in which a famous opera singer, Johanna Wagner, agreed to sing exclusively for Benjamin Lumley, for a three-month period. When another opera company persuaded her to break her contract with Lumley and sing for them instead, Lumley sought and obtained an injunction restraining her from appearing at that concert or any other concert during her contract period with him. The court recognized that while it could not compel her to sing for Lumley, it could "compel her to abstain from the commission of an act which she has bound herself not to do, and thus possibly cause her to fulfil[sic] her engagement."[28]

As is the case with specific performance, a court will not grant injunctive relief to a party where money damages would be adequate. A common example of where injunctive relief is sought as a remedy is in the case of post-employment restraints. In such cases, the employee promises the employer not to compete with the employer after the employment ends. Such restrictive covenants are enforced in cases where the employee's services are special, unique, or extraordinary either because of a special skill or talent or because of special knowledge the employee has gained by working for the employer. Here, the award of money damages would not make the employer whole since the employee could do more harm to the employer's business interests due to the loss of confidential trade secrets or customer lists than could be measured in monetary terms alone. Consequently, an injunction is granted to enforce the non-compete agreement by enjoining the employee from working for a competitor.[29]

---

27. 42 Eng. Rep. 687 (1852).

28. *Id.* at 693.

29. Another common situation where courts enforce agreements in restraints on trade occurs with the sale of businesses. Here the buyer has a need to protect the value of the good will purchased with the business. Without such an agreement, the seller could open a competing enterprise with the one she has just sold.

REVIEW OF REMEDIES UNDER THE UCC

> UCC 1-106, 2-718, 2-719

According to UCC 1–106(1), remedies are to be "liberally administered to the end that the aggrieved party may be put in as good a position as if the other party had fully performed[.]"[30] The basic damage philosophy of the Code is to put the plaintiff in the same economic position performance would have and not in a better one.

Article 2 organizes its statutory formulas for calculating damages into seller's remedies for the buyer's breach and buyer's remedies for the seller's breach. We'll begin by examining the remedies available to the seller of goods when the buyer breaches and then we'll consider the remedies available to the aggrieved buyer when the seller breaches.

You will see as we review available remedies, the Code provides sellers and buyers with a wide range of parallel remedies. The chart below summarizes the functional equivalents between seller's and buyer's remedies.

Parallels between Seller's and Buyer's Remedies

Buyer	Seller	Remedy
2–711	2–703	List of Remedies in General
2–716	2–709	Buyer: right to specific performance or replevin Seller: action for price
2–712	2–706	Buyer: cover; procurement of substitute goods Seller: resale of the goods

---

30. U.C.C. § 1–106(1) (2004). U.C.C. § 1–106 is renumbered § 1–305(a) in revised Article 1.

Buyer	Seller	Remedy
2–713	2–708	Buyer: damages for non-delivery or repudiation Seller: damages for non-acceptance or repudiation
2–715	2–710	Buyer: Incidental and consequential damages Seller: Incidental damages (in revised Article 2, a seller's right to consequential damages is expressly recognized)

Seller's Remedies

UCC 2-703, 2-706, 2-708,
2-709, 2-710

A buyer breaches a sales contract when she wrongfully rejects goods, wrongfully revokes acceptance of goods, fails to make a payment when due, or repudiates with respect to a part or the whole contract. Repudiation is treated separately in Chapter 10 and will not be discussed here.

The seller has four basic damage remedies available to measure the value of the buyer's promised performance: first, bring an action for the price; second, resell the goods and recover the difference between the contract price and the substitute sale; third, seek damages based on the market price of the goods; and fourth, seek damages based on lost profits. As usual, the seller's decision as to which remedy to pursue will depend on the nature of the breach and the actions it takes in response. The following discussion outlines some of the possibilities.

Assuming there has been a breach, the seller may be able to pursue an action for the price under UCC 2–709. When the buyer fails to pay the price as it becomes due, the seller may recover the price of goods accepted. If, however, the buyer has breached before accepting the goods or incurring the risk of loss, the seller is entitled to recover the price only "if the seller is unable after reasonable effort to resell them at a reasonable price or the circumstances reasonably indicate that such effort will be unavailing."[31]

If the seller cannot sue for the price, it may be possible for the seller to seek recovery of damages based on a resale or "substitute transaction" under UCC 2–706. This remedy is similar to the buyer's remedy of cover. It allows the seller to resell the goods and recover the difference between the resale price and the contract price together with any incidental damages under UCC 2–710,[32] but less expenses as a consequence of the buyer's breach.[33] This option presumes that the seller still has the goods in her possession. Further, if the seller makes a profit upon resale, it has no obligation to give it to the buyer.[34]

Whether the goods have been resold or not, the seller has the option to seek damages for "non-acceptance or repudiation" under UCC 2–708.[35] Under subsection (1), the seller can measure its damages by using the contract-market price formula: the difference between the market price at the time and place for tender and the unpaid contract price. Essentially, this provision allows for the seller's recovery based on a hypothetical resale instead of an actual resale.

UCC 2–708(2)[36] offers the seller a unique remedy: recovery of its "lost profits" if the measure of damages provided in UCC 2–706

---

31. U.C.C. § 2–709(1)(b) (2004). There are no significant changes to this section in the 2003 revision of Article 2 except to recognize that a seller may obtain consequential damages.

32. *See* U.C.C. § 2–710 (2004). The 2003 revision to the Code adds subsection (2) to U.C.C. § 2–710 to provide specifically for seller's right to recover consequential damages. The right is limited, however, to commercial transactions and precludes recovery against a consumer. The section defines consequential damages in similar terms to those used for a buyer in § 2–715.

33. U.C.C. § 2–706(1) (2004). Section 2–706 has not significantly changed in the 2003 revision of Article 2 except to recognize that a seller may obtain consequential damages.

34. *Id.* § 2–706(6).

35. U.C.C. § 2–708 (1) (2004). Section 2–708 has not changed significantly in the 2003 revision of Article 2 except to recognize that a seller may obtain consequential damages where appropriate.

36. *Id.* § 2–708(2). The 2003 revision of U.C.C. § 2–708(2) clarifies that when the resale remedy under § 2–706 is inadequate, lost profits can also be claimed under this section.

or UCC 2–708(1) is inadequate to put the seller in as good a position as performance would have done. A lost volume seller is one with a predictable and finite number of customers and has the capacity to sell to all new buyers or to make the one additional sale represented by the resale after the breach. For such a seller who would have made the post-breach resale anyway, damages measured by the difference between the contract price and the market price do not put the seller in as good a position as it would have been in had the buyer performed because the breach cost the seller a profit. Recovery of lost profits by a lost volume seller is predicated not only on the seller's ability to produce the additional units it would have had to produce but for the breach, but also on the profitability of the production of the extra unit.

Under UCC 2–710, an aggrieved seller is entitled to recover its incidental damages, i.e., those "commercially reasonable charges, expenses or commissions incurred in stopping delivery, in the transportation, care and custody of goods after the buyer's breach, in connection with return or resale of the goods or otherwise resulting from the breach."[37] Noticeably absent is the seller's right to recover consequential damages. The question is whether the seller is entitled to recover such damages when they are not specified for the seller and they are specifically granted to the buyer under section 2–715. Section 1–106(1) states that consequential damages or other such damages are not available unless they are specifically provided for "in this Act or by other rule of law."[38] By reading the specific grant in section 2–715 together with the restriction in section 1–106, courts have found that the Code's drafters did not intend to give sellers consequential damages.[39]

However, according to White and Summers, sellers should be able to recover consequential damages where appropriate, using sections 1–106 and 1–103 to support this result.[40] Section 1–103 incorporates general rules of contract law. As we have seen, section

---

37. U.C.C. § 2–710 (2004). U.C.C. § 2–710 is unchanged in the 2003 revision.

38. U.C.C. § 1–106(1).

39. James J. White & Robert S. Summers,

Uniform Commercial Code, § 7–16(b) (5th ed. 2000). *See also id.*, at § 7.16 n.8.

40. *Id.* § 716.

1–106 allows recovery of consequential damages if they are authorized by this act or "by other rule of law." General contract law provides for such recovery by a seller under Restatement Second § 347(b) where any "injured party" may recover "any other loss, including incidental or consequential loss, caused by the breach[.]"[41] According to comment b, the terms used to describe the type of loss, such as "incidental" or "consequential," are not "controlling," and that "the general principle is that all losses, however described, are recoverable."[42]

This conflict is resolved in the 2003 amendments to the Code which specifically allow a seller to recovery consequential damages in non-consumer contracts.

Buyer's Remedies

> UCC 2-711, 2-712, 2-713, 2-714,
> 2-715

A seller breaches when she repudiates, fails to deliver, or tenders non-conforming goods. When there has been a delivery of non-conforming goods, the buyer may rightfully reject or revoke acceptance.[43] Once again, repudiation is treated separately in Chapter 10 and will not be discussed here.

Typically, upon breach by the seller, the buyer is most concerned with replacing the goods or compelling the seller to perform. Accordingly, if the goods have not been tendered, the buyer's most critical remedies will be specific performance or cover and the recovery of incidental and consequential damages. Like the common law, the remedy of specific performance is an exceptional remedy and limited to cases where the goods are unique or in other circumstances the court deems proper.

Cover and Market Damages

Cover is one of the buyer's most important remedies. Under UCC 2–712(1), a buyer may " 'cover' by making in good faith and

---

41. Restatement (Second) of Contracts   **43.** U.C.C. § 2–711 (2004).
§ 347(b).

42. *Id.* § 347 cmt. b.

without unreasonable delay any reasonable purchase of or contract to purchase goods in substitution for those due from the seller."[44] If appropriate, the buyer may recover from the seller as damages the difference between the cost of cover and the contract price together with any incidental or consequential damages, less expenses saved as a result of seller's breach.[45]

The buyer is not obligated to seek cover but may choose instead a market measure of damages under UCC 2–713.[46] In this case, the measure of damages is the difference between the market price when the buyer learned of the breach and the contract price together with any incidental or consequential damages but less expenses saved as a result of the breach. Official Comment 5 makes clear that this remedy is an alternative to cover and applies only when the buyer has not covered.

Warranty—Accepting Non–Conforming Goods

In some cases, the buyer accepts non-conforming goods. Provided that the buyer provides timely notice, she may claim damages for the seller's breach under a warranty theory. Under UCC 2–714(2), the "measure of damages for breach of warranty is the difference at the time and place of acceptance between the value of the goods accepted and the value they would have had if they had been as warranted[.]"[47] The buyer may also recover incidental and consequential damages if appropriate.

Consequential and Incidental Damages

In some cases, a party will suffer damages beyond those that are a direct result of the breach. Here, the usual damages measured by the contract price and either the market price or the cost of cover will be insufficient compensation. In this case, the buyer will seek to recover its consequential or incidental damages or both.

---

44. U.C.C. § 2–712(1) (2004).

45. *Id.* § 2–712(2). Section 2–712 has not changed significantly in the 2003 revision of Article 2.

46. U.C.C. § 2–713 (2004). U.C.C. § 2–713 has not changed significantly in the 2003 revision of Article 2; one change is that it now uses the same standard for determining market price for both buyers and sellers—the time and place for tender.

47. U.C.C. § 2–714 (2004). U.C.C. § 2–714 has not changed significantly in the 2003 revision of Article 2.

Recovery of consequential damages is subject to the same limitations we discussed with respect to the common law: the loss must result from or be caused by the breach; the loss must result "from general or particular requirements and needs" of the buyer "of which the seller at the time of contracting had reason to know"; the loss must be one "which could not reasonably be prevented by cover or otherwise";[48] the loss must be proved with reasonable certainty.

Incidental damages are recoverable as well. They are those damages the buyer incurs as a result of dealing with the breach such as expenses "reasonably incurred in inspection, receipt, transportation and care and custody of goods rightfully rejected" as well as any reasonable charges or expenses in connection "with effecting cover and any other reasonable expense incident to the delay or other breach."[49]

Liquidated Damages

The Code is virtually identical to the common law with respect to the right of the parties to agree to damages in the event of breach. They are free to limit or modify remedies to suit their particular needs as long as "there be at least a fair quantum of remedy for breach of the obligations or duties outlined in the contract."[50] The parties may agree to liquidated damages but "only at an amount which is reasonable in the light of the anticipated or actual harm caused by the breach[.]"[51] Like the common law, an unreasonably large amount of liquidated damages would be void as a penalty. In addition to defining damages, the parties may agree to limit to limit the buyer's remedies to return of the goods and repayment of the price or to repair and replacement of the

---

48. U.C.C. § 2–715(2)(a) (2004).

49. U.C.C § 2–715(1) (2004). This section is unchanged in the 2003 revision of Article 2.

50. U.C.C. § 2–719 cmt. 1 (2004). Section 2–719 is unchanged in the 2003 revision of Article 2.

51. U.C.C. § 2–718(1) (2004). The 2003 revision to Article 2 limits the requirement that the anticipated or actual harm be difficult to prove or that an adequate remedy might not otherwise be available to cases of consumer contracts. Under revised § 2–718, the only question in a non-consumer contract is whether the pre-agreed amount was reasonable in view of the anticipated loss.

non-conforming goods.[52] They may also agree to limit or exclude consequential damages "unless the limitation or exclusion is unconscionable."[53] In this case, the limiting clause is "subject to deletion" and the remedies generally available under the Code "are applicable as if the stricken clause had never existed."[54]

Although the Code is flexible in allowing parties to provide their own remedial scheme, it recognizes the possibility that it might result in the case where a party is deprived of the substantial value of its bargain. In such a case where "circumstances cause an exclusive or limited remedy to fail of its essential purpose," a party may have "remedy as provided in this Act."[55]

REMEDIES CHECKLIST

Here is a checklist for analyzing problems presenting questions regarding remedies. As always when beginning a contracts problem analysis, you must begin by asking whether the transaction involves the sale of goods or the common law. If the transaction involves the sale of goods, then Article 2 and the Code's provisions apply. Proceed to Section II. If the common law controls, proceed with Section I.

I. Common Law

Assuming that the threshold question of a breach of a valid contract has been established, the next question is, "what is the appropriate remedy and damages?"

A. **Expectation Damages**— can the injured party recover the "benefit of her bargain"? Expectation damages put the non-breaching party in as good a position as she would have been in had the contract been performed. If the breach was the cause-in-fact of the party's loss, then she is entitled to recover expectation damages subject to certain limitation. Consider the following:

---

52. *See* U.C.C § 2–719(1)(a).

53. *Id.* § 2–713(3).

54. *Id.* § 2–719 cmt. 1.

55. *Id.* § 2–719(2).

1. **Foreseeability**—were the losses caused by the breach reasonably foreseeable at the time of contract by the party in breach?

   a. **Yes.** If so, then continue to the next question.

   b. **No.** If not, then expectation damages are not available but a party may be able to recover reliance damages. Proceed to Part I.B.

2. **Certainty**—can the non-breaching party establish the amount of the loss with "reasonable certainty"?

   a. **Yes.** If so, then continue to the next question.

   b. **No.** If the losses are too speculative and cannot be calculated with reasonable certainty, then they are not recoverable. For example, the lost profits of a new business may be very difficult to calculate since there is no past history of operations. However, if a party cannot recover expectation damages, she may be able to recover reliance damages. Proceed to Part I.B.

3. **Mitigation/Avoidability**—did the non-breaching party make reasonable and appropriate efforts after the breach to avoid unnecessary damages?

   a. **No.** If not, the injured party is not entitled to any damages which she could have reasonably avoided.

   b. **Yes.** If so, and the answer to all the previous questions was also "yes," then the party may recover expectation damages. Proceed to the next question for measuring this amount.

4. **Measuring Expectation Damages**—what is the measure of a party's expectation interest? There are various ways to measure a party's expectation damages; any formula is only a set of principles to follow. *The basic guideline is to determine the difference between what the injured party reasonably expected to receive under the contract and what she actually received.*

   a. **When Neither Party Has Performed**—has a party breached by failing to perform and the aggrieved party has withheld her own performance? If so, then one of the following formulations may be appropriate in calculating damages:

i. **Substitute Performance/Transaction**—has the aggrieved party entered into a substitute or "cover" performance or would be entitled to do so?

- **Yes.** If so, then she is entitled to sue for loss based on the difference between the contract price and the substitute performance or its market price, subject to the duty to mitigate in making a reasonable substitute transaction.

- **No.** This measure is either not possible or does not adequately compensate the plaintiff's loss. Proceed to the next question.

ii. **Lost Income**—has the breach resulted in lost income? If so, then ask the following:

- **Substitute Performance Impossible?** If the contract was for services and there was no cost to the plaintiff other than her services and she was not able to secure a substitute performance, then she will have lost her entire expectation interest in the event of breach. She would be entitled to recover the full amount due under the contract.

- **Lost Income but also Savings?** If the breach resulted in lost income but also saved the plaintiff costs in not having to perform, then damages are measured by deducting the savings from the expected earnings. With respect to what is deductible, consider:

    — **Direct or Variable Costs**—did the plaintiff incur costs solely for the purpose of performing the contract? If so, then they would be saved by the breach and should be deducted from gains to measure the true expectation interest. However, there are exceptions. Ask:

    — Has the plaintiff entered into another contract in reliance on the contract with the defendant which cannot be canceled without liability? If so, then such costs incurred as a result of the defendant's breach would not be deducted.

— **Fixed or Overhead Costs**—does the plaintiff have costs or expenditures (i.e., rent) which have to be paid whether or not she performed this contract? If so, then such costs would have to be paid whether or not she performed the contract. They are the fixed costs of doing business and are not saved by virtue of the breach. They are not deducted from the damages.

- **Consequential Damages?** Did the plaintiff incur losses beyond those which generally arise from the breach?

  — **Yes.** If so, and such losses were foreseeable at the time of contract to the breaching party as a consequence of her breach, then such damages are recoverable.

  — **No.** Such damages were not foreseeable and therefore are not recoverable.

- **Incidental Damages?** Did the plaintiff incur incidental damages associated with the breach such as packing, shipping, or other such costs?

  — **Yes.** If so, such damages are recoverable.

  — **No.** If not, they are not recoverable.

b. **Part Performance**—has a party breached by rendering an incomplete or defective performance?

   i. **Substantial Performance**—has there been a trivial and innocent breach such that the cost of redoing the performance would be disproportionate to the actual loss suffered by the promisee and impose an unfair forfeiture on the breaching party?

   - **Yes.** If so, then the proper measure of damages is the **diminution in value** which is the "difference in value" between what was promised and what was received.

   - **No.** If not, proceed to the next question.

   ii. **Cost of Completion or Repair**—has there been a breach resulting in defective or unfinished construction and the loss in value is not proved with reasonable certainty? If so, then the owner is not limited to the diminution in value but may recover the cost to complete or repair the defective performance unless such damages would be considered "economic waste." Economic waste occurs when the cost to remedy the defective performance would be disproportionate to the probable loss in value to the injured party.

B. **Reliance Damages**—can the injured party recover damages based on her reliance interest? Has the promisee changed position to her detriment in reliance on the contract?

 1. **Yes.** If so, the injured party may recover such damages as are necessary to restore her to the *status quo ante*—the position she would have been in had no contract been made—but they may not exceed the full contract price. This includes "expenditures made in preparation for performance or in performance, less any loss that the party in breach can prove with reasonable certainty the injured party would have suffered had the contract been performed." R2d § 349.

 2. **No.** If not, then reliance damages are not available. Proceed to the next question.

C. **Restitution Damages**—can a party with a claim for damages recover in restitution as an alternative remedy? Has one party obtained a benefit at the other party's expense?

 1. **No.** If not, then restitutionary damages are not available.

 2. **Yes.** If so, then ask, "would it be unfair for the recipient to retain that benefit without compensating the other party?"

  a. **No.** If not, then restitutionary damages are not available.

  b. **Yes.** If so, then the party has been unjustly enriched and plaintiff is entitled to restitution. Proceed to the next question for measuring this amount.

 3. **Measuring the Restitution Interest**—what is the measure of a party's restitution interest? Consider the following:

    a.   **Sum of Money?** If a sum of money is awarded to protect a party's restitution interest, it may as justice requires be measured by the market value of the services provided (*quantum meruit*) or the extent to which the other party's property has been increased in value. R2d § 371.

    b.   **Specific Restitution?** If the benefit is something that can be returned to the injured party, then a court will grant specific restitution to a party who is entitled to restitution. Specific restitution may be appropriate where the return promise is to do something other than to pay money, such as in contracts to transfer land. R2d § 372 cmt.b.

D. Agreed Remedies—have the parties set their own remedies in the event of a breach?

    1. Liquidated Damages—is there a liquidated damages provision in the agreement in which the parties have set an amount or identified a formula to determine damages in the event of a breach?

        a.   **No.** If the parties did not include such a provision, then liquidated damages are not available.

        b.   **Yes.** If so, then ask, "was the amount set by the parties reasonable in light of the anticipated or actual loss caused by the breach"? In answering this question, consider two factors: the difficulty of proving the loss and the reasonableness of the estimated amount of loss:

            i.   **Yes.** If so, then the provision is enforceable and damages are limited to the sum stated.

            ii.   **No.** If not, the provision is unenforceable because the provision was either punitive in relation to the loss to be suffered and/or the loss was one that was possible of calculation and a liquidated damages provision was not necessary.

    2. Limited Remedies—have the parties put a cap on damages or otherwise specified the types of remedies that are available, for example, precluding the recovery of consequential damages?

        a.   **Yes.** If so, then a term limiting damages is enforceable unless it is unconscionable.

b. **No.** If the parties did not include such a provision, then the aggrieved party has a right to all available remedies.

E. **Equitable Remedies**—will the award of money damages not compensate the aggrieved party for its loss? If so, the following may be available:

1. **Specific Performance**—is the plaintiff entitled to a court order commanding the defendant to perform the contract as promised? If so, then the court would order a mandatory injunction. In answering this question, consider the following:

   a. **Is a Substitute Available?** If the contract is for something unique such as the sale of land or a patent or copyright or where the subject of the contract involves matters of taste or heirlooms, then no substitute is available to compensate the aggrieved party and specific performance is the only way to do so.

   b. **Are the Contract Terms Definite and Certain?** The terms of the contract must be sufficiently definite to allow the court to determine with certainty what it must order each party to do to carry out the agreement.

   c. **Is Enforcement Feasible?** Specific performance will not be granted where the burdens on enforcement or supervision of the order "would be disproportionate to the advantages to be gained."[56] For example, the difficulty of judging the quality of a performance or supervising a performance over an extended period of time.

   d. **Is the Breaching Party Insolvent?** If the breaching party is insolvent and the contract is unperformed on both sides and provides for a fair exchange, then a court might grant specific performance.[57]

   e. **Is it a Personal Service Contract?** A court will not grant an order requiring a service that is personal in nature due to difficulties in enforcement, supervision and evaluation. If specific performance is denied, injunctive relief might be granted. Proceed to Part I.C.2.b.

---

56. Farnsworth, *Contracts* at § 12.7.   **57.** *Id.* at § 12.6.

2. **Injunctive Relief**—is the plaintiff entitled to a court order for an injunction?

    a. **Mandatory Injunction**—is the plaintiff entitled to compel the defendant to render the performance promised in the contract? This is really just a form of specific performance. If the answer is "yes" to sub-questions a–d in Part 1.E.1, then a mandatory injunction is appropriate.

    b. **Prohibitory Injunction**—is the plaintiff entitled to prohibit the defendant from performing a specified act? If an injunction would provide substantial protection to the injured party without offending the policies against requiring specific performance, then the court will order a "negative injunction." For example, this would be the remedy in the case of a restrictive covenant where the employee possesses unique skills or trade secrets—the employee would be "enjoined" from working for the competitor.

3. **Other Relief**—is the injured party entitled to any other relief? Was the grant of specific performance or injunctive relief sufficient? Even if a court awards specific performance, it may also award money damages if the performance is not identical to what was promised or there are damages resulting from a delay in rendering the ordered performance.[58]

II. Sale of Goods

A. Seller's Remedies—what is necessary to put the aggrieved seller in as good a position as if the buyer had fully performed?

1. **Breach**—has the buyer breached her obligations under the sales contract in one of the following ways:

    a. Wrongfully rejected the goods?

    b. Wrongfully revoked acceptance of the goods?

    c. Failed to make a payment due on or before delivery?

If the answer is "yes" to any of the above, then there has been a breach and the seller is entitled to seek a remedy.

---

58. Farnsworth, *Contracts*, at § 12.5.

2. **Action for the Price**—should the seller pursue an action for the price under UCC 2–709?

   a. **Goods Accepted?** Has the buyer failed to pay the price when it became due? If so, the seller may recover the price of goods accepted.

   b. **Breach before Acceptance?** Has the buyer breached before accepting the goods or incurring the risk of loss? If so, the seller is entitled to recover the price only "if the seller is unable after reasonable effort to resell them at a reasonable price or the circumstances reasonably indicate that such an effort will be unavailing." UCC 2–709(b).

3. **Resale of the Goods**—should the seller seek recovery of damages based upon a resale of the goods under UCC 2–706?

   a. **Yes.** If the seller has the goods in her possession, then she can resell them and recover the difference between the resale price and the contract price together with any incidental damages but less expenses saved as a consequence of the buyer's breach.

   b. **No.** This measure of damages would be inadequate to put the seller in as good a position as performance would have done. Proceed to Part II. A.5.

4. **"Hypothetical Resale"**—can the seller recover the difference between the market price and the contract price together with any incidental damages but less expenses saved in consequence of the buyer's breach?

   a. **Yes.** This is an alternative to an actual resale and measures loss by the difference between the market price and the contract price. This may be a viable choice if the seller chooses not to resell the goods upon the buyer's breach.

   b. **No.** This measure of damages would be inadequate to put the seller in as good a position as performance would have done. Proceed to the next question.

5. **Lost Volume Seller**—is the measure of damages through resale or the difference between the market price and the unpaid contract price inadequate to put the seller in as good a position as performance would have done? If so, the seller is a

lost volume seller and entitled to the profit from the post-breach resale. The second sale is not a "substitute" for the first sale because even though the seller lost the first sale, it would have made the second sale anyway.

6. **Incidental Damages**—did the buyer incur incidental damages associated with the breach such as packing, shipping, or other such costs?

   a. **Yes.** If so, such damages are recoverable.

   b. **No.** If not, they are not recoverable.

B. **Buyer's Remedies**—what is necessary to put the aggrieved buyer in as good a position as if the seller had fully performed?

   1. **Breach**—has the seller breached her obligations under the sales contract by failing to deliver the goods, tendering non-conforming goods or goods with a latent defect? Under these circumstances, the buyer is entitled to recover damages based on the lost value of the goods. Proceed to the next question.

   2. **Specific Performance**—are the promised goods unique such that money damages cannot adequately compensate the buyer?

      a. **Yes.** If so, then the buyer should seek specific performance under UCC 2–716. Generally, specific performance is available if the goods are unique in some way, if damages are difficult to estimate as in the case of output contracts for a long term, or where an equivalent substitute performance is either unavailable or can be procured only with great inconvenience or hardship.

      b. **No.** If not, then proceed to the next question.

   3. **Cover**—can the buyer purchase substitute goods? Ask the following:

      • Has the seller failed to make delivery or repudiated?

      • Has the buyer rightfully rejected the goods?

      • Has the buyer justifiably revoked acceptance?

      a. **Yes.** If the answer is "yes" to any of the above, then the buyer can recover the difference between the cost of the substitute goods and the original contract price, plus any incidental or consequential damages, but less expenses saved as a result of seller's breach. If the buyer chooses not to cover, she can use the market price as the basis of recovery. Proceed to the next question.

b. **No.** If none of the above are applicable, then cover is not available.

4. **"Hypothetical Repurchase"**—can the buyer recover damages based on the market price?

a. **Yes.** This option is available "only when and to the extent that the buyer has not covered." UCC 2–713 cmt. 5. The buyer may recover the difference between the market price at the time the buyer learned of the breach and the contract price together with any incidental and consequential damages but less expenses saved in consequence of seller's breach.

b. **No,** the buyer is not entitled to this remedy if she can cover.[59]

5. **Breach of Warranty**—did the buyer accept the goods despite a breach of warranty?

a. **Yes.** If so, then she is entitled to damages based on the difference in value between the goods as accepted and as warranted.

b. **No.**

6. **Consequential Damages**—did the buyer incur losses beyond those which generally arise as a consequence of the breach such as lost profits? Consider the following:

a. **Reason to Know**—did the loss result from general or particular requirements and needs of which the seller at the time of contracting had reason to know? UCC 2–715(2)(a).

---

59. Farnsworth, *Contracts*, at § 12.11 n.16. As Professor Farnsworth explains, although "UCC 2–713 cmt. 3 says that the buyer 'is always free to choose' between cover and damages based on market price, this appears to be said in the context of whether the buyer can recover damages based on market price after failing to cover, not of whether the buyer can recover such damages after covering."

   b. **Preventable**—was the loss one which could not reasonably be prevented by cover or otherwise? UCC 2–715(2)(a).

   c. **Reasonable Certainty**—has the buyer proven the type and amount of loss with reasonable certainty?

   d. **Causation**—with respect to a breach of warranty claim, was the breach the substantial cause in fact of the loss? UCC 2–715(2(b).

If the answer is "yes" to all of the above, then the buyer is entitled to recover consequential damages.

7. **Incidental Damages**—has the buyer reasonably incurred expenses in the inspection, receipt, transportation, and care and custody of goods rightfully rejected? UCC 2–715(1).

   a. **Yes.** If so, any such reasonable commercial "charges, expenses or commissions in connection with effecting cover and any other reasonable expense incident to the delay or other breach" are recoverable as incidental damages.

   b. **No.** If not, they are not recoverable.

ILLUSTRATIVE PROBLEMS

Consider the following problems. Here is an opportunity to apply the checklist to resolve remedies questions.

■ PROBLEM 12.1 ■

In October, Jill agreed to build an addition to Meredith's store so she would have space to add a whole new line of shoes, handbags, and accessories. Meredith also wanted Jill to do some remodeling in the existing store because she wanted it to blend with the new addition. Meredith's store was very successful and carried only the trendiest merchandise. Business had grown tremendously after it was reported that a celebrity stylist shopped there to dress the characters on "Gossip Girl," a hugely popular television series. Meredith was certain that by enlarging the store and adding accessories, the store would be even more successful.

The contract between Jill and Meredith provided, in relevant part, that the addition would have a hardwood floor and that the remodeling portion would include re-carpeting and repainting the entire store. Meredith also wanted wood molding trim on the ceilings to match the hardwood floors. Jill said it would be no trouble to cut the strips from the same wood used on the floor and installation would be very simple to do after the painting had been completed. Meredith selected the flooring, cabinetry, and lighting for the addition and the carpeting and paint color for the remodeling. During negotiations, Meredith told Jill that she needed the work to be completed by Wednesday, November 25, which was the day before Thanksgiving. Meredith wanted the store ready for a grand re-opening on "Black Friday" so she could be fully operational during the entire Christmas selling season. Jill promised that she would have the work completed on time.

After full and fair negotiations, Jill and Meredith entered into a written contract. The contract price was $200,000, with $150,000 for the addition and $50,000 for the remodeling of the existing store. Meredith was to pay $50,000 upon execution of the contract and the balance upon completion of the project. Meredith paid Jill $50,000 upon signing the contract. Among other things, the agreement contained the following provisions in numbered paragraphs:

10.   The specifications for the hardwood floor in the store addition "shall be classified clear grade, free of all defects with varying natural color, with no knots except small pin knots of the grade known as American Hardwood."

11.   In the event that the contractor fails to complete all necessary work by Wednesday, November 25, the day before Thanksgiving, she will be liable for damages in the amount of $1000 per day until the work is completed in accordance with the contract.

On November 20, Jill notified Meredith that the project was completed. When Meredith inspected the work, she realized that Jill had not installed the clear grade flooring she had requested. Meredith could detect slight variations in the wood coloring and occasional light markings. An untrained eye would not be able to detect these very slight imperfections, but Meredith was a perfectionist. Jill also forgot to install the wood molding trim although she had completed the rest of the installation and remodeling which was the substantial portion of the job. The rest of the work, which included the re-carpeting and repainting was completed in full accordance with the contract's specifications.

Meredith immediately summoned Jill and demanded that she remove the flooring and replace it. Jill said that the failure to install the hardwood floor as specified was purely innocent and the grade she installed was substantially equivalent to the clear grade Meredith had requested. Jill claimed that the value of the addition to her store was unchanged by the error but Meredith still objected to the slight variations in the wood coloring. She also noted Jill's failure to install the wood molding trim on the ceiling.

Jill said that it would cost about $150,000 to rip up and replace the floor because the flooring was the most expensive and labor-intensive part of the entire job. She said that she would immediately put up the wood trim which was simply an innocent oversight. Also, if she had to rip up and replace the flooring, it would delay the store's re-opening by three weeks, which would be almost the entire Christmas selling season. Jill installed the wood trim moldings by Monday, November 23. When she asked Meredith for the $100,000 balance of the contract price, she refused to pay. Instead, she said that Jill had breached the contract by not providing the proper flooring and that she was bringing suit for breach of contract and $1000 per day in damages pursuant to paragraph 11 of the contract.

Jill contacts you to represent her in this action. What result?

Analysis

Jill committed a breach of contract by rendering a defective performance when she installed the incorrect flooring. Even Jill admits that the wood floor that she installed was not the clear grade hardwood required by the contract. The question, however, is whether Meredith is entitled to the difference in value between what was promised and what was received, or the cost to repair the defective performance.

In this case, Jill can claim that she rendered substantial performance and that the breach was innocent and trivial. While it is true that the difference in flooring was noticeable to Meredith and she has a right to receive what she contracted for, in this case doing so would result in an unfair forfeiture for Jill. Jill completed the entire addition to the store and the remodeling in full compliance with the contract's specifications. Jill's breach in installing the incorrect flooring was not material because it was "purely innocent," the grade she installed was substantially equivalent to the clear grade she should have installed, and the value of the addition to Meredith's store was "unchanged" by the error. Further, as soon as she realized that she had forgotten to mount the wood moldings, she immediately did so.

If Jill were required to rip out and replace the flooring, it would be a tremendous forfeiture for her because it would cost $150,000 to do so and there would be no difference in value to Meredith's store. The entire cost of the job was only $200,000 so to expend $150,000 to redo that which was already done would be a pure economic waste. Since the cost of redoing the performance would be disproportionate to the actual loss suffered by the promisee (which was nominal at most) and would impose an unfair forfeiture on the breaching party, it is unlikely that the court would require Jill to take this action. Instead, it is more likely that the court would find that the proper measure of damages would be difference in value, if any, between the store with the hardwood floor as promised and its value with the one that was installed.

Further, since it is unlikely that a court would compel Jill to specifically perform by replacing the wood flooring, Meredith would not be entitled to receive the liquidated damages award of $1000 per day. Jill completed the addition and renovation by Monday, November 23 when she installed the wood trim molding, which was two days before the contract's required completion date of November 25. Consequently, the store was ready for the public on "Black Friday," which was Meredith's goal in redoing the store.

Assuming, however, that the court found that Meredith was entitled to receive the "benefit of her bargain"—which would require the precise wood flooring that she contracted for—then it would not be possible to have it installed in time to meet the contract deadline. While it is unlikely that a court would order Jill to render the performance because it would be difficult to supervise or evaluate such a performance and now personal feelings are involved, another contractor could be hired and Jill would be liable for the costs involved in replacing the floor. She would also be liable for the $1000 per day in damages pursuant to paragraph 11 of the contract.

The parties included a liquidated damages provision in their contract to specify what the damages would be in the event of a breach. Parties are entitled to set an amount for damages as long as that amount is reasonable in light of the anticipated loss caused by the breach. However, if the agreed-to amount is significantly larger than necessary to compensate the injured party for its loss, a court will consider the provision to be punitive in nature and not enforce it. In this case, it is possible that the $1000 per day in damages is reasonable because the facts indicate that the store was successful and did a great deal of business. It is very likely that daily sales receipts would be in excess of $1000 per day so that this amount would be deemed reasonable in light of the anticipated loss. Finally, since this was an established business, it would be easy enough to verify whether this amount was a typical day's sales receipts. If so, then the court would surely enforce the provision.

■ PROBLEM 12.2 ■

On June 1, Jessica contracts with Molly to be her production assistant for $75,000 on a new television series with work to begin on September 1. The contract is for six months. Thrilled to have this wonderful opportunity to work with Jessica, Molly turns down another offer she received for an internship in educational television for $50,000 for the same six month period. This job was in the same building where Molly will work with Jessica.

On August 15, Jessica calls Molly and tells her that she won't be needing her services because plans for the new series have fallen through. Molly is devastated. She reasonably spends $500 in fees attempting to find other suitable employment through appropriate agencies, but with no luck. Finally, she finds another job working at a local television station but it only pays $25,000 for the same six month period. Apparently, all the production jobs are taken because it is so late in the season. Fortunately, Molly saves on the transportation costs of $200 per month she would have had to spend to commute to her job with Jessica because this job is near her home. Molly brings suit against Jessica for breach of contract. What result?

Analysis

As the injured party, Molly is entitled to recover damages based on her actual loss caused by the breach. Molly expected to earn $75,000 for working for six months and will now earn only $25,000. Unfortunately, the only suitable job she could find still results in a loss of $50,000 in expected earnings. If she brings a claim based on her expectation interest, Molly is entitled to receive the benefit of her bargain less any expenses saved by the breach. Here, she would save $200 per month for six months by not having to commute to her job with Jessica for a total of $1200. This amount would be deducted from her recovery. However, she would be entitled to recover the $500 she spent in trying to find another job. This would be considered an incidental expense incurred as a result of the breach. This claim would amount to $49,300.

Molly could consider a claim based on her reliance interest based on the internship offer in educational television for $50,000 that she gave up in reliance on Jessica's offer. Since this job was in the same location as the one she would have had with Jessica, she would have incurred the same transportation expenses, thus requiring a deduction of $200 per month for six months for a total of $48,800.

However, since Molly has a duty to mitigate her losses and she found another suitable job, it is required that she take it—which she did. Therefore, it is likely that a court would award the $50,000 in lost income minus the $1200 saved in transportation costs plus the $500 in incidental damages for a total of $49,300.

■ PROBLEM 12.3 ■

Nathan contracts to remodel the master bathroom in Georgette's house for $50,000 but repudiates the contract after doing part of the work and having been paid $10,000. Other contractors would charge Georgette $30,000 to finish the bathroom but luckily she finds one who is willing to do it for $20,000. Nathan brings suit for damages. What is his likelihood of success?

Analysis

Although Nathan is the breaching party, he may be entitled to recover in restitution if he conferred a benefit on Georgette by virtue of his performance. Georgette expected to pay $50,000 to get her bathroom remodeled. She paid $10,000 to Nathan and then $20,000 to someone else to complete the job for a total expenditure of $30,000. Georgette is required to pay Nathan $20,000 because otherwise she would be unjustly enriched at his expense by this amount because then she would have paid only $30,000 for a bathroom for which she expected to pay $50,000. Even if she had not be so lucky as to find a contractor to complete the work for $20,000 and had to pay $30,000, she would not have been able to save this money—she would have had to pay Nathan $10,000.

■ PROBLEM 12.4 ■

Mike, a farmer who grows strawberries, contracts to sell to Steve, a manufacturer of strawberry preserves, 10,000 bushels of berries at $20 per bushel, for delivery at the end of the growing season in late June. Steve tells Mike at the time of contract, "Your strawberries are the essential ingredient in my strawberry preserves and without them, I would not have been able to get the contract to sell to Aunt Jenny's Jams and Jellies." Apparently, Aunt Jenny is the largest manufacturer and distributor of jams and jellies in the United States. In reliance on the contract, Steve substantially expands his plant and hires additional employees.

On June 1, Mike repudiates the contract, deciding to keep the berries for his own use. Because it is so late in the growing season, Steve finds strawberries from another farmer, Sam, but has to pay $45 per bushel. Also, Steve has to pay $500 in shipping charges because Sam's farm is located much further from Steve's factory than Mike's farm had been.

Two months later, Steve gets an angry phone call from Nancy, the chief operating officer at Aunt Jenny's. Apparently, their customers have been returning the strawberry preserves because they leave a bitter aftertaste. Steve has the returned jars tested and finds that the berries were not as sweet from Sam's farm because the soil was more alkaline than the soil in Mike's farm. Now Aunt Jenny is sending back all the jars she still has on the shelves and expects a refund of $50,000 from Steve. This represents the entire profit that Steve was making from his contract with Aunt Jenny. Steve is also worried that he will lose any future business from Aunt Jenny since she has had such a bad experience with this contract.

Steve has hired you to bring an action against Mike. What is the likely result?

Analysis

Since this contract involves the sale of strawberries, which is a "good" according to the UCC definition where goods are all things which are moveable at the time of identification to the contract and includes growing crops, Article 2 is the applicable law. Mike repudiated the contract when he decided to keep the strawberries for himself and not deliver them to Steve. Typically upon breach by the seller, the buyer is most concerned with replacing the goods, as Steve was in this case since he had a factory and employees ready to process the strawberries. He was entitled to seek cover under UCC 2–712 by going out into the market and making a good faith substitute purchase. He did so by buying strawberries from Sam. Steve is entitled to recover from Mike as damages the difference between the cost of cover and the contract price together with any incidental or consequential damages, less expenses saved as a result of the seller's breach. This means that Steve is entitled to recover the extra $25 per bushel he had to pay to purchase 10,000 bushels from Sam for a total of $250,000. Steve is also entitled to recover as incidental damages the $500 cost of shipping as costs incurred incidental to the breach.

The next question is whether Steve is entitled to recover the $50,000 he has to refund Aunt Jenny. These would be considered consequential damages since they represent losses suffered by the non-breaching party beyond the mere loss in value of the promised performance. If such losses were foreseeable at the time of contract to the breaching party as a consequence of her breach, then such damages are recoverable. Here, Mike knew that Steve had a contract with Aunt Jenny for using Mike's strawberries since Steve told him at the time of contract that, "your strawberries are the essential ingredient in my strawberry preserves and without them, I would not have been able to get the contract to sell to Aunt Jenny's Jams and Jellies." Consequently, Mike would be liable for this loss. While Steve tried to prevent the loss by covering with strawberries from another farmer, the type of loss which he sustained was not preventable by cover since the flavor of the berries was different based on the different soil content. Mike cannot escape liability for Steve's additional $50,000 loss in profit.

Arguably, Steve might have a claim based on a loss of future business with Aunt Jenny since she was so dissatisfied with his performance on this contract and it was due to Mike's breach. However, at this point, it might not be possible to calculate with reasonable certainty the value of a lost opportunity to sell to Aunt Jenny. Steve had no prior business dealings with the company and we have no facts to indicate his success with other companies of similar size and reputation. Without additional facts, the loss would be too speculative on which to base a recovery.

POINTS TO REMEMBER

- The basic principle of contract remedies is to make the injured party whole through compensation for the loss caused by the breach.

- Breaching parties are not "punished" and punitive damages are not awarded since the goal of contract remedies is not compulsion of the promisor to perform the promise but compensation of the promisee for the loss resulting from the breach. However, since the concern is with economic loss, if a non-breaching party suffers no actual financial loss, there is no entitlement to damages beyond an award for nominal damages.

- Contract damages are usually based on the injured party's expectation interest and are intended to give her the "benefit of her bargain" by awarding a sum of money that will, to the extent possible, put her in as good a position as she would have been in had the contract been performed.

- Reliance damages are a lesser measure of recovery than expectation damages and allow the injured party to recover damages incurred in preparing to perform, in performing, or in foregoing opportunities to make other contracts.

- Restitution damages may be granted to prevent unjust enrichment where a party has not only changed position in reliance on the contract but has also conferred a benefit on the other party.

- Specific performance will not be granted where money damages are an adequate substitute for the injured party.

- A party has a duty to mitigate her damages by taking reasonable action following a breach. A defendant will not be liable for those losses which the plaintiff could have avoided by taking appropriate measures.

- Remember that to be recoverable, damages must be proven with reasonable certainty. This is most difficult in recovering consequential damages since they often involve lost profits or opportunities. The problem may be the ability to show a direct causal link between the breach and the loss or it may be in establishing the basis and amount of the loss. In such cases, the injured party is left with recovery of her reliance damages because she is able to show with certainty what she expended in reliance on the contract.

Formation ➡	Avoiding ➡ the Deal	Performance ➡	Third ➡ Parties	Remedies
Do we have a deal?	We have a deal, but	Who has to do what and when, or maybe not	Is there a third party to the deal?	Someone failed to perform when required, now what?
Mutual Assent + Consideration				

Excerpts of Contracts Time-line

THIRD PARTIES
IS THERE ANOTHER PARTY TO THE DEAL?

At formation?	**Subsequently?**
3rd Pty Beneficiary	Assignment
• Intended	Delegation
• Incidental	Novation

Close-up on Third Parties

CHAPTER 13

Third Party Interests

The introduction of third parties into the usual two party dynamic of contractual relationships is often a source of confusion—but this need not be the case. By keeping some basic principles in mind, you will be able to determine the rights of the parties—even when it's no longer "just the two of us."

REVIEW OF THIRD PARTY BENEFICIARIES

> R2d § 302, 304, 305, 310, 311
> UCC 2-318

Distinguishing Between Intended and Incidental Beneficiaries

Generally, privity of contract is required to provide a party with standing to sue and enforce contractual rights. This is because contract rights and duties exist only between the contracting parties and do not extend to those who are not parties to the contract. However, third party beneficiaries are an exception to this rule. In some circumstances, third parties may be able to sue on their own behalf to enforce the agreement.

In determining whether a third party has acquired the right of enforcement, the critical factor is whether the contract was made for the benefit of the third party. The contracting parties must have intended the contract to benefit the third party at the time of the contract's formation. While beneficiaries may be "incidental" or "intended," only intended beneficiaries have the right of enforcement.

An incidental beneficiary is one who may benefit in some way from the contract between the parties, but the contract was not made expressly for that party and so she has no legally enforceable rights. For example, while an employee may expect to enjoy the advantages from using the new computer equipment the employer ordered for the office, the employee does not have the right to sue the manufacturer should the equipment malfunction. Although the employer clearly intended the employee to use the equipment, it did not intend when entering the contract to provide the employee with the right to bring its own action against the manufacturer. Here, the employer alone has this right as the purchaser of the equipment.

On the other hand, an intended beneficiary, whether a donee or creditor beneficiary, has the right to enforce the contract. While Restatement Second § 302 does not distinguish between donee and creditor beneficiaries, it is useful to understand the difference between them. A donee beneficiary is one who receives the right gratuitously having given nothing to the promisee in exchange for the benefit. For example, suppose Amy agrees to tutor her law school friend Robyn for $100 and tells Robyn to give the money she earns to Amy's friend, Ashley. Ashley is a donee beneficiary in the contract between Amy and Robyn.

Now let's change the facts a bit and turn Ashley into a creditor beneficiary. Suppose Amy was short of cash one day and needed to buy a Contracts casebook for class. Ashley gave Amy $100 to buy the book. Now when Amy tells Robyn to give the $100 to Ashley, Ashley is a creditor beneficiary because Amy had a pre-existing obligation to her.

Before we move on to consider the next topic, let's take a moment and clarify the terms. Looking at things from the point of view of the third-party beneficiary, the "promisor" is the contracting party who is to render the performance to the beneficiary and the "promisee" is the contracting party whose right to performance has been conferred on the beneficiary. In the above example, Robyn is the "promisor" because she is to pay the $100 directly to Ashley to settle Amy's debt. Amy is the "promisee" because her right to Robyn's performance has been conferred on the beneficiary (in this case, Ashley).

When a contract confers the status of beneficiary on a third party, it means two things: first, that the performance must be rendered to or for the third party's benefit and, second, that the parties intended to grant the beneficiary an independent right to enforce the promise. The beneficiary's right to enforce the contract is of critical importance. It means that Ashley has the right to sue Robyn, the promisor, if she fails to perform her promise. If Ashley did not have this right against Robyn, Ashley could bring suit only against Amy under the pre-existing debt. Now, as an intended beneficiary of the Amy–Robyn contract, Ashley has rights against two parties against whom she can seek recourse. Now whether Ashley can do this at all depends on whether her rights under the contract have "vested."

Requirement of Vesting

While an intended beneficiary has the right to sue the promisor directly, this right does not arise until it has "vested." Before the right has vested, the original parties can modify or even rescind the agreement without concern for the third party. However, once the right has vested—that is, accrued to the beneficiary— the contracting parties no longer have the power to change or eliminate the contract without first obtaining the beneficiary's consent. Of course the contracting parties can always agree otherwise in their contract—they can reserve the power to change the rights given to the beneficiary even after vesting has occurred—but they must be certain to do so or they will lose them as soon as vesting occurs.

The Restatement does not distinguish between creditor and donee beneficiaries in determining when the beneficiary's rights vest. According to Restatement § 311(3), a beneficiary's rights vest when she *manifests assent* to it at the request of one of the parties, or she *sues on it*, or she materially changes position in *justifiable reliance* on it.

Rights of Parties

The relative rights of the parties in a contract for the benefit of a third party can be complicated because three parties are involved instead of the usual two. We begin with the rights of the beneficiary (C) against the promisor (A) and then against the promisee (B).

Beneficiary's Rights Against the Promisor

Once the rights of a creditor or donee beneficiary have vested, she can sue the promisor on the contract and collect damages for the promisor's failure to perform.[1] This is because the intended beneficiary's rights are based on the contract between the promisor and promisee and are therefore measured by the terms of that contact.

It is also the case, therefore, that the beneficiary takes subject to any defenses the promisor could assert had she been sued directly by the promisee. The promisee cannot create in the third party beneficiary rights greater than she has herself. For example, if the contract had been formed by a misunderstanding, or induced by duress or a misrepresentation, or the promisee rendered a defective performance, then the promisor can allege these defenses in a suit brought by the beneficiary.

Beneficiary's Rights Against the Promisee

In addition to a right against the promisor, the beneficiary retains any right against the promisee that she held against the promisee before the contract between the promisor and promisee was made. This is the case in which the beneficiary is a creditor beneficiary where the promisee already owed a duty to the beneficiary. Here, the contract with the promisor and the benefi-

---

1. Restatement (Second) of Contracts § 304 (1979).

ciary's acceptance of it did not discharge the promisee's original duty. Quite the opposite—now there are two duties owed to the beneficiary: one owed by the promisor and the original owed by the promisee. The beneficiary can seek judgment against both although she is entitled to only one satisfaction.[2]

The case of a donor beneficiary is different. A donor beneficiary typically has no rights against the promisee because there is no prior obligation owed from the promisee to the beneficiary and the promisee undertakes no obligation to the beneficiary by virtue of the contract. However, under Restatement Second § 311(4), where the promisee receives consideration for a promise to discharge or modify the promisor's duty, a donee beneficiary may have an interest in the consideration received by the promisee.

Promisee's Rights Against Promisor

The promisee as well as the beneficiary has a right against the promisor. The availability of damages and specific performance depends, however, on whether the beneficiary is a donee or creditor beneficiary. If the promisee's intent was to make a gift of the promised performance to the beneficiary, then the promisee will typically suffer no economic loss if the promisor fails to perform. If the promisee were to sue for damages, she could recover only nominal damages.

REVIEW OF ASSIGNMENT AND DELEGATION

Assignment: R2d § 317, 322
Delegation: R2d § 318, 328
UCC 2-210

Assignment and delegation involve introducing new parties to the contract *after* its formation. Unlike third party beneficiaries who acquire their interest at the time the original contract is formed,

---

2. Restatement (Second) of Contracts § 310(1) (1979).

assignees and delegates acquire their rights through a later transaction with one of the original contracting parties. The transfer of
a right is an "assignment," and the transfer of a duty is a
"delegation." An "assignment of the contract" requires both the
assignment of rights and the delegation of duties.

Assignment of Rights

An assignment is a transfer of a contractual right or benefit.
The party who transfers the right is the "obligee" under the
original contract and, upon assignment, is called the "assignor."
The party who acquires the right is called the "assignee." The party
who owes the right under the original contract and now owes it to
the assignee is called the "obligor."

An assignment is a present transfer of the right and so
extinguishes the right in the obligee and sets it up exclusively in the
assignee. This gives the assignee a direct right against the obligor
under the contract. The obligor, however, must be **notified** of the
assignment before she is legally bound to pay the assignee rather
than the original promisee, now the assignor. If notice is not given
to the obligor, she can continue to render her performance to the
promisee. Therefore, if she renders performance to the assignor
before being notified of the assignment, her obligations are discharged and she does not have to perform again to the assignee.
However, once notified of a valid assignment, the assignee is
substituted for the assignor and only performance to the assignee
discharges the obligor's duty.

In sum, the assignment extinguishes the assignor's right to
enforce the same contractual right and the assignee alone may now
enforce the contract. The assignee becomes the real party in
interest insofar as that right is concerned and she may sue the
obligor directly. However, the suit is subject to all the defenses and
counterclaims arising out of the contract which the obligor could
have asserted against the obligee, i.e., the assignee "stands in the
shoes" of the obligee.

What Constitutes an Effective Assignment?

Any manifested intention by the obligee under a contract to
make a present transfer of her rights to another will constitute an

assignment. The obligee must intend to vest in the assignee a present (rather than a future) right to the thing assigned. An effective assignment requires that the right be adequately described and that present words of assignment be used. The test is whether the language used manifests an apparent intent by the assignor to divest herself completely and immediately of the right in question and to establish it in the assignee. The word "assign" need not be used; words such as sell, transfer, convey, give, etc., are adequate. Unless there is a controlling statute, a writing is not required for an effective assignment.

Limitations on Assignability

The general rule is that contract rights are freely assignable.[3] A contractual right can be assigned unless the contract itself validly precludes assignment or the assignment is prohibited by statute or otherwise violates public policy. However, the right to receive the personal services of another is not assignable. Nor may a right be assigned where it would materially change the duty of the obligor, or materially increase the burden or risk imposed on her by her contract, or materially impair her chance of obtaining return performance or materially reduce its value to her.[4]

Similarly, under UCC 2–210(2),[5] all rights of either the seller or the buyer can be assigned except where the assignment would materially change the duty of the other party, or increase materially the burden or risk imposed on her by her contract, or impair materially her chance of obtaining return performance.

Anti–Assignment Clauses

Sometimes the parties will include a specific provision in the contract prohibiting assignment. The question is the validity and effect of such clauses. The general rule is that when parties include

---

3. Restatement (Second) of Contracts § 317(1) (1979).

4. *Id.* § 317(2).

5. U.C.C. § 2–210(2) (2004). U.C.C. § 2–210 has been redrafted in the 2003 revisions to the Code and the changes are far too extensive to discuss in a footnote and well beyond the scope of this book. Note, however, that the basic concept in 2–210(2) is maintained in revised 2–210(1)(a).

a specific prohibition against assignment in the language of their contract as when it stipulates that any such assignment would be void, then courts will enforce it. Such a provision is said to destroy both the obligee's right and power to assign so that no assignment in violation of the contract is enforceable. This is different, however, from a promise by the obligee not to assign which only destroys the obligee's right, not the power, to make an assignment. In this case, an assignment would be valid but the obligor would have a right to damages for breach of contract.[6]

Under UCC 2–210(2), an anti-assignment provision is ineffective where the rights are no longer executory—such as an assignment of a right to damages for breach or a right to payment for delivered goods.[7] These rights may be assigned even though the agreement prohibits assignment.

Delegation of Duties

Restatement Second § 318 and UCC 2–210 define the basic principles of delegation: an obligor is entitled to delegate her contractual duties unless this violates the contract or public policy. The transfer of a duty due under a contract is called a delegation. The person who transfers the duty is called a "delegator" and the person to whom the duty is transferred is called the "delegate." The party to whom the delegated duty is owed under the original contract is called the "obligee."

By a delegation, the obligor empowers a delegate to perform a duty that the delegating party owed to an obligee. Any contractual duty may be delegated to another, unless the obligee has a substantial interest in having the original obligor perform personally because it involves the personal service or skill of the obligor. This is usually the case in contracts involving artistic performances. Also, delegation is prohibited where the obligee is forced to accept a material increase in burden or risk.

The delegation of duties under a contract is different from the assignment of rights. In most cases, the assignment of rights under

---

6. Restatement (Second) of Contracts § 322(2)(b) (1979).　　**7.** U.C.C. § 2—210 cmt. 3.

a contract is likely to have only a minimal impact on the other party to the contract because all that happens is that she is to render her performance to the newly designated person. For example, it makes no difference to me whether I write out a check to pay the mortgage on my home to the bank with whom I originally took out the mortgage or to the new lender who has been assigned my mortgage. It is the same check.

However, the delegation of one party's duties to another can have a significant impact on the other party to the contract. For example, suppose Seth purchases a fitness center for his home from Brands Fitness Center. One of the terms of the Seth–Brands contract was that Brands would provide training, service, and maintenance from its team of renowned fitness professionals. Seth chose to purchase the equipment from Brands for this reason. Shortly after signing the contract, Brands assigned the Seth–Brands contract to another fitness center, Shape–Up. However, Shape–Up's equipment training and service is provided by its regular sales staff. While competent, they are not professionals. Seth would not be obligated to accept Shape–Up's performance of the Seth–Brands contract because the same services were not being provided.

Delegation differs from assignment is another respect: unlike an assignment of rights, a delegation of duties does not result in a complete substitution of the delegate for the obligor. Instead, the obligor remains liable for any breach. Even though a delegation of duties is permissible unless it violates the contract or public policy, the obligor remains accountable and can be sued by the obligee for breach if the delegate fails to perform or renders a defective performance.

The general rule is that if the delegate fails to perform or renders a defective performance, then the obligee has a cause of action against the obligor. As usual, there is an exception: if the duty is delegated *by a contract* between the obligor and the delegate, then the delegate's promise to the obligor to perform the obligor's duty is viewed as a contract for the benefit of the obligee, who now enjoys the status of a third party beneficiary. And, as would any intended third party beneficiary, the obligee has the direct right of enforcement against the delegate.

REVIEW OF NOVATION

If, on the other hand, the obligor did not want to remain liable to the obligee, then it would seek a "novation." A novation is a new contract wherein the obligee discharges the obligor from her duties under the contract and agrees to accept the delegate as a complete substitute. In effect, there are two new parties to the contract and the original obligor is no longer the party in privity. The term "novation" is therefore often used to describe a substituted contract.

THIRD PARTY INTERESTS CHECKLIST

With this review in mind, here is the checklist for analyzing problems presenting questions regarding third party beneficiaries and assignment and delegation:

A. **Third Party Beneficiary**—was a third party to the contract identified at the time the contract was formed? If the promisee of a contractual promise intends that her performance benefit someone outside the contract, then that person is an intended third party beneficiary. If not, then there is no third party beneficiary issue. However, if new parties are introduced after the original contract is formed, then it may be a question of assignment or delegation. If so, proceed to Part B.

    1. **Benefit**—was the contract made for the benefit of the third party? The contracting parties must clearly intend and specify in the contract that a third party receive rights or benefits from the performance of the contract.

        a. **No.** If not, then there is no third party interest to consider.

        b. **Yes.** If so, then proceed to the next question.

    2. **Type of Beneficiary**—was the beneficiary an incidental or intended beneficiary?

a. **Incidental Beneficiary**—was the beneficiary an incidental beneficiary? If so, then the contract was not made expressly for that party and she has no legally enforceable rights.

b. **Intended Beneficiary**—was the beneficiary an "intended" beneficiary? Only an intended beneficiary has the right of enforcement and can sue the promisor directly. If the party was an intended beneficiary, then ask what kind of intended beneficiary:

   i. **Donee Beneficiary?**—Did the beneficiary receive the contract right gratuitously from the promisee?

   ii. **Creditor Beneficiary?**—Did the promisee owe a debt to the third party?

3. **Vesting**—has the intended beneficiary's rights vested? Until the beneficiary's rights vest, the contracting parties may modify or rescind the contract without regard for the beneficiary. Once rights vest, the beneficiary has the right of enforcement. Rights may vest in any one of the following ways:

   a. **Assent**—has the beneficiary manifested assent to the promise at the request of the promisor or promisee?

   b. **Suit**—has the beneficiary brought suit to enforce the promise?

   c. **Reliance**—has the beneficiary materially changed position in justifiable reliance?

B. **Assignment and Delegation**—has one of the contract parties purported to transfer her rights or delegate her duties under the contract to someone who was not an original party to the contract?

1. **Assignment of Rights**—has there been a present transfer of a contract right? An assignment extinguishes the right in the obligee and sets it up exclusively in the assignee. This gives the assignee a direct right against the obligor under the contract. To determine whether the assignment was valid and enforceable, ask the following:

   a. **Effective**—was it an effective assignment? An effective assignment requires the owner of the right to use words of present intent and to describe the right to be transferred adequately. Ask: does the language manifest an apparent intent by the assignor to divest herself completely and immediately of the right and establish it in the assignee? While the word "assign" need not be used, were such words as "sell," "transfer," "convey," or "give," used?

   i. **No**. If not, then it was only an attempted or purported assignment and was ineffective.

   ii. **Yes**. If so, then proceed to the next question.

b. **Type of Right**—is it the type of right that may be assigned? A contractual right may be assigned unless it would materially alter the other party's duty, risk, or likelihood of receiving the promised return performance. Ask:

   i. **Public Policy**—would the purported assignment violate public policy?

   ii. **Adverse Effect**—would the purported assignment materially change or materially increase the risk or burden of the obligor's duty? In cases where the obligor's duty depends on the obligee's personal discretion, substituting an assignee for the obligee might result in a material change in the obligor's duty. If so, a court might find the assignment ineffective. The same is true in cases where the obligor's risk or burden under the contract is materially affected as in insurance contracts.

c. **Preventing Assignment**—is there a term in the parties' contract preventing assignment?

   i. **Yes.** If so, then absent a statute, most courts would uphold the provision depending on the precise contract language. Ask:

     • Does the contract language indicate that "assignment of rights under this contract is prohibited"? If so, then while an assignment would be a breach of contract and the obligor could seek damages, the transfer of rights would itself be effective.

     • Does the contract language indicate that "assignment of rights under this contract is void"? If so, then the assignment is ineffective.

- Does the contract language indicate that "assignment of the contract is prohibited"? If so, this should be construed to bar only the delegation of duties and not the assignment of rights unless a contrary intent is indicated.

ii. **No.** If there is no prohibition, then contract rights can be assigned because the general policy is free assignability.

d. **Notice**—has the obligor been given notice of the assignment?

i. **Yes.** If so, then she is bound to render performance to the assignee instead of the assignor.

ii. **No.** If not, then she has no reason to know that her performance is due to the assignee. If she renders her performance to the assignor before receiving notice of the assignment, her obligations are discharged and she does not have to perform again for the assignee.

2. **Delegation of Duties**—has there been a transfer of a duty due under the contract to another party? The law with respect to delegation is similar to that of assignment and an obligor is free to delegate her contractual duties as long as it does not violate an express provision of the contract, the reasonable expectations of the obligee, or public policy. Ask: is it the type of duty that can be delegated?

a. **Personal**—is the duty one that is "personal" in nature such that it involves the party's taste, skill, or discretion?

i. **Yes.** If the performance involves unique skills or the personal services of professionals like lawyers, doctors, and portrait painters, then it is non-delegable. In these cases, the obligee should not be required to accept performance from anyone other than the original obligor.

ii. **No.** If the performance is impersonal, then it can be delegated unless it materially alters performance.

b. **Public Policy**—would the delegation violate public policy? If so, then it is non-delegable.

3. **Novation**—has there been a substitution of the original parties to the contract? To determine whether there has been a novation, ask: has the obligee agreed to accept the delegate as a complete substitute for the obligor and release the obligor from her duties under the contract?

   a. **Yes**. If the obligee accepts the delegate in the place of the obligor, then there has been a novation and the obligor is no longer liable to the obligee should the delegate fail to perform or render a defective performance.

   b. **No**. If the obligee does not expressly manifest intent to enter into a novation, then one is not implied from the fact that the obligee accepts the delegate's performance. In this case, the obligor remains liable on the contract.

ILLUSTRATIVE PROBLEMS

Here are some problems that will let us see how the checklist can be used to resolve issues regarding third parties.

■ PROBLEM 13.1 ■

Deb, who owned a dry cleaning store, hired Jake to keep the sidewalks and parking lot cleared of ice and snow during the winter months for $2500. At the time they signed the contract in November, Jake told Deb to make the $2500 payment to his mechanic, Mike, because he owed him that amount. Deb agreed. Two days later, Mike called Jake asking about the money he owed him. Jake told him he would get paid from Deb in February. Mike, counting on the money he was to receive, placed an order for new tools for his garage.

Things were not going so well for Jake and he needed the money he was earning from Deb. He called her in January and asked her to pay him instead of Mike. Deb agreed. Does Mike have a valid basis for an action to collect the $2500?

Analysis

Whether Mike can collect the $2500 depends on whether Mike is an intended third party beneficiary of the Deb–Jake contract. When two parties form a contract, there are two kinds of beneficiaries which may be created: intended and incidental beneficiaries. Only intended beneficiaries have enforceable rights under the contract. There are two classes of intended beneficiaries: creditor and donee beneficiaries. A creditor beneficiary is one to whom the promisee owes a pre-existing duty which the promisor's performance will fulfill. A donee beneficiary is one to whom the promisee intends to make a gift of the performance. Here, Mike was a creditor beneficiary of the Deb–Jake contract because they intended at the time of contract that Deb's performance would flow to Mike to satisfy a debt that Jake owed Mike.

The next question is whether Jake and Deb could modify their agreement to change the payment term from Mike to Jake. The rule is that once a third party beneficiary's rights under the contract have vested, the contract cannot be changed without the beneficiary's consent. According to Restatement Second § 311(3), a beneficiary's rights vest when she manifests assent to it at the request of one of the parties, or she sues on it, or she materially changes position in justifiable reliance on it. Here, Mike's rights vested when Jake informed him that he would receive payment from Deb in February and he materially relied on the promised payment by going out and buying tools. Once Mike's rights vested, the power of Deb and Jake to modify their agreement terminated, absent Mike's consent. Mike is entitled to recover the $2500 owed to him and can bring suit against either Deb or Jake.

■ PROBLEM 13.2 ■

Heather owned a successful decorating business known for its unique designs. She designed on a grand scale—huge country houses, sea-side mansions, and penthouse apartments. She specialized in creating grand, dramatic spaces for her celebrity clients.

Heather entered into a written agreement with the famous come-
dian, Terry Kreinfeld, to design his new country estate and, subject
to his approval of the design plan, to decorate and select the
furnishings for the home's interior for a fixed fee.

Before Heather began work on the Kreinfeld project, she
accepted an offer to sell her business to her friend, Robyn. Heather
had received an opportunity to star in her own reality television
series and could not pass up the opportunity. She knew that Robyn
was a very talented designer and had studied architecture and fine
arts in Paris. As part of the agreement for the sale of the business,
Heather assigned to Robyn and Robyn agreed to complete, the
Heather–Kreinfeld contract. Robyn notified Kreinfeld of the assignment and provided information about her financial stability
and prior decorating awards and achievements.

When Terry received notification of the assignment from
Robyn, his shouts could be heard a mile away: "I don't care if
Robyn designed the Eiffel Tower. She is not designing
KreinfeldAcre." If Robyn brings suit because Terry refuses to allow
her to perform, will she be successful?

Analysis

Whether Robyn's suit for breach of contract would be successful depends on whether the performances promised under the
Heather–Kreinfeld contract were delegable. Unfortunately for
Robyn, contracts involving the performance of artistic services are
non-delegable and therefore judgment would be for Terry.

Delegation is a transfer of one's duties under a contract. If a
party wishes to have another person perform her duties under a
contract, she delegates them. Most duties are delegable except
those which call for the promisor's unique skills or talents.
Typically, contracts involving artistic performances or professional
services are non-delegable.

In this case, Heather was famous for her unique home
designs. This is the reason that Terry hired her to design and

decorate his country estate. The rule that performances requiring the artistic skills of the promisor cannot be delegated would be applicable in this case. Consequently, when Heather sold her decorating business to Robyn, she was assuming the risk that her clients would accept the services of another designer, even one with excellent credentials who had won decorating awards. Terry is not obligated to allow Robyn to perform the contract.

■ PROBLEM 13.3 ■

Same facts as above. Suppose that Terry agreed to let Robyn perform the contract and approved her design plan but Robyn failed without excuse to complete the job as agreed. Against whom does Terry have a valid claim for breach of contract?

Analysis

Terry would be able to bring suit against either Heather or Robyn. Even when a performance is delegated, the delegator remains liable. Here, Terry has a breach of contract action against Heather because Heather's delegation to Robyn did not terminate Heather's liability under the Heather–Terry contract. Terry also has a contract claim against Robyn because Terry was the intended beneficiary of the Heather–Robyn agreement where he was to receive the performance of designing and decorating his home. Therefore, he has status as a third party beneficiary of Robyn's promise to perform the contract.

If Heather did not want to remain liable under the Heather–Terry contract, she should have sought a novation. A novation is a new contract wherein the obligee discharges the obligor from her duties under the contract and agrees to accept the delegate as a complete substitute. However, this would have required Terry's consent to accept Robyn as a new party to the contract, something which did not occur in these facts. Consequently, both Heather and Robyn are liable.

POINTS TO REMEMBER

- Only intended beneficiaries have enforceable rights and a beneficiary's rights are not enforceable until they have vested.

- Before a third party beneficiary's rights have vested, the parties to the contract may modify or even rescind the contract without concern for the beneficiary.

- Courts interpret anti-assignment clauses as narrowly as possible since the law favors the assignability of rights and the delegation of duties.

- An obligor is entitled to delegate her contractual duties unless it violates the contract or public policy.

- Contracts involving the promisor's own special or unique skills are non-delegable. This usually includes artistic performances and professional services.

- When the performance of a duty is delegated, the delegator remains liable under the contract.

- A novation substitutes a new party to the contract and discharges one of the original parties by agreement of all parties.

Conclusion:
General Examination Tips

Now that you have the full set of checklists for each of the topics that you will encounter on your examination, here is some final advice to help you ace your contracts exam.

PREPARING FOR YOUR EXAM

- In law school, the secret is to learn the material over time. In addition to sequencing your outlining as you proceed daily and weekly though the semester, it's essential to incorporate practice problems into your study plan.

- You should practice answering hypotheticals on individual topics as soon as you've covered them in class. Never wait until you've completed the course and you're studying for the final exam. Working with rules as you learn them by applying them in the context of new factual situations is the most effective way to find out whether you truly understand them while you still have time to find answers to questions that naturally arise as you learn new material. This is the main reason that there are illustrative problems in every chapter of this book.

- Meet with your professors to answer any questions you have as you work your way through the course material. In addition to answering the questions in this book, you should answer any past exam questions your professor has made available to you. By working with your professor's questions, you'll become familiar with the structure, substance, and style of her exam and get a pretty good sense of what to expect. Of course there's no guarantee that just because your professor followed a particular exam format in the past, it will be replicated on your exam. Still, while question structure may vary, language and presentation generally remain the same.

- Take practice exams so that the whole process of reading and answering the questions becomes automatic. By doing everything you can possibly do to learn the material, you'll approach the exam in the optimum position for success. Not only does it help to minimize anxiety to know that you've done everything you can to prepare, but it pretty much assures that you've seen how most if not all of the issues are likely to arise.

- It is also important to practice complete exams to see how all the individual issues are likely to appear together. The summary checklists in the Appendix will be helpful to guide you through an exam question with multiple issues.

- The last weeks of the semester should be spent completing your reading and your outlines. Then when classes are finally over, you're ready to focus solely on memorizing the rules and acquiring the deeper understanding of the material that you need to do more than just issue-spot on the exam. Instead, you'll be able to identify problems, analyze the facts, and explain your answers with sophistication and a nuanced knowledge of the law.

- Certain types of essay exam formats emphasize some skills over others. Long, involved fact patterns with multiple parties test organizational abilities in addition to substantive knowledge. Single-issue essays seek to determine your responsiveness to the question which is another means of testing your ability to follow directions and maintain focus.

- Because open-book and take-home exams allow access to your study materials, rote memorization is not the issue but the need for proper preparation remains essential. Even if it's a take-home exam, you're still working under time constraints and the last thing you need to do is learn the material as you race the clock to answer the questions. What this means is that you must prepare as much for an open-book exam as you do for a closed-book exam.

- When studying, aim for a mastery of the material which requires a deep understanding of the material. "Knowing the law" means that you internalize the material in such a way that you truly "own" it. It must become such a part of your understanding that you're able to see connections between and among concepts.

TAKING THE EXAM

- Be in the moment. No matter how much you've studied, how many practice exams you've taken, and how carefully you've outlined and considered what's likely to be tested, once you get to the exam, you must be prepared to let go and "be in the moment." This means that you respond to what the professor asks of you and not what you want to tell the professor you know. Professors craft exam questions to test you on the material you should have mastered in class; if you turn questions around or avoid answering the ones that are asked, you're thwarting the professor's agenda and substituting your own. Trust me—there's no better way to ensure a poor grade than to ignore what's asked of you. By answering the professor's question, you'll be showing what you know.

- If you've prepared properly and you're willing to surrender to the professor's questions, the moment will come when you are in the "exam zone." Like a "runner's high," it's a feeling that there is only "the now." It's where you're on auto-pilot and your training has taken over. You've connected with whatever it was you were working to achieve: for the athlete, it's that connection of mind and body that allows for peak performance; for the law student, it's that command of the material that lets you see the issues in the facts and connect it with the rule and allows you to write with clarity and cogency. Your thinking and writing come together—it flows because you flow.

- Law school exams test your ability to "think like a lawyer." This means mastery of the fundamentals of IRAC, the "Issue, Rule,

Application, Conclusion" structure of legal analysis. All professors share the same expectation of a student essay: a well-reasoned argument based on an analysis of the relevant issues and an application of the law to the facts. The ability to reason in a logical, lawyer-like manner is critical. The value of an answer depends not as much upon the conclusion as upon the demonstrated understanding of the facts, a recognition of the issues, an explanation of the applicable rules, and the reasoning by which the conclusion is reached.

- Only clear, organized thoughts can give rise to coherent, comprehensible answers. After you've completed reading the essay question, and before you write your answer, you must organize your ideas into an outline based on a consideration of the relevant issues. Resist the impulse to start writing immediately—it doesn't matter what others around you are doing—it's worth the few minutes it will take to think through the problem and plan your response. If you take the time to organize your thinking and draft an outline around the relevant issues, you'll have the beginnings of an "A" essay.

- Your ability to find the legal question in the facts is the single most important element in the analysis because you need to know enough law to find the issue. It's not enough to master the substantive rules of law: you need to know when a particular rule is implicated by the facts. This is the critical connection: if you miss the issue, whether or not you know the rule doesn't matter—you never get to the rule if you don't see the issue.

- Even after you've identified the issue, it remains a critical factor in the development of your discussion. Faithfulness to the legal question as you proceed allows you to distinguish between relevant and irrelevant facts and avoid being led astray. Further, it ensures that you'll be on the right path in your analysis, leading to an essay that connects the rules with the questions presented rather than one that rambles and follows a "kitchen sink" approach.

- Never discuss issues that are not in controversy. Not only is it a waste of precious time, but it indicates that you're unable to distinguish between what is relevant and what isn't—and that's a serious problem. It's simply wrong to discuss something that's not in controversy.

- Follow an IRAC-based structure in your answer. At its core, it's an organizing principle—a way to help structure your thinking and your writing—nothing more. Still, it's enormously useful and while it won't guarantee an "A" paper, students who learn to structure their analyses and write well tend to receive good grades. I would be remiss if I didn't tell you that some of your professors will object to IRAC and insist that you refrain from using it on their exams. They have reasons for feeling as they do, since like anything else, IRAC can be abused. The objection is not so much to the concept but to a tortured application. Remember: IRAC is only a tool to aid in the organization of analysis, not a formula. Each problem is different and will proceed from a different issue based on the question that is posed in the facts.

- Your discussion of the applicable law is an essential part of your exam answer: it lets your professor know that you have identified the legal problem (in many cases you can avoid or compensate for an incomplete issue statement if you go directly to the relevant rule) and it shows that you know the law. While your job on an exam is not to regurgitate the rules or provide lengthy treatises, you must discuss the relevant rules in a manner sufficient to analyze the problem and to do so in a concise and coherent manner.

- Once you've identified and explained the controlling rule, your next task is to examine the inferences and implications of each fact in light of the rule. The analysis or application is the heart of the discussion. As you write your analysis, you'll work from your articulation of the rule to guide your application of the facts. Your statement of the rule provides a blueprint to follow to discuss the facts.

- A hallmark of a solid analysis is one that identifies and addresses the ambiguities in the facts. That's the essence of analysis—seeing the possible ways to interpret a fact scenario and then explaining the consequences which flow from each interpretation. Be certain to present and evaluate counter-arguments—which is usually referred to as "arguing both sides." Typically, there is more than one way to look at anything—and you can be certain of that on a law school exam.

- No legal analysis would be complete without consideration of public policy concerns. Sometimes an exam question will ask you to evaluate competing policy interests, recommend whether a jurisdiction should adopt a particular rule, or consider how implementation of a particular rule will affect a given population. To be responsive to the question, you must raise and address policy issues.

- You should offer a conclusion with respect to each issue. The conclusion need only be suggestive of a possible outcome—rarely, if ever, definitive. After all, the factfinder makes the ultimate decision, not you. But for purposes of completing your discussion of the topic, you should venture some assessment of the strengths of the arguments you've just put forth and offer a resolution.

AFTER THE EXAM

- Go directly home. Do not stop to chat with friends and discuss the exam. Do not relive the exam by thinking of what you did or did not do. Move on to the next exam where there is something you can still do to affect the outcome.

    ## ESSAY WRITING CHECKLIST

Here is a checklist for taking the exam. It's a blueprint to guide you through practice sessions and to use on test day. If you know what you're going to do and practice the routine sufficiently, it becomes second nature. On exam day, you can count on the routine to take over and prevent you from freezing up. You'll soon be in the "exam zone."

A. Allocating your Time

1. Do you have your watch in plain view?

2. Did you set up a timetable on your scrap paper after allocating the time for each question based on point value?

B. Reading the Question

1. Did you begin by reading the call-of-the question?

2. Did you skim through to get a sense of the problem?

3. On your second read, did you read "actively"?

    a) Have you identified the area of law and the legal relationship between the parties?

    b) Have you circled amounts of money, dates, locations, quantities, and ages?

    c) Have you noted the words "oral" and "written"?

    d) Are you perfectly clear about *who is doing what to whom?*

C. Outlining your Answer

1. Have you set up a mini-outline by identifying the rules you need to discuss based on the issues raised in the problem?

2. Have you compiled the building blocks for the rule of law by considering,

    a) elements?

    b) definitions?

    c) exceptions to the general rule?

    d) distinctions?

3. Have you followed a hierarchy of concepts by,

    a) moving from the general to the specific?

    b) defining each legal term of art?

D. Writing the Essay

1. Does your statement of each issue include the word **"when"** to ensure that you include the relevant facts?

2. Does your statement of the rule identify the controlling law: common law, federal rule, state-specific statute, etc.?

3. Did you use "**Here**" or "**In this case**" to introduce your application?

4. Did you use "**because**" to make the connection between rule and fact?

5. Did you match a "fact" with each "element" or "definition" in your rule of law?

6. Did you address the ambiguities in the facts?

7. Did you articulate the arguments and counter-arguments?

8. Did you consider questions of public policy?

9. Have you answered the question you were asked?

10. Did you draw a logical conclusion before moving on to the next issue?

APPENDIX:

Summary–Checklists

In this Appendix, you will find two checklists: one for the common law and one for the sale of goods. Each is an analytical outline of leading questions to guide you through analysis of a problem. The framework of questions moves from one issue to the next as though you were answering a hypothetical that raised every possible issue covered in the course, from formation through remedies for breach.

Use these checklists to accomplish the following:

- Provide a summary outline for a final review

- Finalize a framework for the overall structure of the course

- Create a topic checklist for issue-spotting on the exam

As you know, it is beyond the scope of this book to discuss all the rules under UCC Article 2. Consequently, the sales checklist covers only the basic topics likely to be found on a general contracts exam but not one dealing specifically with the Uniform Commercial Code. Please do not rely on the checklist for this purpose since it does not cover all the possible topics in the level of detail required for such a course.

COMMON LAW CHECKLIST

A. Was there mutual assent?

1. **Was there an offer?** In determining whether a party made an offer capable of acceptance as opposed to preliminary negotiations or mere inquiries, ask the following:

   a. Was there a manifestation of present contractual intent?

   b. Were the terms definite and certain?

   c. Was it communicated to one capable of acceptance?

2. **If there was an offer, was it accepted?**

   a. Did the proper party accept the offer? Was it the party with the "power of acceptance"?

   b. Has the offeree accepted in the manner required by the offer?

      i. Was it an offer that called for acceptance by return promise or performance?

      ii. Did the offeree still have the power of acceptance or was it terminated in one of the following ways?

         • By revocation? If revoked, then ask:

            — Was the revocation received?

            — Was it an indirect revocation?

            — Was it the revocation of a general offer?

         • By death or insanity?

         • By intervening illegality?

         • By rejection/counter-offer?

         • By lapse of time?

         • By destruction of the subject matter?

      iii. Was there an acceptance by silence?

iv. Was the offeree required to give notice of acceptance to the offeror?

v. When did acceptance become effective?

- Was it an instantaneous communication?

- Was it by mail?

- Was it in the manner invited by the offer so as to be effective upon dispatch (mailbox rule)?

- Was it acceptance of an option contract?

3. **Was there an option contract or an irrevocable offer?** Was there a promise to keep an offer open for a stated period of time? Ask the following:

   a. Was there consideration?

   b. Was there a statute?

   c. Does the jurisdiction follow the Restatement rule? (writing signed by the offeror, recites consideration, and proposes a fair exchange within a reasonable time?)

   d. Was there an offer for a unilateral contract? Has the offeree partially performed the requested performance? Ask the following:

      i. Common law rule? If so, the offer may be revoked at any time before completion of the requested act.

      ii. Restatement (Second)? Did the offeree begin performance of the requested act so as to make the offer irrevocable? Did the offeree begin the actual performance or was it mere preparations to perform?

      iii. Reliance that is not part performance? Did the offeror make an offer which she should reasonably expect to induce reliance on the part of the offeree before acceptance and which did induce such reliance?

B. Was there consideration?

    1. Was there a "bargained for" exchange? If the promise was not sought by the promisor and given by the promisee in exchange for that promise, then what type of promise was it?

        a. Gratuitous promise?

        b. Past consideration?

        c. Illusory promise?

            i. Requirements–Output Contract?

            ii. Exclusive dealings?

        d. Conditional Promise?

            i. On an event?

            ii. On personal satisfaction?

    2. Was there reliance? Are the elements for promissory estoppel as set forth in Restatement Second § 90 satisfied?

        a. Promise?

        b. Foreseeability of reliance?

        c. Actual, justified reliance?

        d. Enforcement of promise necessary to avoid injustice?

    3. Was there a modification? Is there consideration to support a promise modifying a duty under a contract not fully performed by either party?

        a. Pre-existing duty?

        b. Modern trend? Does the jurisdiction depart from the pre-existing duty rule and enforce a modification absent consideration if the following requirements are met:

            i. Voluntary? Did the parties voluntarily agree?

    ii. Executory? Is the contract still executory on both sides?

    iii. Unanticipated circumstances? Was the basis of modification unanticipated by the parties?

    iv. Fair and equitable?

C. Was there a defense or basis on which to avoid the contract?

1. **Misunderstanding?** Did the parties express assent to the same words or terms, but attach materially different meanings to what they said?

2. **Statute of frauds?** Was it the type of contract which needed to be in writing to be enforceable?

    a. One year provision?

    b. Contract in consideration of marriage?

    c. Sale of an interest in land?

        i. Part performance exception?

    d. Sale of goods over $500? (see the Sale of Goods checklist)

    e. Guaranty contracts (suretyship provision)?

        i. Main purpose rule exception?

    f. Executor to answer for the duty of their decedents?

    g. Exceptions:

        i. Was it a unilateral contract?

        ii. Promissory Estoppel?

3. **Capacity?** Did the party have capacity to form a contract?

    a. Infancy?

    b. Mental Incapacity?

4. **Mistake?** Did one or both of the parties hold an erroneous assumption about the facts that existed at the time of contracting?

   a. Unilateral mistake?

   b. Mutual mistake?

   c. Scrivener's error? Was there an error in recording the parties' agreement?

5. **Misrepresentation?** Was there an assertion not in accord with the facts?

   a. Was it fraudulent or material?

   b. Was it an opinion?

   c. Was it a failure to disclose or concealment of a material fact?

6. **Duress or undue influence?** Did one party improperly/wrongfully pressure the other party into giving assent? Did one party take advantage of the relationship with the other to induce assent?

7. **Unconscionability?** Was the contract manifestly unfair or oppressive?

   a. Substantive unconscionability?

   b. Procedural unconscionability?

8. **Illegality and public policy concerns?** Was either the consideration or the object of the contract is illegal? Did the agreement offend public policy?

D. **Was there a dispute during the performance phase of the contract?**

   1. **Parol Evidence?** Was there a dispute regarding the scope and content of the deal? Is one party introducing evidence of a prior or contemporaneous agreement to show that the terms of the parties' written agreement are other than as shown in the writing?

a. Integrated or unintegrated?

    i. Merger clause?

b. Completely or partially integrated?

2. **Interpretation?** Do the parties disagree as to the meaning of the terms in their agreement? Is evidence admissible to interpret the parties' agreement?

3. **Promise or condition or both?**

a. Was it a condition of performance?

    i. Condition Precedent?

    ii. Concurrent Conditions?

    iii. Condition Subsequent?

    iv. Express Condition?

    v. Constructive Conditions?

b. If so, was the condition excused or waived?

c. Was it a promise?

d. Was it a promissory condition?

4. **Changed circumstances?** Have drastically changed circumstances made the obligor's performance impracticable or has the purpose in performing the contract been frustrated?

a. Existing or supervening impracticability?

b. Frustration of purpose?

E. **Was there a breach of contract?** Did a promisor, without justification or excuse, fail to tender a promised performance when performance was due or tendered a defective performance?

1. **Anticipatory repudiation?** Has one party to the contract expressed the intent, either through words or conduct, that

a promised performance will not be forthcoming? Has this occurred before the actual time set for performance?

a. Was it a clear, unequivocal refusal to perform?

b. Adequate assurances? If there was doubt, did the aggrieved party seek adequate assurances of performance?

c. Retraction? Was there a retraction of the repudiation? Did it occur before the aggrieved party relied on the repudiation?

2. **Material breach or substantial performance?** Did the party commit a material breach or substantially perform?

a. Consider the following factors:

   i. To what extent has the breaching party already performed?

   ii. Was the breach wilful, negligent, or purely innocent?

   iii. What is the extent to which the injured party will be deprived of the actual benefit of the contract?

   iv. To what extent will the breaching party suffer a forfeiture?

      • Is the contract divisible?

   v. To what extent has the injured party obtained or will obtain the substantial benefit for which she bargained?

   vi. To what extent can the injured party be compensated for the defective performance by damages?

b. Cure? If the breach is material, can it be cured before it is a total breach?

F. Remedies?

  1. Expectation interest? Can the injured party recover the benefit of her bargain?

   a. Measuring the interest?

    i. Has neither party performed?

    ii. Has there been part performance?

     • Diminution in value?

     • Cost of completion or repair?

   b. Are there limitations on recovery?

    i. Foreseeability?

    ii. Mitigation/avoidability?

    iii. Certainty?

  2. Reliance interest? Was the injured party's loss caused by reliance on the contract? Can she be put in as good a position as she would have been in had the contract not been made?

  3. Restitution interest? Has the plaintiff conferred a benefit on the other party so that it would be unjustly enriched at the plaintiff's expense?

  4. Agreed remedies? Have the parties defined their own remedies in the event of breach?

   a. Liquidated damages?

   b. Restriction on remedies?

  5. Equitable remedies? Will the award of money damages not compensate the injured party for her loss?

   a. Specific performance?

   b. Injunctive relief?

G. Third Party Interests? Was there a third party to the deal?

  1. Third party beneficiary?

    a. What type of beneficiary?

        i. Intended?

- Creditor?

- Donee?

       ii. Incidental beneficiary?

    b. Vested? Has the intended beneficiary's rights vested so that the beneficiary has acquired the right of enforcement?

        i. Assent? Has the beneficiary manifested assent to the promise at the request of the promisor or promisee?

       ii. Suit? Has the beneficiary brought suit to enforce the promise?

      iii. Reliance? Has the beneficiary materially changed position in justifiable reliance?

2. Assignment and delegation? Has one of the contract parties purported to transfer her rights or delegate her duties under the contract to someone else who was not an original party to the contract?

    a. Assignment of rights?

        i. Are there any limits on assignability?

- Personal services?

- Material change or material increase in risk or burden to obligor's duty?

- Public policy?

       ii. Is there an anti-assignment clause?

    b. Delegation of duties?

3. Novation? Has there been a substitution of the original parties to the contract?

SALE OF GOODS CHECKLIST

A. Do the provisions of Article 2 apply?

1. Is it a transaction involving the sale of goods or services?

2. Is it a hybrid? If so, are goods the predominant purpose?

3. Are one or both of the parties to the agreement "merchants" so as to fall within the Code's merchant provisions where applicable?

B. Was there an agreement or "bargain of the parties in fact"?

1. Was there an offer and acceptance?

2. Was there a dispute over contract terms because of additional or different terms in the acceptance, i.e., "battle of the forms"?

3. Was there a "firm offer"? Did a merchant offer to buy or sell goods in a signed writing which promised to hold the offer open?

C. What are the terms of the agreement?

1. Are "gap fillers" necessary to fill in terms left open by the parties, except for the quantity term which is required?

2. Is it an requirements/output contract or one for exclusive dealings?

D. Statute of frauds? Was it a contract for the sale of goods over $500 such that a writing would be required? Does an exception apply?

1. Specially manufactured goods?

2. Admissions?

3. Goods paid for and accepted, or received and accepted?

4. Merchant memo? Has a merchant sent a written confirmation to another merchant who has reason to know its contents and it is in a form sufficient to bind the sender? If

so, then the writing requirement is satisfied unless written notice of objection is given within 10 days of receipt.

E. Parol evidence? Is one party introducing evidence of a prior or contemporaneous agreement to show that the terms of the parties' written agreement are other than as shown in the writing?

1. Integrated?

2. Partially or completely integrated?

3. Explained or supplemented by course of dealing or usage of trade or by course of performance?

F. Modification?

1. Good faith? Although consideration is not necessary, was the modification made in good faith?

2. Statute of frauds? If the contract as modified falls within the statute, have its requirements been met?

3. Waiver? If it was not a modification, could it be a waiver?

G. Impracticability? Can performance be excused by a "failure of presupposed conditions"?

H. Warranty?

1. Warranty of title?

2. Warranties of quality? Has the seller made a representation of quality to which the goods must conform at the time of delivery?

   a. Implied warranties?

      i. Warranty of merchantability? Goods sold by a merchant?

      ii. Warranty of fitness for a particular purpose? Did the seller have reason to know of the buyer's particular purpose, know or have reason to know that the buyer was relying on the seller's skill to furnish appropriate goods, and the buyer relied on the seller to select the goods?

   b. Express warranty?

      i. Was there an affirmation of fact or promise"?

      ii. Was there a description of the goods?

      iii. Was there a sample or model?

      iv. Were there post-sale statements?

3. Exclusion or disclaimer of warranties?

   a. Express warranties? Would it be inherently inconsistent?
      Implied warranties?

      i. Warranty of merchantability? Did the language mention the word "merchantability" and, if in writing, was it conspicuous?

      ii. Warranty of fitness for a particular purpose? Has the seller excluded or modified the warranty in a writing which is conspicuous?

   c. Modification or limitation of remedies?

      i. Exclusive remedy? Was the limited remedy "expressly agreed to be exclusive?"

      ii. Essential purpose? Was the seller unwilling or unable to repair the defective goods within a reasonable time or willing and able to repair but repairs cannot be done?

I. Performance?

1. Perfect tender? Has the seller tendered non-conforming goods?

2. Right to cure? Has the non-conforming tender or delivery occurred before the contract's specified delivery date so that the seller has time to cure?

J. Breach?

1. Did the buyer breach?

    a. Wrongfully rejected the goods?

    b. Wrongfully revoked acceptance of the goods?

    c. Failed to make a payment when due?

    d. Repudiated a part or the whole contract?

        i. Was repudiation by statements? (overt communication)

        ii. Was repudiation by conduct? (an action)

        iii. Was repudiation by failure to give adequate assurances?

    e. Was it the breach of an installment contract? Can the buyer reject an installment?

        i. Was it non-conforming, and

        ii. Did the non-conformity substantially impair the value of that installment, and

        iii. Can the seller cure the non-conformity?

        iv. If there was a breach of an installment, was it a breach of the whole?

2. Did the seller breach?

    a. Repudiated the contract?

    b. Failed to deliver the goods?

    c. Tendered non-conforming goods? (perfect tender rule)?

K. Remedies?

1. What are the seller's remedies for the buyer's breach?

    a. Action for the price?

     b. Resale of the goods?

     c. Hypothetical resale?

     d. Lost volume seller?

     e. Incidental damages?[1]

2. What are the buyer's remedies for the seller's breach?

     a. Specific performance or replevin?

     b. Right to cover?

     c. Hypothetical repurchase?

     d. Breach of warranty? Can the buyer claim breach of warranty?

         i. Did the seller made some warranty, express or implied?

         ii. Was the warranty breached?

         iii. Was the breach the cause of the damages sought?

         iv. Was there a disclaimer of warranties?

            • Was the disclaimer unconscionable?

     e. Incidental damages?

     f. Consequential damages?

         i. Causation?

         ii. Reason to know?

         iii. Preventable?

         iv. Reasonable certainty"?

†

---

[1]. The 2003 revision to the Code provides specifically for seller's right to recover conse-quential damages in similar terms to the rights of the buyer.